BRINGING ASTROLOGY DOWN TO EARTH

(BOOK 1)

THE INTIMATE STORY OF YOU

—•((●●●●))•—

Kyle Ryan Ukes

Hastings House Publishers

A Division of Newhouse Creative Group

Bringing Astrology Down to Earth Book 1: The Intimate Story of You
By Kyle Ryan Ukes

Hastings House Publishers
Orlando, Florida
NewhouseCreativeGroup.com
©2025, Kyle Ryan Ukes

Names: Ukes, Kyle Ryan.
Title: Bringing Astrology Down to Earth / by Kyle Ryan Ukes
Description: Orlando, FL | Hastings House Publishers, 2025. | Series: Bringing Astrology Down to Earth | Summary: Rede ining astrology in a new light.
Identi iers: ISBN 978-1-945493-87-4 (paperback)
Subjects: LCSH: Astrology. | Astrology and health. |New age. |Metaphysical. | Personal growth.
Classification: LCC BF1724.U34 Bri 2025(print)

All charts and ephemerides were compiled using software designed and owned by Astrodienst AG at the website ASTRO.COM. Written permission has been granted for commercial use.

Dedicated to John Marchesella, whose "meat and potatoes"
astrology has kept me satiated all these years.

——————•（（●●●））•——————

CONTENTS

"The heavens themselves, the planets, and this center
Observe degree, priority, and place,
Insisture, course, proportion, season, form,
Office, and custom, in all line of order."

-William Shakespeare from Troilus and Cressida, Act I, Scene 3

INTRODUCTION

Astrology in a Whole New Light!

I know what you're thinking. Just another one of a thousand other astrology books. You're expecting it to be filled to the brim with pages upon pages of word salad — clichés like "watery Pisces" or "airy Gemini." No doubt you are already envisioning the obligatory phrases about how Chiron is known as the "wounded healer" and other timeworn narratives. Groundbreaking, right?

Nope. This isn't your typical astrology book. This book series is going to put legitimacy back into astrology. Gone are the days where all you get is watered down astrology that provides no sustenance or insight into your own journey. This book series is different.

It's time to approach astrology from a new perspective by reformatting our understanding and refining common definitions and theories. This will be accomplished by integrating the genius of astrologers from the twentieth century all the way back to the dawn of time. We are going to learn not only how astrology works, but more importantly, we will uncover why it works.

Before we begin exploring why astrology works, we first need to address what people mean when they tell us it doesn't. These critics are getting louder by the day. They feel emboldened because, in many ways, astrology has lost its way. This book is going to change all of that.

Our format is based in critical thinking, scientific data, and the metaphysical and psychological philosophies of the twentieth century. Through this unique approach, we become equipped to counter and falsify every single argument a skeptic can throw at astrology.

Marcus Cicero: The Ultimate Buzzkill

Marcus Cicero, the first-century Roman skeptic, first devised this thorn in astrology's proverbial side two thousand years ago when he uttered,

> . . .*[individuals] who were born at the very same instant are unlike in character, career, and destiny. [Therefore,] the time of birth has nothing to do in determining [an individual's] course in life.*[1]

This Occam's razor conclusion has become the crux of astrology's curtailment from an acceptable study to a point of near extinction in today's modern world. Ironically, astrology's popularity is currently at an all-time high.[2] Practically as soon as Cicero made his statement, cynics began embracing it as their secret weapon to slowly chip away at astrology's validity and reputation. It's time to put an end to the belittling of astrology and make a valid counterpoint to Cicero once and for all. We are going to dissect and scrutinize Cicero's assertion one line at a time, using the same tools skeptics use to disprove astrology.

Let us start by addressing the first segment of Cicero's statement, ". . . *[individuals] who were born at the very same instant . . .*", and develop a few experiments based upon actual data which confront this first issue. Now, bear with me, we're gonna have to get a little nerdy here. Remember, this isn't a typical astrology book. We must bring astrology back to its roots. To do this, we need to integrate parts of astrology that have been sorely missing. Astrology is full of logical reasoning, mathematics, and existential introspection. It has always been this way. Astrologers have simply lost sight of these practices. So let us act like credible astrologers and discuss why Cicero is full of crap.

---

1   Marcus Tulius Cicero, *De Senectute De Amicita De Divinatinoe*, trans. William Armistead Falconer (Harvard University Press, 1923), 479

2   *The Economist*, "Astrology is Booming, Thanks to Technology and Younger Enthusiasts," January 15, 2025, https://www.economist.com/culture/2025/01/15/astrology-is-booming-thanks-to-technology-and-younger-enthusiasts.

Cicero Asks the Impossible

Cicero's stipulation has one gigantic fatal flaw. When he says the individuals have to be born *at the very same instant,* he is referring to an astronomically rare occurrence.

Here's what I mean. UNICEF gives an average estimate of 255 births per minute globally.[3] Although we cannot assume that every one of these births occurred within a hospital, let us assume that all 255 took place inside one. According to a study, there are around 164,500 hospitals worldwide[4] indicating that the probability of two strangers being born at the same exact moment and the same exact location is approximately 0.00024 percent.

In other words, Cicero's context where two individual strangers are born at the same location and time up to the minute is immensely improbable to a negligible degree. In non-nerd speak, people being born at the very same instant is a rare and unlikely occurrence.

But What About Twins?

By now, I'm sure the skeptic is jumping up and down and shouting—wanting to remind me that there are such things as twins and they are birthed at the same location and time. They would think that their epic gotcha moment is social media worthy, but let us not celebrate too soon and take a step back. Remember, Cicero wants us to refer to moments when people are born at the very same instant. Even twins are usually born at slightly different times.

According to a statistical study, twins have a 61 percent chance of being born within fifteen minutes or less and a thirty-nine percent chance of being born at an interval longer than fifteen minutes, with a mean time of twenty-one

---

3   *The World Counts,* "How Many Babies are Born Each Day?" 2025, https://www.theworldcounts.com/stories/how-many-babies-are-born-each-day.

4   "Ranking Web of World Hospitals," Cybermetrics Lab, archived 2015 at https://web.archive.org/web/20150206120833/http://hospitals.webometrics.info/.

minutes.[5] This means the distribution is more or less bell-shaped, indicating that the probability of two individuals being born at the exact minute, as in Cicero's argument, is likewise be substantially low. Again, in non-nerd speak, the chances of twins being born at the same exact moment is extremely rare. Furthermore, a mean time of twenty-one minutes is still enough of a range to produce two distinct and unique charts; even in the case of twins. This has to do with the relatively fast daily rotation of planet Earth.

All of the planets in astrology travel around the sky above our heads along a circular band we call the zodiac, and astronomers call this band the ecliptic. This 360° wheel circles around our sky once every twenty-four hours. The twelve signs of astrology divide the zodiac wheel into twelve equal parts of 30° each. The zodiac and the planets have been doing this since the dawn of time and will continue to do so eons after our own time.

And now some math: If the 360° of the zodiac traverses our sky once a day, and there are 1440 minutes in a day, this means our view of the ecliptic changes approximately 0.25° per minute of time. Now remember the twins? If a set of twins were born at the mean time of twenty-one minutes, this indicates that the ecliptic in the sky would have shifted approximately 5° from birth to birth. This might not seem like a lot, but 5° is all it takes to derive a completely different chart. Take, for example, the two pairs of theoretical twins below born at the same location, but within a time difference of twenty minutes (Fig. INT-1).

---

5   William F. Rayburn et al., "Multiple Gestation: Time Interval Between Delivery of the First and Second Twins," *Obstetrics & Gynecology*, 63(4), April 1984, 502–6. https://journals.lww.com/greenjournal/abstract/1984/04000/multiple_gestation__time_interval_between_delivery.12.aspx.

FIGURE INT-1. Two Sets of twins born 20 minutes apart from one another.

Th., 4 November 1976   Time: 1:00 p.m.
Vancouver, BC (CAN)   Univ. Time: 21:00
123w07, 49n16   Sid. Time: 15:44:26
Natal Chart
Method: Web Style / Placidus
Sun sign: Scorpio
Ascendant: Capricorn

⊙ Sun   12 Sco 34' 38"
☽ Moon   19 Ari 57' 54"
☿ Mercury   11 Sco 0' 56"
♀ Venus   18 Sag 25' 24"
♂ Mars   18 Sco 36' 9"
♃ Jupiter   27 Tau 55' 14" r
♄ Saturn   16 Leo 23' 23"
♅ Uranus   7 Sco 47' 56"
♆ Neptune   12 Sag 33' 59"
♇ Pluto   12 Lib 46' 17"
⚴ True Node   3 Sco 35' 38" d
⚷ Chiron   28 Ari 58' 43" r
AC 28 Cap 15' 2: 23 Pis 38' 3: 3 Tau 22'
MC 28 Sco 21' 11: 17 Sag 26' 12: 5 Cap 35'

♀ Person B
Th., 4 November 1976   Time: 1:20 p.m.
Vancouver, BC (CAN)   Univ. Time: 21:20
123w07, 49n16   Sid. Time: 16:04:30
Natal Chart
Method: Web Style / Placidus
Sun sign: Scorpio
Ascendant: Aquarius

⊙ Sun   12 Sco 35' 29"
☽ Moon   20 Ari 7' 46"
☿ Mercury   11 Sco 2' 17"
♀ Venus   18 Sag 26' 25"
♂ Mars   18 Sco 36' 44"
♃ Jupiter   27 Tau 55' 7" r
♄ Saturn   16 Leo 23' 25"
♅ Uranus   7 Sco 47' 59"
♆ Neptune   12 Sag 34' 1"
♇ Pluto   12 Lib 48' 19"
⚴ True Node   3 Sco 35' 39" d
⚷ Chiron   28 Ari 58' 41" r
AC 5 Aqu 16' 2: 1 Ari 51' 3: 9 Tau 24'
MC 3 Sag 10' 11: 21 Sag 54' 12: 10 Cap 29'

Type: 2 GW 2-Jan-2021

♀ Person C
Mo., 30 June 1997 Time: 9:30 a.m.
Manila, PHIL   Univ.Time: 1:30
121e00, 14n35   Sid. Time: 4:06:39

Natal Chart
Method: Web Style / Placidus
Sun sign: Cancer
Ascendant: Virgo

⊙	Sun	8 Can 18'40"
☽	Moon	10 Tau 52'42"
☿	Mercury	13 Can 28'26"
♀	Venus	1 Leo 33'49"
♂	Mars	4 Lib 54'22"
♃	Jupiter	21 Aqu 18'29"r
♄	Saturn	19 Ari 27'49"
♅	Uranus	7 Aqu 48'53"r
♆	Neptune	29 Cap 7'37"r
♇	Pluto	3 Sag 19'45"r
☊	True Node	23 Vir 0'13"
⚷	Chiron	25 Lib 42'54"

AC 2 Vir 29' 2: 1 Lib 41' 3: 2 Sco 46'
MC 3 Gem 40' 11: 3 Can 30' 12: 2 Leo 54'

Type 2 GW 2-Jan-2021

♀ Person D
Mo., 30 June 1997 Time: 9:10 a.m.
Manila, PHIL   Univ.Time: 1:10
121e00, 14n35   Sid. Time: 3:46:36

Natal Chart
Method: Web Style / Placidus
Sun sign: Cancer
Ascendant: Leo

⊙	Sun	8 Can 17'52"
☽	Moon	10 Tau 41'22"
☿	Mercury	13 Can 26'39"
♀	Venus	1 Leo 32'48"
♂	Mars	4 Lib 53'58"
♃	Jupiter	21 Aqu 18'32"r
♄	Saturn	19 Ari 27'47"
♅	Uranus	7 Aqu 48'55"r
♆	Neptune	29 Cap 7'38"r
♇	Pluto	3 Sag 19'47"r
☊	True Node	23 Vir 0'17"
⚷	Chiron	25 Lib 42'53"

AC 27 Leo 42' 2: 26 Vir 36' 3: 27 Lib 42'
MC 28 Tau 52' 11: 28 Gem 54' 12: 28 Can 16'

Type 2 GW 2-Jan-2021

Although the changes within these charts are subtle, once they are spotted, each chart conveys a drastically different picture. Chart interpretation will be explained further in Book II. For now, understand that two factors cause the planets to manifest in different ways. The first is the location of the planets within the various subdivisions of the zodiac, which we call signs, and the second factor is the subdivisions of the sky map, which we call houses.

For example, Person A's Venus is in the 11th house, while their twin's Venus (Person B) is located in the 10th house. This means that Venus will be expressed within different avenues of their life experience along with any other planet that is located in a different house. Furthermore, it is important to note that the cardinal points, the thicker black lines within the chart, also emphasize different manifestations unique to the individual. For example, Person C is a Virgo Rising, which means their Mercury is a heavily emphasized planet within their chart. Conversely, their twin, Person D, is a Leo rising, which means the Sun in their chart is weighed just as heavily as their twin's Mercury. This subtle difference emphasizes two radically unique manifestations of the planets whose locations around the zodiac are nevertheless shared by both twins.

A Swing and a Miss

The reason astrology wasn't foiled by Cicero is because astrology is not so one-dimensional as Cicero would have us believe. The computations that go into an astrology chart include multiple parameters such as one's birth time, birth date, and the global longitude and latitude in which it took place. This is how astrology charts can take on such unique qualities even if they were created twenty minutes apart, as in the example above. (Fig. INT-1).

Take these four charts below as another example. All four of these individuals were born at the same exact moment, but at different parts of the world (Fig. INT-2).

FIGURE INT-2. Four individuals born April 17, 2004 11:26 UTC at various locations around the world.

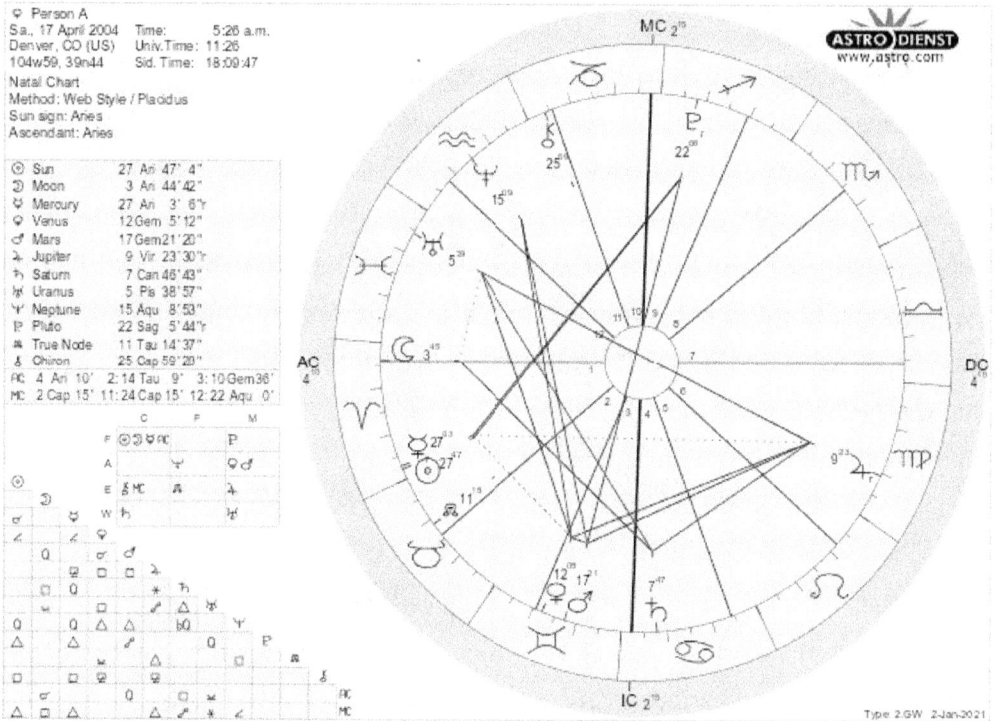

♀ Person A
Sa., 17 April 2004   Time: 5:26 a.m.
Denver, CO (US)   Univ.Time: 11:26
104w59, 39n44   Sid. Time: 18:09:47
Natal Chart
Method: Web Style / Placidus
Sun sign: Aries
Ascendant: Aries

⊙ Sun	27 Ari 47' 4"	
☽ Moon	3 Ari 44'42"	
☿ Mercury	27 Ari 3' 6"r	
♀ Venus	12 Gem 5'12"	
♂ Mars	17 Gem 21'20"	
♃ Jupiter	9 Vir 23'30"r	
♄ Saturn	7 Can 46'43"	
♅ Uranus	5 Pis 38'57"	
♆ Neptune	15 Aqu 8'53"	
♇ Pluto	22 Sag 5'44"r	
⚷ True Node	11 Tau 14'37"	
⚷ Chiron	25 Cap 59'29"	

AC 4 Ari 10'   2:14 Tau   9'   3:10 Gem 36'
MC 2 Cap 15'   11:24 Cap 15'   12:22 Aqu 0'

Type 2.GW 2-Jan-2021

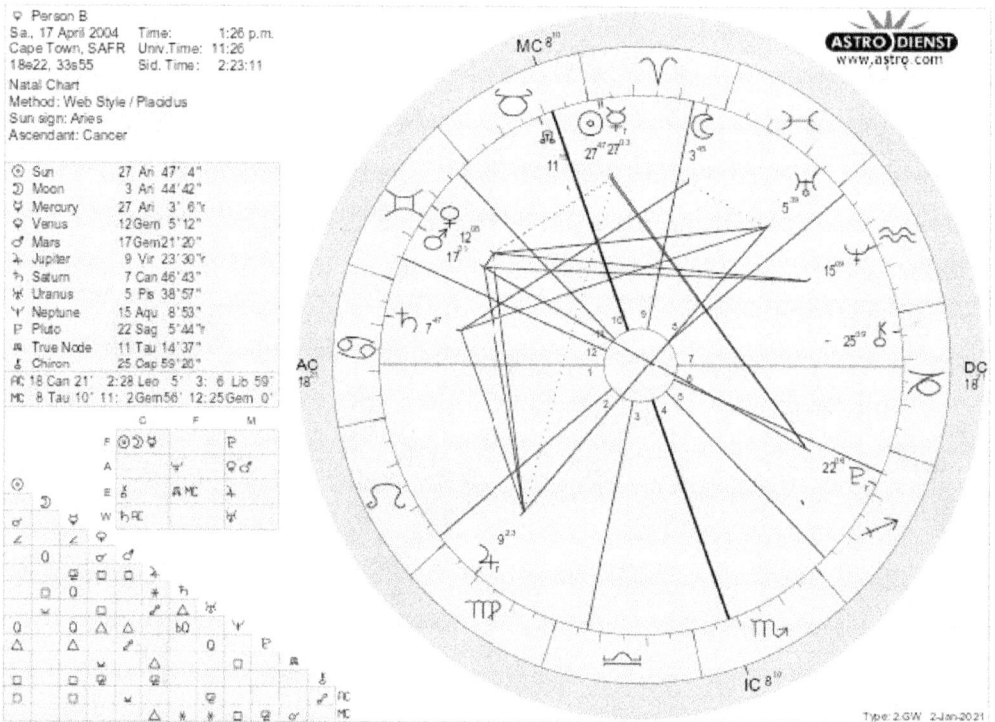

♀ Person B
Sa., 17 April 2004   Time: 1:26 p.m.
Cape Town, SAFR   Univ.Time: 11:26
18e22, 33s55   Sid. Time: 2:23:11
Natal Chart
Method: Web Style / Placidus
Sun sign: Aries
Ascendant: Cancer

⊙ Sun	27 Ari 47' 4"	
☽ Moon	3 Ari 44'42"	
☿ Mercury	27 Ari 3' 6"r	
♀ Venus	12 Gem 5'12"	
♂ Mars	17 Gem 21'20"	
♃ Jupiter	9 Vir 23'30"r	
♄ Saturn	7 Can 46'43"	
♅ Uranus	5 Pis 38'57"	
♆ Neptune	15 Aqu 8'53"	
♇ Pluto	22 Sag 5'44"r	
⚷ True Node	11 Tau 14'37"	
⚷ Chiron	25 Cap 59'28"	

AC 18 Can 21'   2:28 Leo   5'   3: 6 Lib 59'
MC 8 Tau 10'   11: 2 Gem 56'   12:25 Gem 0'

Type 2.GW 2-Jan-2021

Person C

Sa., 17 April 2004   Time: 1:26 p.m.
Cairo, EGYPT   Univ.Time: 11:26
31e15, 30n03   Sid. Time: 3:14:43
Natal Chart
Method: Web Style / Placidus
Sun sign: Aries
Ascendant: Leo

☉ Sun	27 Ari 47' 4"	
☽ Moon	3 Ari 44'42"	
☿ Mercury	27 Ari 3' 6"r	
♀ Venus	12 Gem 5'12"	
♂ Mars	17 Gem 21'20"	
♃ Jupiter	9 Vir 23'30"r	
♄ Saturn	7 Can 46'43"	
♅ Uranus	5 Pis 38'57"	
♆ Neptune	15 Aqu 8'53"	
♇ Pluto	22 Sag 5'44"r	
☊ True Node	11 Tau 14'37"	
⚷ Chiron	25 Cap 59'28"	

AC 24 Leo 19'   2: 19 Vir 26'   3: 18 Lib 42'
MC 21 Tau 7'   11: 24 Gem 1'   12: 25 Can 19'

ASTRO DIENST
www.astro.com

Type: 2 GW   2-Jan-2021

Person D

Sa., 17 April 2004   Time: 8:26 p.m.
Tokyo, JAPAN   Univ.Time: 11:26
139e46, 35n42   Sid. Time: 10:28:47
Natal Chart
Method: Web Style / Placidus
Sun sign: Aries
Ascendant: Scorpio

☉ Sun	27 Ari 47' 4"	
☽ Moon	3 Ari 44'42"	
☿ Mercury	27 Ari 3' 6"r	
♀ Venus	12 Gem 5'12"	
♂ Mars	17 Gem 21'20"	
♃ Jupiter	9 Vir 23'30"r	
♄ Saturn	7 Can 46'43"	
♅ Uranus	5 Pis 38'57"	
♆ Neptune	15 Aqu 8'53"	
♇ Pluto	22 Sag 5'44"r	
☊ True Node	11 Tau 14'37"	
⚷ Chiron	25 Cap 59'20"	

AC 25 Sco 10'   2: 25 Sag 32'   3: 29 Cap 55'
MC 5 Vir 23'   11: 7 Lib 6'   12: 3 Sco 15'

ASTRO DIENST
www.astro.com

Type: 2 GW   2-Jan-2021

Without knowing anything about astrology, it is still easy to see how each of these individual charts are oriented differently with their own distinct character.

Nice Try Cicero

We can now finally and definitively rule out Cicero's first quibble about astrology for three main reasons:

(1)   With such a low likelihood of two strangers being born at the same time and location, it is safe to say that this occurrence is essentially nil.

(2)   Even so, two strangers being born "at the very same instant" in astrology is inconsequential because the parameters that determine a chart's appearance are mathematically determined by a person's birth date, time, and location. In those instances when individuals are born at the same time but in a different location, the astrology charts are oriented differently, producing different manifestations.

(3)   There is evidence to suggest that most sets of twins are born within a long enough timespan to significantly alter the astrological chart of one twin compared to the other.

Already, you can start to see that astrology can and should be approached from this type of perspective. When we approach it this way, valid scientific arguments that support astrology can start to be respected and observed. But we're not done yet. There is still more to Cicero's argument that we need to address.

Cicero's Next Point

Cicero's next objection is that people born at the same time are unlike the other in "character, career, and destiny." Looking at the first part of our argument, it should be noted that Cicero's statement is no longer based within probable reality. We have already demonstrated that two people meeting Cicero's standards of being born at the "very same instant" is both statistically improbable and astrologically immaterial. Nevertheless, let us put the next segment of Cicero's paradigm to the test and put him to rest by comparing similar birth days of three different well-known individuals with a Wikipedia page so we can find correlative evidence.

The Butcher, the Baker, the Candlestick Maker

On February 2, 1987, 03:22 Coordinated Universal Time (UTC), international soccer player Gerard Piqué was born in Barcelona, Spain. Eight hours later, at 11:04 UTC, American actor, Martin Spangjers, was born in Tucson, Arizona. Finally, at 16:20 UTC, thirteen hours after Gerard and five hours after Martin, professional motorcyclist Johnathon Rea was born in Ballymena, Ireland. Three distinctly unique individuals from three far-off parts of the world, all born within the first half of February 2, 1987, starting with the subtle breaking of twilight from the night before with Mr. Piqué, and ending with Mr. Rea right when the sun was just about to begin its descent into the horizon. According to Cicero, if astrology has no legitimate basis, then all three of these individuals will be "unlike in character, career, and destiny. . ." Let's see if this is accurate.

We will start with their careers. On the surface, Cicero's parameter holds true as all three of these men work within three completely different fields. However, I would argue that one's cultural influences, which are based upon one's nationality, make available certain professions for some, and a different list of potential paths for another, and should be considered.

For example, soccer is more heavily emphasized within Mr. Piqué's culture having hailed from Spain. Mr. Spanjers, being American, would simply not have had that career path as readily available as it was for Mr. Piqué. Similarly, Mr. Spanjers' proximity to Hollywood gave him the opportunity to become a film actor, which again, is heavily based upon his culture's emphasis toward the film industry, along with his physical proximity to Los Angeles. I would further argue that cultural norms, interests, and opportunities are too diverse to allow for two individuals in question to possess specifically identical jobs. Again, we see a standard from Cicero that seems unreasonable when comparing people from different nationalities.

Still, it is true that there are similar professions that exists within the diverse spectrum of cultures, such as teachers, farmers, and doctors, but I would once again reiterate that all three of the individuals above were not born "at the exact moment" and cannot possibly be born within the same culture (location) based upon our statistical thought experiments that have been previously mentioned. Despite cultural differences, numerous similarities are observed when comparing a soccer player, an actor, and a motorcycle racer. They all:

(1)   Involve performing in front of a crowd.

(2)   Need individual patronage, support, and representation.

(3)   Have a fan base.

(4)   Entail fast-paced environments with high-pressure situations.

(5)   Call for different forms of athleticism/physicality.

(6)   Involve working as a team/ensemble while receiving individual glory.

(7)   Require charisma and ability to work with the public/media.

(8)   Are highly competitive and specialized professions.

(9)   Include unpredictable and unstable job security.

(10)   Recognize personal individuality as part of their public persona.

(11)   Necessitate interacting with the public.

Even though these men were born hours apart from one another, they were born on the same day. The commonalities between all three of these professions cannot be ignored. Therefore, this list disproves Cicero's objection that people born at the same time are unlike in "character, career, and destiny."

Is Life Truly Written in the Stars? Cicero Says, "Hell No!"

The next stipulation Cicero points out is destiny. Indeed, some would argue that the discussion of destiny and astrology's ability to "predict" future events breaches the realm of sorcery. Ok, I give up. Just burn me at the stake already.

But come to think of it, scientists create mathematical models that can "predict" certain outcomes in chemical, biological, and physical reactions all the time. When scientists predict statistically probable events such as these, do we burn them at the stake as heretics? No, because these realms of scientific speculation and exploration are accepted as legitimate within our culture. Astrology, sadly, is not.

However, I would argue that an astrologer's ability to use mathematical data in order to predict future events does not differ from a physicist who can predict the force of an impact, a chemist who can predict the reaction of a compound, or when a biologist can predict how a cell will respond to a certain hormone. In this same light, using astrological methodologies, I will now correlate specifically fated (or destined) events of these three individuals and demonstrate that they not only occurred at the same time, but they manifested very similar circumstances.

(1) 2002-2005. All three individuals were "learning the ropes" of their professions which climaxed in 2005/2006.

    a. Mr. Piqué debuted with Manchester United in 2004, FA Cup Debut in 2005, and his first league start in 2006.

    b. Mr. Spanjers was performing his most notable adolescent role in the show *Eight Simple Rules* from 2002 to 2005, while guest staring in other shows during this time. After 2005, Mr. Spanjers transitioned into more serious adult roles in shows like the substantially popular *Grey's Anatomy* and *True Blood*.

    c. Mr. Rea began on the British circuit in 2003, demonstrating his potential as a legitimate contender finishing sixteenth in 2005.

(2) During this time, all three individuals received a major shift in their career from other people's misfortune or death.

    a. Mr. Piqué's first league start only occurred because starting right-back Gary Neville was injured in 2006.

    b. Three episodes into filming *Eight Simple Rules,* main character John Ritter suddenly died in 2003, drastically altering the overarching plot for the rest of the season.

    c. In 2005, a junior teammate of Mr. Rea died in a crash.

(3) 2011-2012. Two of the three individuals experienced serious romances and marriages.

    a. In 2011, Mr. Piqué began dating singer-songwriter Shakira.

    b. (Mr. Spanjers' only publicly known romance involves Ally Gasparian in 2016.)

    c. Mr. Rea married his wife, Tatia, in 2012.

(4)   2017. All three individuals received national attention and recognition.

   a.   In 2017, Mr. Piqué became heavily involved in the Catalan Independence Referendum and was known as a public face for the movement.

   b.   Mr. Spanjers received eight film awards in 2017; the most he has ever received in a single year.

   c.   In 2017, Mr. Rea was appointed a Member of the Order of the British Empire.

(5)   2019. All three individuals experienced substantial public exposure for better or for worse relating to their countries of birth.

   a.   In 2019, Mr. Piqué had to pay 2.1 million after being exposed for tax fraud in Spain.

   b.   In 2019, Mr. Spanjers became a prominent supporter and activist for political movements such as Medicare for All and the Dakota Access Pipeline in the United States.

   c.   In 2019, Mr. Rea was conferred an honorary doctorate from Queen's University Belfast.

Although these three individuals were born just hours apart on different parts of the globe, all three of them experienced similar events during the same periods of time, proving that astrology not only possess the utility to correctly predict fated events, it also proves that these events are shared by people who possess similar potentialities based upon their proximity in birth time and date.

The statistical probability that all three of these individuals experienced similar events at similar times goes beyond the realm of coincidence, and the scientific approach was used to reach this conclusion.

What About Character?

Again, enter the skeptic, enraged as ever, shaking both fists in a fury as they watch their conceptualizations of astrology break down before their very eyes. They finally retort, "You fool! You cannot possibly demonstrate that all three of these individuals possess the same exact personality due to the uniqueness of the individual." To which I would reply, "You're right."

The caveat of character is admittingly the hardest to prove, even though analyzing one's character is a major reason people are drawn to astrology. As such, one's character can only be confirmed by one's closest confidants, therapists, and the individuals themselves. We are therefore now entering the world of inference. The reason I chose three individuals born on February 2, 1987, is that they were born on the same day as someone I know extremely well—myself. Yes, I too was born on February 2, 1987.

I am certain that if I were to make twenty statements about my own personality and character, there would be an overall agreement between me and these other three individuals. Again, there is no way to prove this hypothesis without actually following through, but this at least shows how one could devise an actual study to determine if similarities do exist. I would absolutely welcome this type of study.

So yes, it is difficult to prove that our characteristics are similar without interviewing all of us in confidence. Nevertheless, we have already observed correlative accuracy when it comes to destiny and career, so it is not a far stretch to say that commonalities also exist between us four in terms of our personality and psychology. To understand how this is possible, let us observe all four of our birth charts side by side and note the commonalities between them (Fig. INT-3).

FIGURE INT-3. Birth Charts of Mr. Piqué, Spanjers, Rea, and myself, all born February 2, 1987 UTC

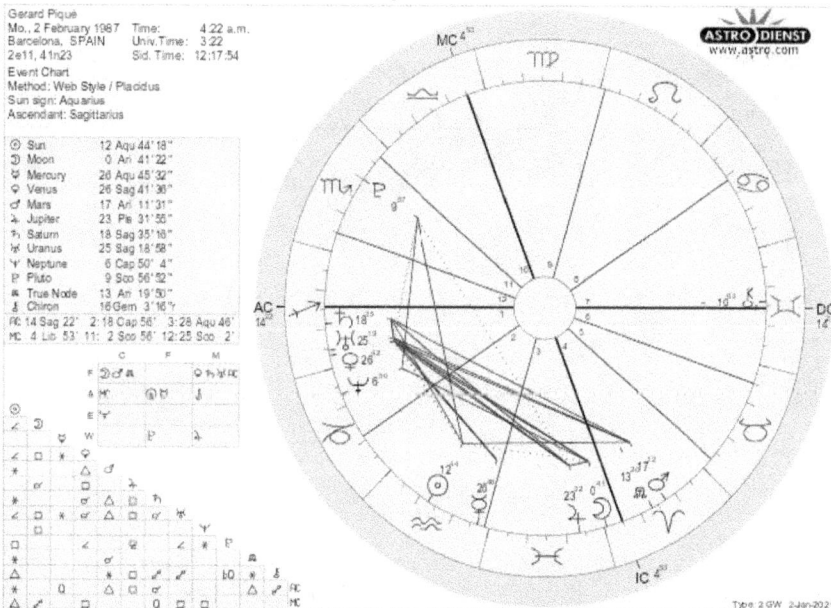

Jonathan Rea
Mo., 2 February 1987   Time: 4:20 p.m.
Ballymena, NIRE (UK)   Univ.Time: 16:20
6w17, 54n52   Sid. Time: 0:44:10
Event Chart
Method: Web Style / Placidus
Sun sign: Aquarius
Ascendant: Leo

☉	Sun	13 Aqu 17'12"
☽	Moon	7 Ari 59'53"
☿	Mercury	27 Aqu 39'40"
♀	Venus	27 Sag 17'21"
♂	Mars	17 Ari 34' 5"
♃	Jupiter	23 Pis 38'48"
♄	Saturn	18 Sag 38' 1"
♅	Uranus	25 Sag 20'27"
♆	Neptune	6 Cap 51' 6"
♇	Pluto	9 Sco 57' 3"
☊	True Node	13 Ari 19'12"
⚷	Chiron	16 Gem 2'29"r

AC 7 Leo 3' 2:22 Leo 32' 3:12 Vir 55'
MC 12 Ari 0' 11:22 Tau 54' 12: 5 Can 43'

ASTRO DIENST
www.astro.com

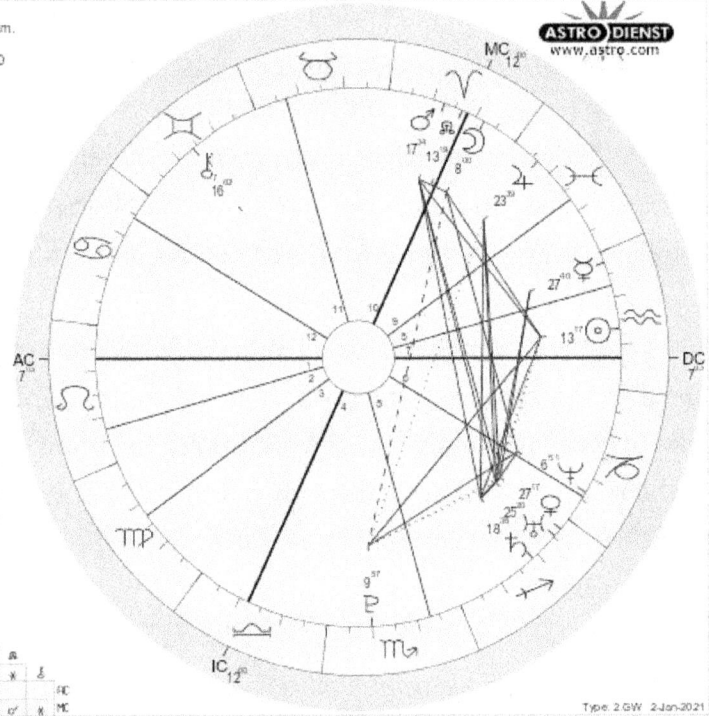

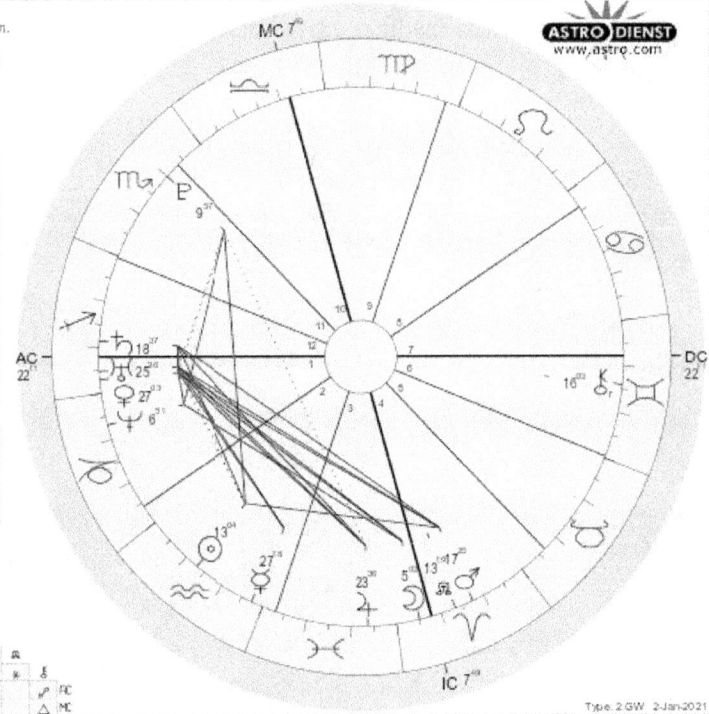

Type: 2.GW 2-Jan-2021

Martin Spanjers
Mo., 2 February 1987   Time: 4:04 a.m.
Tucson, AZ (US)   Univ.Time: 11:04
110w56, 32n13   Sid. Time: 12:28:42
Event Chart
Method: Web Style / Placidus
Sun sign: Aquarius
Ascendant: Sagittarius

☉	Sun	13 Aqu 3'50"
☽	Moon	5 Ari 2'47"
☿	Mercury	27 Aqu 17'44"
♀	Venus	27 Sag 2'49"
♂	Mars	17 Ari 24'55"
♃	Jupiter	23 Pis 36' 0"
♄	Saturn	18 Sag 36'54"
♅	Uranus	25 Sag 19'51"
♆	Neptune	6 Cap 50'41"
♇	Pluto	9 Sco 56'59"
☊	True Node	13 Ari 19'23"
⚷	Chiron	16 Gem 2'48"r

AC 22 Sag 11' 2:25 Cap 52' 3: 3 Pis 1'
MC 7 Lib 49' 11: 6 Sco 33' 12: 0 Sag 23'

ASTRO DIENST
www.astro.com

Type: 2.GW 2-Jan-2021

♂ Myself
Mo., 2 February 1987 Time: 7:21 p.m.
Anaheim, CA (US) Univ. Time: 3:21ᵤₜ
117w55, 33n50 Sid. Time: 4:20:27
Natal Chart
Method: Web Style / Placidus
Sun sign: Aquarius
Ascendant: Virgo

⊙ Sun 13 Aqu 45' 9"
☽ Moon 14 Ari 5'57"
☿ Mercury 28 Aqu 25'18"
♀ Venus 27 Sag 47'46"
♂ Mars 17 Ari 53'16"
♃ Jupiter 23 Pis 44'40"
♄ Saturn 18 Sag 40'19"
♅ Uranus 25 Sag 21'42"
♆ Neptune 6 Cap 51'59"
♇ Pluto 9 Sco 57'12"
⚷ True Node 13 Ari 19' 5"d
⚷ Chiron 16 Gem 1'49"r
AC 9 Vir 3' 2: 4 Lib 40' 3: 4 Sco 25'
MC 6 Gem 57' 11: 9 Can 47' 12: 10 Leo 48'

ASTRO DIENST
www.astro.com

MC 6°⁵⁷'

AC

DC

IC 6°⁵⁷'

Type: 2 GW 2-Jan-2021

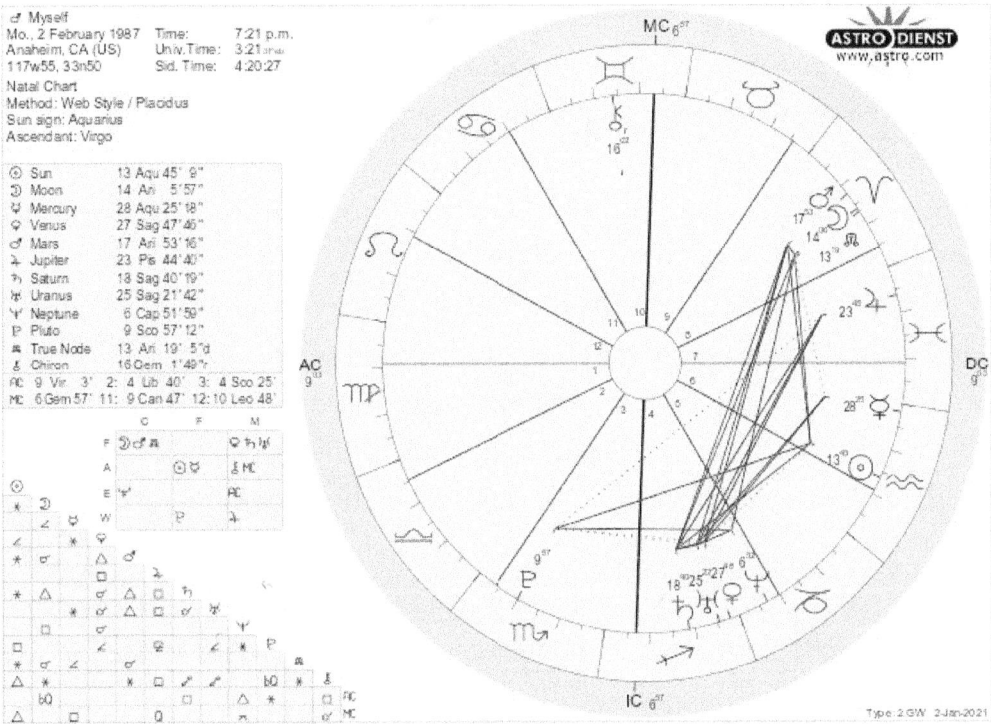

Just as we have observed in our theoretical case studies in Figure INT-1, all four of our charts have completely different orientations due to our various locations around the globe, even though we were all born on the same day. Even so, there are similarities between all four charts that cannot be ignored. Namely, every single one of our planets is oriented at the same location within the zodiac. We each have a Sun in Aquarius (⊙♒), a Moon in Aries (☽♈), a Mercury in Aquarius (☿♒), a Venus, Uranus, and Saturn in Sagittarius (♀♐, ♅♐, ♄♐), a Mars in Aries (♂♈), a Neptune in Capricorn (♆♑), and a Pluto in Scorpio (♇♏). Due to this similarity, the angles that these planets make to one another, which are called aspects, are also the same. This is observed by the grid on the lower left-hand corner of each chart above (FIG. INT-3) called the aspectarian. If you compare all four of our aspectarians to one another, you will find that we possess practically the same exact planetary angles (aspects) which accounts for our similarities both in terms of personality and the timing of events. The difference, as seen in the case studies with the twins in Figure INT-1, comes with how these planets are oriented within the sky map subdivisions, the houses, and the darker lines within the chart, the cardinal points.

For example, Mr. Piqué and Spanjers have their Sun in the 2nd house, but Mr. Rea has his Sun in the 7th house, and I have the Sun in the 6th house. Just as it is with twins, although we possess the same Sun placement relative to the zodiac, these different house placements will cause the Sun's energy to manifest within different realms of our life experiences. Similarly, Mr. Piqué and Spanjers have a Sagittarius rising, Mr. Rea is a Leo rising, and I am a Virgo rising. Just as it was with the twins, this emphasizes certain planets over others, which marks some of the differences in our personalities, physical appearance, and the realms of our lives that are emphasized or deemphasized. Nevertheless, the core foundation as to who we are as individuals, along with the timing of our life events, are similar and accurate due to all of us being born on the same day.

Putting Cicero to Rest

Alright, we've done it. We've devised a strong and formidable argument that explains why astrology works. To reiterate, let us one more time, with immense satisfaction, demonstrate how we fully countered every aspect of Cicero's criticism using the argument we have just presented.

The first issue we addressed was with Cicero's requirement of individuals being born "at the very same instant." Astrological computations consider geographical latitude and longitude in addition to one's birth date and time. Therefore, it is inconsequential if the two individuals in question are born at the very same instant. Even so, using statistical data, it was demonstrated that the probability of two strangers being born at the same exact time and location to be 0.00024%. or nil. In the case of twins, the mean time between births, 21 minutes, is substantial enough to alter the chart's shape and character where two individual personalities are expressed even though similar life events can nevertheless occur.

Next, Cicro claims that people born at similar times are dissimilar in career. Due to the low probability of two strangers being born at the same place and location, it is safe to assume that individuals are raised within different cultures and nationalities. Due to this fact, there are some professions that are readily available in some countries that might not be available in others. Therefore, we cannot expect a high probability of two strangers from two different nationalities to possess similar careers even if they were born at the same moment.

Even though there are professions that do cross national barriers, national and cultural influences cannot be ignored. This is therefore an unrealistic parameter set by Cicero. Still, when comparing individuals who were born on the same day, similarities are observed and correlated when the literal title of the job is removed, and the overall themes of the professions are observed. When this is performed, similarities and consistencies do exist.

Cicero then contends that the lives of individuals born at similar times are dissimilar in destiny. Observing three individuals who were born within a 24-hour time span showed that all three had similarly fated events at the same point in time. The accuracy of the case study regarding four individuals born February 2, 1987, rules out the chances of pure coincidence. The empirical scientific method was used and therefore constitutes as legitimate evidence against Cicero's argument.

Finally, Cicero claims that individuals born at similar times to be dissimilar in character. This is the hardest to prove empirically. The only way to confirm these inferences is to survey the other individuals within the case study. However, given that similarities have already been demonstrated empirically through destined events and similarities in vocation, it is safe to assume that similarities can also exist through character. This was further demonstrated when all four birth charts were compared and similarities in planetary placements along the zodiac and aspect patterns we observed. Additionally, noting the differences in terms of rising signs and house placements still adds individuality to these four similar charts.

Bringing it Home

For probably the first time in an astrology book, we have now presented statistically based thought experiments, including real case studies, theoretical case studies, and empirical correlative evidence, to suggest that one's individual character, destiny, and life goals are indeed heavily influenced not only by one's time and date of birth, but by their location as well.

Individuals who are born within similar time spans have shown to possess strikingly accurate similarities in their careers and destiny. Therefore, the planetary, solar, and lunar energies that exist during one's moment of birth, and their relative locations along the zodiac, firmly binds the individual into an accurately destined timetable along with a pre-determined psychological makeup. Both of these influences are just as profound as they are real, and are just as existential as they are internal.

Finally, two thousand years after the fact, it is finally proven and safe to say that the time of birth has *everything* to do in determining an individual's course in life, effectively nullifying Cicero's paradigm once and for all.

It's Time to Get Real With Y'all

The inherent and assumed skepticism and cynicism that has been focused toward astrology has plagued this study for far too long. Why do people criticize astrology so much? Why do people outright shun what they have not tried themselves? In my opinion, their abject dismissal stems from a fear of control and a fear of the unknown.

Fear of Control

Generally speaking, individuals do not like to be told they are sometimes not the masters of their own destinies. We will discuss free will and fate later in this volume, but it is important to understand that just because an event appears to be fated does not necessarily mean that the individual did not possess any freedom that led them to that "fated" event. In other words, an event can seem fated, but it only seems to be so because the individual was motivated and acted upon their unconscious mind, which constantly begs to be unearthed and understood. This is a core ideal of Jungian psychology and a core principle within astrology.

We experience fear of losing control through fated events such as the death of a loved one, an accident, or a traumatic life event, one always has the free will to react to these external forces as they so desire. Therefore, the issue is not about having free will or autonomy, but how the individual has not been flexible or introspective enough to surrender to the things they cannot control, along with their inability to analyze why they were not able to do so. But then again, how many times has a death, an illness, or hitting rock bottom caused an individual to "wake up" and start to reevaluate their life's priorities and outlook? According to astrological theory, and as we have seen in the three individuals born on the same February 2, 1987 above, yes, certain life events are inevitable and will be felt at specific moments in a person's life. However, the individual's own preparation and understanding can make difficult life experiences easier to comprehend and overcome. With astrology, it pays to be proactive.

Fear of the Unknown

In my opinion, one of the most significant reasons astrology has been shunned is because it is very difficult for an individual to let go of control over their ego and life direction. The study of astrology insists that you be open, flexible, and understanding to the natural ebb and flow of life while constantly striving to improve and understand your true self. That way, fated events are not as severe because the true self, warts and all, is slowly being realized by the individual. It is only the fear of the unknown self and fear of control that immediately deters someone from the healing potential that is latent within astrology.

Fear of the unknown is more prevalent within the minds of individuals who reject astrology than they themselves even realize. Astrology is a journey of self-discovery. Therefore, one cannot explore astrology without also probing into their own personal philosophy when it comes to intense topics like the existence of a soul, God, karma, reincarnation, and even the meaning of life itself.

This is not to say that you need to believe in these sorts of things. Astrology is not a belief system. Still, inquiries and exploration into these incorporeal realms are, nevertheless, unavoidable. In my opinion, it is difficult for individuals to investigate these topics whether or not they believe in their existence. Inevitably, astrology will cause an individual to reevaluate their outlook on life. Instead of taking the dive into these more ethereal topics and being open to new possibilities and personal evolution, most people outrightly shun what they do not fully understand without looking into it firsthand.

This is what I would say to any skeptic: You cannot say it does not work, you cannot say it does not provide any advantages, and you cannot say it is illegitimate without first attempting to explore astrology firsthand. Until that time, any stringent opinion you have about astrology is, in my eyes, invalid until you have put in the objective work yourself.

Now it's your turn

Just as I was able to find certain individuals that share the same birthday as me, you also can look up your own "astro-twins" by using the website astro.com (Table INT-1).

TABLE INT-1. How to find your Astro-twins on astro.com

(1)	Obtain your birth certificate and make sure it displays the time of birth [NOTE: *It is vitally important you do not use any other birth time other than the time on your birth certificate. It does not matter what time your Mom or Dad said you were born. The time that is only important is when the Doctor that delivered you officially declared you alive on this planet.*]
(2)	Go to astro.com and make an account
(3)	Click on the ICON on the upper left corner, then select the FREE HOROSCOPE tab and under HOROSCOPE DRAWINGS & DATA select CHART DRAWING, ASCENDANT
(4)	Click on + ADD to add a new person
(5)	Input your Name and birth information (date, time, and location)
(6)	Click CONTINUE which will then show you your computed birth chart
(7)	On the upper left-hand corner of the chart, confirm that your birth data is correct
(8)	Once again, go to the FREE HOROSCOPE tab and under HOROSCOPE DRAWINGS & DATA select YOUR ASTRO-TWINS
(9)	You will then find an extensive list of individuals that share the same birth data as you with the closest matches on top.

Once you have determined your astro-twins, look up their Wikipedia pages, and see if you can find any correlations around their life events and personality to your own. This is a sure and quick way you can witness and observe astrology in action. If doing this little experiment piqued your interest, the next step is to use the tools and information inside this book series to obtain an even deeper understanding of this wonderful world we like to call: *astrology*.

The Proof Is in the Pudding

This series of books is a culmination of the previous decade and a half of my life. During that time, I became certified in astrology, taught classes, wrote articles, gave lectures, helped clients, read countless books, and studied with some of the best in the profession. You will learn methods that I have personally created and perfected over the years that I use on a daily basis. It is my hope that by the time you have finished Book I, you will understand and possess a core foundational knowledge of astrology that you can use not only in your own life, but in the lives of others if you decide to become an astrologer yourself.

All you need to possess is a willingness to learn, honesty to see your true colors, the tenacity to learn from your mistakes, and an open mind to finally see the true essence and potentiality of astrology, which has mostly been dormant for centuries only to be understood by the select few who have dared to explore the vast workings of our universe and our place within.

This first book is composed of three parts where we learn about the foundational theory, ideas, and energies surrounding astrology. You will also learn how to apply this knowledge into your daily life.

In **Part I,** we will establish a core understanding of astrology by exploring its fundamental theory and methods. We will discuss the main principles within astrology, along with its connection to fate, free will, karma, and the soul. We will also explore the main themes of Jungian psychology and how they are applied into modern-day astrology. Additionally, we will explore and discuss common pitfalls, useful tips, essential books, and necessary tools.

Part II covers the main astrological symbols and archetypes: the signs, planets, houses, aspects, and cardinal points. Traditional rulerships and rules from ancient astrology that are useful in modern-day astrology will also be examined.

Part III covers the use of astrology as a calendar and will cover hourly, daily, monthly, and annual astrological events. This includes the moon cycle, void of course moons, retrogrades, eclipses, and planetary hours.

Time to Ponder

Before we take the deep dive into this world, I would like you to take a moment and ponder a few things. We are already one-quarter of the way into the twenty-first century. That's insane. As a human race, where are we headed? As an individual, where are you headed? What kind of future are we co-creating? What kind of future do we want to create? What kind of future do you want to create? Before we can answer any of these questions, before we can right any of the wrongs of this world and, as we say in the United States, strive for "a more perfect union" between ourselves and each other, we need first to remember what the Persian philosopher Rumi once said all those years ago:

> Yesterday I was so clever, so I wanted to change the world.
> Today, I am wise, so I am changing myself.

Or for a more modern interpretation, what the Klingon warrior Lieutenant Worf from *Star Trek: The Next Generation once said all those years ago:*

> You look for the battles in the wrong places. The true test of a warrior is not without; it is within. Here, here is where we meet the challenge. It is the weaknesses in here a warrior must overcome.

Before we can expect the world to change, we first need to change ourselves. Before we can purge the world of chaos and wrongdoing, we must first purge out our own grosser tendencies and habits and admit the wrongdoings we have done ourselves. Before we have any right to tell anyone how to live their lives, we first need to look at our own life and make sure we are completely conscious and steadfast in our own journey.

This is the true test of the twenty-first century and the test of any true warrior. Pick up your shield, enter the darkness of your unconscious mind, and find the light within yourself. Then, and only then, can you call yourself an astrologer and a true agent of change. I am with you on that battlefield. I have been fighting that fight for over a decade now and still haven't figured it out completely. But it is the work that must be done. This is your birthright. Now go and light the way with truth, forgiveness, and understanding. Once you do this, others will surely follow. This book is simply the torch of knowledge and wisdom that was passed down to me from the lineage of astrologers that came before me. I now humbly pass that torch to you. All I ask is that you strive every day to know yourself, and if you do, the knowledge within these books will be worth its weight in gold.

To the future, which has yet to be written,

PART I

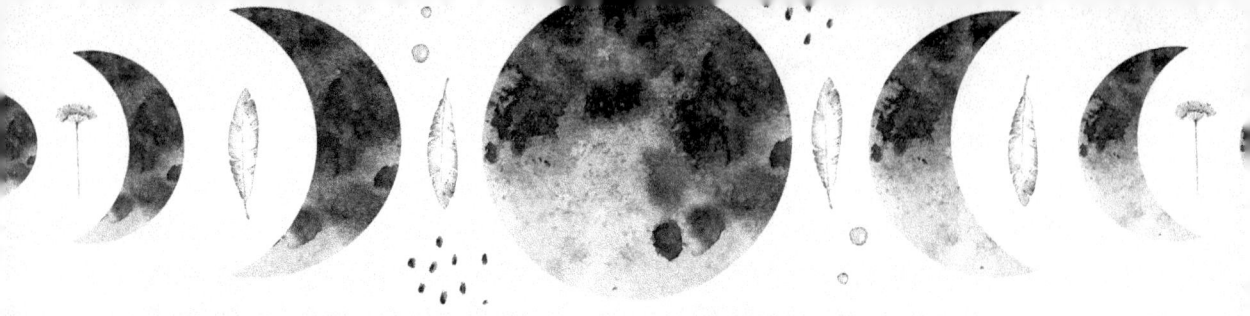

ASTROLOGICAL FRAMEWORK

"Astrology's roots lie in an ancient world-view which perceived the universe as a single living organism, animated by divine order and intelligence"

—Liz Greene, Renowned Astrologer

The Main Framework

There are many types of astrology practices out there, and every one has their own variation on the same theme while contributing something individualistic to the whole. Just take a look at this list of eleven sub-disciplines that exist within astrology (Table I-1).

TABLE I-1. Various Astrological Sub-Disciplines with
Description [NOTE: Not an extensive list.]

SUB-DISCIPLINE	PRIMARY FOCUS
NATAL	The most common study. Natal astrology focuses on one's psychology and life events by examining the natal chart, the transiting chart, and the progressed chart. This study is the primary focus of this book series.
HORARY	Derived for the Latin word meaning "hour", horary is a technique where a question is queried, and the astrologer then erects a chart at that precise moment the question was asked. From the information within that chart, one can discover the answer to their question. Fifteenth-century astrologer, William Lilly, was paramount in distilling this ancient tradition into a newer framework. There are stories where he would have his friends hide certain items and would then erect a horary chart to find their location.
MEDICAL	The study of predicting and healing physical ailments by observing the natal and transit chart through an interpretive lens of the various parts of the body and their respective planetary and sign rulerships.
ELECTIONAL	Deriving from the Latin word for "to pick out," electional astrology consists of determining specific times, dates, and locations for significant events such as weddings, the starting of a business, and filing a lawsuit.

SUB-DISCIPLINE	PRIMARY FOCUS
ASTROECONOMICS	This branch observes correlations to the stock market along with the birth chart of businesses in order to predict when the market will become bearish or bullish, or when a business is about to enter a time of financial success or failure. If you think big business does not use this to their advantage, remember it was J.P. Morgan who once famously said, "Millionaires do not use astrologers; billionaires do."
ASTROCARTOGRAPHY	As the planets travel around the planet, they make certain path lines all around the globe. These specific lines can indicate places where an individual could find more success, difficulty, a community, or just a place for a good vacation.
JYOTISH	Three thousand years older than the Western tradition, Jyotish is an astrological system that is conservatively estimated to have developed in India about five thousand years ago.[6]
ASTROGEOGRAPHY	More recently, astrological scientists have been trying to create predictive models of astrology that can determine the timing of geographical phenomena such as earthquakes, tsunamis, and tornadoes.
RELATIONSHIP	This field focuses on the strengths, weaknesses, and longevity of individuals that are in a relationship whether it be romantic, business, or familial. This Is mostly done by working with the composite and bi-wheel charts.
ARCHETYPAL	This tradition sprang out of the 1970s with astrological authors like Liz Greene, Robert Hand, Steven Arroyo, and academic Joseph Campbell. This branch is heavily focused on Jungian psychological theory in that planetary archetypes and mythologies are echoed in both the individual and global psychology.

6   Shyamasundara Dasa, *A Brief History of Jyotish*, 2021, https://shyamasund-aradasa.com/jyotish/what_is_jyotish/jyotish_history.html.

SUB-DISCIPLINE	PRIMARY FOCUS
EVOLUTIONARY	According to evolutionary astrology founders Steven Forrest and Jeffery Wolf Green, this branch is less of a technical methodology and more of a philosophical framework that assumes some metaphysical rules such as reincarnation, a soul's evolutionary journey from one lifetime to the next, and that the individual possesses a high degree of external and internal autonomy.[7]

When it comes to the framework of this book, it is based upon the fundamental rules of natal astrology with the philosophical backing of archetypal and evolutionary theories. Mainly, that the natal chart does indicate a predetermined psychology based upon Jungian archetypes and that one's individual psychology encounters specifically timed events. Additionally, my astrological approach also considers the idea that one's psychology is meant to be understood and improved upon from these events in order to be the primary objective for the individual during their lifetime. My methods also incorporate realms of traditional astrology. We will be discussing traditional rulerships and rules later.

As you can see, the astrologer has a multitude of tools within their toolbox to choose from when it comes to approaching an astrology chart. This book is simply my own method that I have created by mixing and matching what works for me, and I would encourage you to do the same over time. In the meantime, it is my hope that this book series acts as a foundational cornerstone as you begin your exploration into this vast and vibrant study. So, without further ado, let us get into our first topic.

---

7   Steven Forrest. *What is Evolutionary Astrology?* 2021, https://www.forrestastrology.com/pages/what-is-evolutionary-astrology.

SECTION 1—ASTROLOGY AS A HUMAN TRADITION

Before Time was Time

What we now call astrology, or more specifically western astrology, is a culmination of various cultures, mythologies, and systems that span as far east as India and Egypt, as far West as Rome and Greece, and everything in between. It also spans as far as the earliest of humanity thirty-two thousand years into our past where the first seeds of astrological concepts such as animism and celestial tracking were born. Let us now go on a journey and see how astrology came to be from its inception to the present day.

Pre-Civilization: 32,000 BC–3000 BC The Paleolithic Astrologer

One of the earliest archeological evidence of the human race tracking celestial bodies in the form of a calendar is derived from the lunar trackers of European Aurignacians, c. 32,000 BC. Due to the lack of a formal writing system during this period, there is only so much scientists can deduce in regards to the mindset of this early human society. Nevertheless, the discovery of these lunar trackers, which have been etched into stone and animal rib bones, have allowed scientists to recognize and study early calendar systems.

. . . that there are phases of the moon and seasons of the year that can be counted—that should be counted because they are important – is profound. . .What [archeologists] uncovered is the intuitive discovery of mathematical sets and the application of those sets to the construction of a calendar.[8]

For the longest time, scientists have assumed that the earliest humans were nothing more than an evolved animal with no real capacity for advanced mental processes. These archeological findings have now made it safe to say that early humans not only had the ability for such processes, they were using their skills to correlate human activity with some form of a working celestial calendar.

---

8   "The Oldest Lunar Colanders," 2021 Solar System Exploration Research Virtual Institute, 2021, https://sservi.nasa.gov/articles/oldest-lunar-calendars/.

Our earliest ancestors recorded these events because they recognized their importance. Rather than relying on formal logic or reasoning, they drew upon their intuitive knowing and empirical observation. Instinctively, they understood that these celestial patterns were indeed relevant to their lives here on Earth. With these archeological discoveries, it has now become scientific and archeological fact that our earliest ancestors have been working with celestial time systems for tens of thousands of years.

Sadly, our modern mindset and perception on human history has decided to flatly reject and deny this historical truth due to the explicit bias the academic community has established toward astrology. When we deny this past, we are not only ignoring historical and scientific facts, we are also cutting ourselves off from some of our oldest human heritage.

We must also recall that ancient temples being constructed at that time were aligned to significant celestial events, producing our oldest examples of solar (annual) calendars. For example, construction of Stonehenge started in approximately 31,00 BC, and was aligned to the sunset of the winter solstice and the opposing sunrise of the summer solstice. These two points during the year were significant to early humans because it was essential for them to know when the days would get shorter and colder, or when the days would get longer and warmer, so that they could survive and plan accordingly.

In addition to this practical use, monuments like Stonehenge allowed for humanity to establish a mythology around the Sun and other celestial bodies. Attributing spiritual energies to objects such as these initiated one of the oldest religious and philosophical ideals: animism. This ideology involves the universal concept that every living and nonliving thing, from the birds in the sky to a grain of sand on the beach, is alive and connected through one gigantic web of life.

This cosmic bond between humanity and nature was so strong and universally understood that practically all early developing cultures possessed this concept as a primary foundation within their society. As these cultures evolved, these bonds only became stronger and more complex in tandem with astrology, which similarly developed in complexity and scientific accuracy.

Mesopotamia: 2300 BC–AD 141
Astrology as a System is Formed

Ancient Mesopotamia developed one of the first working astrological systems, c. 1800 BC–1200 BC, because to them, understanding and predicting earthly events was essential to their king's ability to rule. This paved the way for astrology to become a fundamental pillar within Mesopotamian society and governance. Mesopotamian priests handled the documentation and interpretation of celestial phenomena, which was then communicated to the king so that his people could live happier lives.

These priests developed a scientifically sound record system that objectively observed and correlated celestial events to earthly events through a series of tablets called the *Enuma Anu Enlil*. These tablets contained celestial correlations to Mesopotamian life, such as floods, deaths, poor crops, and so forth. Modern academics compare the *Enuma Anu Enlil* to aspects of modern science.

. . . it shares some of the defining traits of modern science: it is objective and value-free, it operates according to known rules, and its data are considered universally valid and can be looked up in written tabulations.[9]

Astrology, even in its earliest form, was deeply rooted in the collection, observation, and analysis of celestial data. Here is an example of an entry:

If the moon becomes visible on the first day: reliable speech; the land will be happy. If the day reaches its normal length: a reign of long days. If the moon at its appearance wears a crown: the king will reach the highest rank.[10]

The Mesopotamians also created mythologies around the seven traditional planets in astrology, giving humanity one of our initial understandings into the nature of the planets and their influences within the Western tradition. As Mesopotamian culture progressed, so did their mathematical measurements. By 400 BC, they were creating the first versions of ephemerides, which catalogued

---

9   Ulla Koch-Westenholz, *Mesopotamian Astrology*, vol.19, (Museum Tusculanum Press, 1995), 13.

10   Hermann Hunger, ed., State Archives of Assyria, *Astrological reports to Assyrian kings*, vol. 8, (State Archives of Assyria, 1992).

future planetary placements with astounding accuracy.[11] The Mesopotamians also created a vast star map, where we can observe the primary outline of the zodiac along with other surrounding constellations. However, during this time, there was no Libra constellation. Instead, Libra was considered to be an extension of the claws of the scorpion associated with the sign Scorpio.

Western Astrology is a Mixed Bag

Western astrology is an amalgam of various ancient cultures (both Eastern and Western) beginning with the Mesopotamians and ending with present-day Western philosophy and psychology. Nevertheless, through advancements in technology and culture, the Mesopotamians took the biggest steps into creating a scientific, mythological, and cohesive approach to what we now call western astrology. All subsequent ancient civilizations expanded on the ideas in this foundation and established a more refined and specialized approach. Consequently, more branches of astrological interpretation and application were developed and created over time.

Ancient Greece: 1250 BC – 30 BC
The Bridge to the Ancient World

The conquests of Alexander the Great exposed the Greeks to the cultures and traditions of central Asia, Babylon, Persia, and Syria, which allowed for astrology to migrate from the east to the west, where it was further developed in ancient Greece and Hellenistic Egypt.

The most significant event that led to this melting pot occurred c. 280 BC, when the Babylonian priest Berossus moved to the Greek island of Kos and taught astrology, along with Babylonian culture, to the Greeks. Over time, in ancient Greece, a form of astrology known as Theurgic Astrology was devised. This type of astrology aligned with the Hermetic philosophy, which involved personal transformation and forming an intimate dialogue with the

---

11   K.P. Moesgaard, "Ancient Ephemeris Time in Babylonian Astronomy," *Journal for the History of Astronomy*, 1983, 14(1):47–60, https://doi.org/10.1177/002182868301400104.

divine. Simultaneously, further development into astrology occurred within Hellenistic Egypt.

Hellenistic Egypt: 300 BC–200 BC
The Calendar Becomes Refined

During this time in history, we begin to observe the merging of five great ancient cultures: Egypt, Babylon, the Middle East, India, and Greece, which occurred from the death of Alexander the Great (323 BC) to the emergence of the Roman Empire (31 BC). At the conquest of Egypt by Alexander the Great, the scholarly city Alexandria was founded and became the source of this melting pot. Prior to this event, ancient Egypt had its own working form of a celestial calendar known as the Dendera zodiac.

The Dendera zodiac includes all twelve zodiacal constellations, including Libra, and also includes a division system of thirty-six decans of ten days each. This is the first time we see the astrological year, containing 360 days instead of 365. The number 360 to form one year is more in tune with the annual rotation of the Earth around the Sun. Furthermore, 360 is the number of degrees in a perfect circle, thereby creating a more synchronistic calendar that not only parallels Earth's true annual orbit but also the natural flow of the Sun around the zodiac.

During this time, mostly in the city of Alexandria, the mixture of Mesopotamian, Egyptian, and Greek systems convalesce into what we call Horoscopic (Natal) Astrology. In this system, rules of Horoscopic Astrology mixed with the philosophical approach of Greek Theurgic Astrology. We can declare this hybrid approach to be the first generation of Western Natal Astrology, the most common astrology studied in today's Western world and the tradition explained within this book.

The First Astrology Books

The meshing of these systems and their diverse applications were compiled within the book *Tetrabiblos*, written by the Alexandrian astrologer and astronomer, Claudius Ptolemy. At this point in our story, we sadly see a severe divergence in the modern telling and conceptualization of ancient history.

Astronomers today will attribute a lot of their history to that of Ptolemy, but will refuse to recognize his contributions to the astrological world as well. This is not only inappropriate but also historically inaccurate. Once again, we see the explicit bias toward astrology causing academics to rewrite history to their own terms instead of relying on the objective truths which have already been historically documented and analyzed.

From ancient history up to the European Renaissance, astronomy and astrology were not only interchangeable terms, they were taught to students simultaneously.[12] If you were to read the history lessons provided in a college astronomy textbook today, you would find that authors deliberately attempt to deny and distance this association by discrediting astrology as nothing more than a mere carnival trick. This kind of inaccurate telling has contributed to the severe discrediting of astrology as a serious study. Which, as you have been discovering during this survey of history, couldn't be further from the truth.

Ptolemy's book *Tetrabilos* was the first time western astrology was catalogued and categorized onto a physical record. This work also provided a sound philosophical case for the study of astrology, which was used many times over to justify astrology as a study during the less-enlightened times of the Dark Age. Up until then, the ancient and profound connection between astrology and society was unquestioned, as it was always a part of ancient culture and studied throughout many ancient civilizations.

The damaging schism and criticism toward astrology began when the Roman Empire took its seat as the Western world's superpower. This is when we witness the first among many attempts to disprove astrology with figures like our good old friend Cicero, as well as the waning of astrology's place within philosophical thought and governmental decisions.

---

12   Kenneth Bartlett, *"Education in the Renaissance," The Great Courses Daily*, 2016. https://web.archive.org/web/20170601225458/http://www.thegreatcoursesdaily.com/education-in-the-renaissance/.

Ancient Rome: 753 BC–AD 57
Romans Stop Astrology's Momentum

Rome was exposed to astrology through the Greeks. At the start of the Roman Empire, the new aristocracy embraced astrology. Emperor Tiberius used his birth astrology as a propaganda tool, along with surrounding himself with astrologers, as rulers had been doing for centuries past.[13]

Toward the start of Roman rule, astrology was coupled with the concept of "Chaldean wisdom," which was the Roman vernacular for all things foreign and mystic. At one point in time, astrology was so popular that Roman satirist Juvenal once said, "there are people who cannot appear in public, dine, or bathe, without having first consulted an ephemeris." Sadly, this developing interest and cultivation began to diminish through a campaign whose primary goal was to eliminate astrology and astrologers at all cost.

During the rule of Emperor Claudius, philosophers vigorously attempted to debunk astrology by proposing the theoretical twin scenario as a way to prove astrology as invalid. In fact, there is historical proof that astrology was banned up to eight times.[14] This is the moment in history when Cicero's paradigm went into full effect, because his arguments seemed like a logical conclusion for astrology's supposed ineffectiveness.

Another way Roman propaganda tried to squash astrology within its culture was by portraying astrology as an insignificant and childish hobby of housewives, and nothing a true Roman man would dare bother to consider.[15] Sadly and amazingly, this stereotype is still prevalent today. Eventually, Roman society's outlook on astrology became so unwelcoming and intolerant that astrologers were hunted down and killed.

---

13   Pauline Ripat, "Expelling Misconceptions: Astrologers at Rome." *Journal of Classical Philosophy* 106, no. 2, (2011):115-54. https://www.journals.uchicago.edu/doi/10.1086/659835.

14   Frederick Cramer, *Astrology in Roman Law and Politics* (American Philosophical Society, 1954), 232-48

15   Ripat, "Expelling Misconceptions," 2011.

The Dark Ages: AD 300–AD 1000
Astrology's Hermitage to the East

The traumatic fall of the once encompassing Roman Empire caused complete disarray in Europe. Old knowledge and wisdom vanished from cognizance. It would seem that during this time, the art of western astrology could have been completely lost to the sands of time, but thankfully, this is not the case. Indeed, western astrology owes an enormous debt of gratitude to the cultures of Islam and India during the dark ages. Western astrology was not only preserved by these two cultures, it was further developed and explored.[16]

We are sometimes taught to believe that the Western world developed in some sort of isolated bubble with no real influences from other cultures of the time. However, with the vast trade routes of the first century AD, commonly known as the Silk Road, knowledge was transported and preserved throughout all of Europe, Eurasia, and Asia. It is not hyperbolic to say if it were not for the Eastern cultures preserving western astrology, the previous centuries of development into this science could have been lost forever. Vedic scholars would have no quarrels with preserving this knowledge as they themselves already had a working astrological system approximately 3,000 years older before western astrology even came into existence with the Babylonians.

Likewise, in Islamic culture, western astrology's ability to deal with the future stirred up much debate within Islamic philosophy, causing two camps of thought to emerge.[17] The more traditional philosophy dealt with the concept that God is the only one that is aware of the future, and man is not able to predict or comprehend God's will. The other camp, with the aid of using western astrology as proof, debated this long-standing belief in Islamic thought by stating that it is possible to understand God's will and doing so was not blasphemy, but an adoration of this higher knowledge. Just as how western astrology obtained the nodes from Vedic Astrology, certain Islamic points like the point of fortune were also added into western astrology.

---

16   Nicholas Campion, *A History of Western Astrology, Volume 1: The Ancient Word* (Continuum International Publishing Group, 2008), 291.

17   George Saliba, *A History of Arabic Astronomy: Planetary Theories During the Golden Age of Islam,* (New York University Press, 1994). 67-69.

Medieval Europe: AD 500–AD 1500
Astrology Hides in Plain Sight

In Medieval Europe, the Roman Catholic Church became the all-encompassing superpower along with their stringent religious philosophy which did not permit astrology's existence. The Catholic Church needed to maintain absolutism with all things spiritual for the sake of their power. Therefore, the church considered themselves to be the one and only vessel that possessed any truth or divine understanding toward God and personal salvation. Any system or person that claimed they could comprehend God outside of the church was considered blasphemous and incredibly dangerous. Regardless, astrology was able to adapt within these constrictions and a new branch of astrology developed and emerged: medical astrology.

During this time in history, the outlawing of human dissection severely limited medical understanding of the human body and diseases. Astrology was used as a reliable system where doctors carried around special almanacs, allowing them to check the positions of the stars before making a diagnosis. Ancient studies of astrology were translated from Arabic to Latin in the twelfth and thirteenth centuries and soon became a part of everyday medical practice in Europe. These astrological theories incorporated Galenic medicine, which was inherited from the Greek physiologist Galen (AD 129–216).[18] Using astrology within medieval medicine became so prominent that by the end of the 1500s, physicians across Europe were required by law to calculate the position of the moon before carrying out complicated medical procedures such as surgery or bloodletting. It could be deduced that because this form of astrology does not address questions regarding spirituality or the soul's salvation, it was permissible, or at least tolerated, by the Roman Catholic Church.

Still, one of the biggest ironies during the medieval era is that although those in power highly condemned astrology, they themselves were using astrology on a daily basis, just as ancient rulers had done for centuries before them.

---

18 "Astrology and Medicine," *Science and Its Times: Understanding the Social Significance of Scientific Discovery*, Lois Magner, 2000. https://www.encyclopedia.com/science/encyclopedias-almanacs-transcripts-and-maps/astrology-and-medicine.

The most influential astrologer (and astronomer) during this time was Guido Bonatti. He was the personal advisor to Holy Roman Emperor Frederick II and other monarchs of that time who were in direct conflict with the Pope in Rome.[19] In fact, Bonatti was specifically targeted in Dante's *Divine Comedy*, where he is depicted as residing in hell as punishment for using astrology.

Bonatti's famous book, *Liber Astronomiae* (The Book of Astronomy), was written in AD1277 and remained a classic astrology textbook for the next two centuries.[20] Thankfully, Bonatti preserved and expanded upon astrological philosophy and defended the argument contained within the pages of his textbook in public arenas. Bonatti is famously known for winning formal public debates against members of the priesthood. He upheld the validity of astrology as a serious academic study along with its utility for understanding the workings of the universe and the creator. Astrologers like Bonatti maintained a firm ground within European culture during this darker period. Thankfully, with the advent of the Renaissance two hundred years later, astrology's popularity once again reached an all-time high.

European Renaissance: AD 1400 – AD 1650 Astrology Goes on a Journey

The European Renaissance (literally meaning *rebirth*) created an upheaval within social and individual priorities and philosophies. The once prominent focus on the church and salvation that had existed for five hundred years shifted to a focus on humanitarianism, self-awareness, and the arts. In academia during this time, students were taught seven liberal arts, correlating to the seven traditional planets, including astrology.

Classical Greek mythology became an important subject within the arts, cementing the importance of these stories and archetypes into the human culture. Greek influences and inspirations are still observed within the stories we

---

19   *Science Source*, Guido Bonatti: Italian Astronomer and Astrologer, 2025. https://www.sciencesource.com/2009908-guido-bonatti-italian-astronomer-and-astrologer-stock-image-rights-managed.html.

20   Nicholas Campion, *An Introduction to the History of Astrology*, (ISCWA, 1982), 46.

tell in today's world. To this point, a new genre emerged during this era called opera. This new genre initiated a tradition of retelling traditional Greek myths for the stage and continues to this day. According to scholars like Carl Jung and Joseph Campbell, the reason these stories are still preserved within our culture today is because their morals, characters, and themes are just as relevant to our life experiences now as they were for our ancient ancestors and for centuries before they were written.

The most famous, some during his time would say infamous, astrologer of this era was William Lilly, a highly influential individual. William Lilly even played a significant part in the English Civil War of 1644. He was either admired or hated by many members of English parliament, and correctly predicted the 1666 Great Fire of London so accurately, that an investigation committee was established to see if it was Mr. Lilly who had started the fire in the first place.[21]

Mr. Lilly composed an annual almanac that sold thousands of copies a year and wrote a renowned staple within the astrological repertoire: *Christian Astrology*. In this work, Mr. Lilly explores the study of horary astrology, the study of asking a question, erecting a chart at the time of questioning, and discovering an answer based upon that chart. In fact, just for the fun of it, Mr. Lilly would challenge his colleagues by having them hide something of his, and he would then find the item using horary techniques.

Although horary is an ancient study, many ideas from horary continue to be utilized within natal astrology today. Concepts like planetary strengths and weaknesses (dignities and debilities), the natural temperaments of the planets, and the importance of the cardinal points, are all subjects that are helpful to the study of natal astrology and will be covered later in this book.

As astrology continued to advance and develop, so did other scientific studies such as astronomy, along with technologies like the telescope, and methodologies like the scientific method. For the first time, humanity was introduced to the heliocentric (sun-centered) model of the solar system demonstrated by Copernicus c.1543. Due to the more enlightened viewpoint of this time, it was

21   Maurice McCann, "The Secret of William Lilly's Prediction of the Fire of London," *Astrological Journal* 32, no.1(1990).

becoming more widely accepted that the Sun, not the Earth, was the center of the universe.

Although this scientific fact is indeed the true format of our solar system and humanity is better off for understanding this truism, it unfortunately became a major focal argument toward the invalidity of astrology during this time. Scientists began to conclude that because the Earth was not the center of the universe (the geocentric model), then astrology is therefore neither true nor accurate. Just like Cicero thousands of years prior, scientists yet again missed the point due to their lack of understanding when it comes to astrological theory.

Yes, it is true that the solar system does revolve around the Sun. There is not one modern astrologer that would disagree with this statement. Similarly, today's astrologers also know that the Sun and the Moon are not true planets in an astronomical sense, even though we refer to them as *planets* within our vernacular.

We should be reminded that astrology is not the study of the solar system's journey around the Sun, it is the study of human experience here on Earth. It is here on this planet that humanity is indeed the center of the universe because the entire human story exists and persists on this planet alone. Therefore, calculating astrology on a geocentric model makes sense.

Another scientific discovery that downplayed astrology as a study was the realization of the fading intensity of stars. Due to advancements in technology, early European scientists were able to observe that the intensity of a star's light faded over time. From this observation, they began to deduce that if stars were not permanent in state, then humanity is therefore not tied down to the destiny of the stars portrayed within astrology because they themselves are not perfect or static in state.[22] As with other anti-astrology arguments, this one contains an imperfect logic and misunderstanding toward how astrology operates. When it comes to astrological studies, star placement and intensity are not factors that are considered within analysis.

In actuality, astronomical entities like the planets are observed, not the stars. Planetary bodies, along with solar and lunar movements, follow along

22   Anna Herlihy, "Renaissance Star Charts" in *History of Cartography* (University of Chicago Press, 1998), vol. 3, 99–122.

stable and predictable paths and brightness. These movements, since the time of Mesopotamia, have proven to be steady and mathematically predictable through ephemerides. Furthermore, even though the brightness of a star does decay over time, their location within the sky remains unwavering, with a very slow perception of movement over long periods of time.

As scientific advancement and thought began to superimpose their conclusions onto the study of astrology, this trend only continued for centuries thereafter. Scientific and industrial advancement became the hallmark of human prestige for the next three hundred years.

The Industrial Revolution: AD 1712 – AD 1900 Astrology Takes a Back Seat

This time in history, which includes the discovery of the planet Uranus in 1781, became the age of revolutions. Although the outer planets — Uranus, Neptune, and Pluto, are common to modern astrologers, it is important to remember that these outer planets were not discovered until the eighteenth century and onward. For millennia prior, astrological systems used the seven traditional planets that ended with Saturn. Again, throughout this book, we will consider traditional rules and concepts as needed simply because they have been part of the astrological tradition for numerous generations.

The discovery of Uranus brought a time of change and upheaval both political with the French and American revolutions, and societal, including the industrial revolution, scientific and labor movements, and women's suffrage. These events removed age-long boundaries of status and wealth by not only acknowledging the equality of humanity in theory but also in practice; as the middle class grew, the *rights of man* became law, and entrepreneurial commoners were finding themselves alongside *old money*.

Uranus also brought the scientific age of enlightenment, where superstition and religious rhetoric were replaced with objectivity, deductive logic, and Darwinism. As important as these scientific advancements were and still are, astrology was becoming even more distant from its roots as a respectable study.

Academia seemed to be separating itself even further from their own history and heritage.

Consequently, humanity's priorities began to shift from self-reflection and understanding to profits and industry. Income and social status were used to define an individual's self-worth. Spirituality, along with astrology, was becoming less of a priority. However, exploring these types of realms slowly began to make a comeback with the discovery of Neptune in the nineteenth century.

The Metaphysical Movement: AD 1800–AD 1960 Ethereal Ideas Inspire Astrology

Neptune, discovered in 1846, brought with it the age of mysticism, hypnotherapy, and Eastern thought. This was the era of Pamela Colman Smith, the artist of the Rider-Waite tarot deck, occultists such as Helena Blavatsky who co-founded the Theosophical Society in 1875, along with the scientific genius Nikola Tesla.

During this time, séances, psychics, and examining the unknown and hidden world through new psychological and metaphysical means were at the forefront of entertainment and healing. This is also the era of academics such as Sigmund Freud, Carl Jung, and James Braid. These three figures were interested in the subconscious and hidden psychological forces that motivate our ego expression, external perceptions, and internal motivations, all of which are part of the core theory taught within this book.

The Western world also engaged further with Eastern concepts such as reincarnation, yoga, karma, and universal oneness, which was brought to their shores through Indian gurus such as Swami Vivekananda, Paramahansa Yogananda, and spiritualist Alice A. Bailey. In a way, religion underwent a transformation from creed in the Medieval era, to critical thinking in the Industrial era, and then back to spiritualism in the1800s. It is as though Uranus first introduced the illogical inconsistencies within religious doctrine, and Neptune then picked up the pieces, offering new answers to age-old questions.

However, it would seem that during the 1700s and 1800s, astrology nevertheless fell further into the background. It was no longer considered legitimate enough to be a science and simultaneously not ethereal enough to be part of the mysticism movement. Be that as it may, the spiritual and psychological concepts that were being explored during this time have made a firm impression within astrology and the Western consciousness of today. Jung's psychological theories, Yogananda's ideas of self-realization, and Helena Blavatsky's exposure of occultism were paving the way for a completely new psychological and spiritual approach to astrology, which emerged during the latter half of the twentieth century.

The Astrology Renaissance: AD 1960 – AD 2000 Modern Astrology is Born

Explorations into otherworldly and psychological practices during the first half of the twentieth century culminated during the latter half of the twentieth century when astrology seemed to experience an immense rebirth. As such, a new branch made its way into the foreground: Psychological/Archetypal Astrology. This movement was mostly spearheaded by the writings of Robert Hand, Liz Greene, and Steven Arroyo, who to this day are noted as a reputable academic researcher, author, and psychological counselor respectively.

Within their writings, they combined old concepts of mythological archetypes with the ideas of Jungian psychology, which demonstrated how these archetypes are a reflection of our personal perception of our outer world through the eyes of our inner psychological makeup. Astrology has been a tool for self-discovery ever since the ancient Greeks with Theurgic Astrology. In the late twentieth century, authors took newer psychological and archetypal concepts and adapted them within modern-day thinking, cultural context, and complexities.

Consequently, an explosion of astrological literature, organizations, and even academic studies emerged, as some colleges would once again offer astrology as a legitimate discipline.[23] Sadly, this rebirth did not last for very long. It slowly became saturated and discredited as part of the "new age movement," which only further dissipated astrology's legitimacy. The scientific community

---

23   "Kepler's History," Kepler College, archived June 19, 2021 at https://web. archive.org/web/20210619041944/https://www.keplercollege.org/index.php/ about/history.

also became even more absolute, cynical, and skeptical with their own opinions toward astrology, jettisoning the study into the point of near extinction. As the Western world proceeded into the twenty-first century, the skeptics only grew louder, and astrology became more of "that which it hates." Namely, over time, astrology began to commercialize, delegitimizing itself into nothing more than obscure daily horoscopes one could find on the back of a newspaper.

The Present: AD 2000–Present
Astrology Becomes Commercialized and Diluted

After observing the further dilution of astrology both in terms of legitimacy and understanding, it is no surprise to find that the majority of astrology in existence today is frivolous and inaccurate. Although respectable astrological organizations, journals, practitioners, and authors do exist and have been trying their hardest to maintain some form of legitimacy to the astrological sciences, these efforts are quickly quashed by the overwhelming saturation of daily horoscopes, blogs, and YouTube and TikTok videos by people whose understanding of the subject is superficial and really more of a means to an end in obtaining celebrity status.

As hard as organizations have been trying, this cannot be helped, because there are no requirements or academic thresholds that an individual must demonstrate in order to be considered qualified to dispense astrological knowledge. Before a surgeon can put a scalpel to a body, or before a lawyer can defend someone in court, they need to be educated, tested, and certified. This kind of institutional confidence is simply not observed in astrology, even though it does exist. How can you tell the legitimate astrologers from the soothsayers? I have composed a list of some common red flags that can easily demonstrate if an astrologer is legitimate or not.

TABLE I-2. Common Red-Flags of Astrologers who have
a superficial understanding of the science.

- They possess no certification of any kind. This shows that the astrologer has not been tested on specific and required astrological techniques. It also demonstrates that the astrologer is not tied to any sort of ethical regulation that most certified professional astrologers obey.

- Astrologers that do not follow astrology. This is more common than you think. I cannot count the number of times I have sat in board meetings for astrological organizations and watched leaders plan meetings and events during inauspicious moments. Any astrologer that tells you to do or not do something but does not follow their own advice is a hypocrite and a fraud.

- The astrologer has not been published in any form of legitimate peer-reviewed astrological journal, book, or organization. If all they have to their name is their own website or channel, you should be skeptical of their opinions because they have never been countered by other astrologers in the field. I have had to defend my position many times at conferences and through journal writings. If the astrologer has never encountered any counter arguments to their own thinking, it means that they work in a bubble of their own ideas that have never been contested and therefore they assume that they are always right.

- Any astrologer who always tells you that now is a good time or that this year is a good year without providing any warnings or pitfalls is misleading you. Even if you do have great things happening to you, there will also be pitfalls and down points to be mindful of. There is no such thing as a perfect year.

- Any astrologer who says an eclipse period is a good time to do anything is a big red flag. Or, if they provide any advice that goes against common astrological knowledge like saying signing a contract is OK during a Mercury retrograde when it most certainly is not. The eclipse is never a good time to do anything. Period. This shows you right away that the astrologer has no idea what they are talking about.

- If the astrologer uses flowery language like "watery Pisces" or "earthy Taurus" or only uses key words or phrases like "Neptune is all about the unknown" or "Chiron is known as the wounded healer." They are merely recycling shallow talking points that have been repeated *ad nauseam*.

- Any astrologer that mentions absolutes within your chart with no solution only serves to increase your anxiety without helping you to solve real problems you may be facing.

- If an astrologer cannot provide specific dates by consulting an ephemeris, or if they do not even possess an ephemeris, they are not worth your time or money.

- Any astrologer that promotes pseudo new age talking points like "all you need to do is be more positive and you will attract positivity" or "Your soulmate is right around the corner if you believe hard enough" have no real understanding of the metaphysical makeup of this universe. They are using emotional manipulation to swindle you.

- The astrologer should possess a library of sorts, should be constantly reading astrology books to a point where they are able to list at least ten books they have read from cover to cover.

Pointing out these red flags is not done to condemn anyone for their way of making a living. However, I think it is important that the astrological community begin to point out the fraud and illegitimacy of our own profession, not only for our own sake but for the sake of individuals who are sincerely seeking advice and wisdom—and pay good money to do so.

For anyone truly interested in learning and becoming an astrologer, certification tests are available to obtain the appropriate credentials. Additionally, by contributing to legitimate academic journals and organizations current and future astrologers have multiple opportunities to demonstrate their knowledge and abilities. To this point, one of the founders of the astrological movement of the twentieth century, Robert Hand, has this to say about modern astrology:

> *My only criticism of it is that in the hands of some of its less competent practitioners it has been an extremely mushy sort of astrology where anything can be made to mean anything, depending on the emotional frame of mind of the client and the astrologer. The language of 20th century astrology as a language tends to be imprecise, vague, inarticulate, and unclear. But the goals of 20th century astrology are absolutely commendable.[24]*

My analysis is simply a reflection of this same criticism. It is time the astrological community begins to legitimize itself. Personally, I have been published in peer-reviewed journals four times, I am certified through NCGR-PAA, I have a library of countless astrological books, I have sat on the boards of astrological institutions, participated in astrological conferences, and am now writing a book series for you, the gracious reader.

The Ball's in Your Court

Now that you have gained a thorough understanding of astrology's history, you are equipped with some ammunition in your pocket when you encounter a naysayer. The next time someone begins to criticize astrology's legitimacy, mention the prehistoric calendars of ancient cave dwellers, or the scientifically accurate books of the Mesopotamians, or the various other treatises written by prominent astronomers that contain legitimate defenses for astrology, such as those of Bonatti, Ptolemy, and Lilly. Remember, everything I have just mentioned in this survey is founded upon historical, archeological, and anthropological fact, and has been appropriately sourced. It is okay to see astrology within an academic context. It is not okay to deny historical fact for fiction, and anyone who is passionate about astrology has a part to play in setting the record straight.

---

24   Robert Hand, *Towards a Post-Modern Astrology*, 2005. https://www.astro.com/astrology/in_postmodern_e.htm.

SECTION 2—THE PRINCIPLES OF ASTROLOGY

It's Time to Evolve

In order to apply astrology to the fullest, we need to understand how astrology operates. I found that these principles organically unveiled themselves to me as a natural consequence of simply studying astrology. Astrology asks you to ponder deep existential and spiritual questions, and I've found that this sort of philosophical exploration helped me to better my understanding of cosmic truths about life, the self, and our universe.

Astrology inevitably presents to you important questions about the workings of nature which are hard to ignore because astrology is indeed the study of how the universe operates within the microcosm of our consciousness and through the macrocosm of our place within the world. The friction that comes from this kind of introspection is real, but the rewards to your well-being are also just as real and profound.

PRINCIPLE #1: Self-awareness is a key component of astrology

Mirror, Mirror, on the Wall

Astrology is an effective system to help you realize your true self. This entails understanding who we truly are and getting rid of the parts of our personality that are not really us. (More on this topic in Part I-Section 3.) The closer we get to this goal, the closer we become the embodiment of our fullest individual expression within this lifetime.

Many of us do not accomplish the evolutionary goals we were set out to complete in this world due to our lack of self-understanding. This causes ignorance toward the power of the ego, which creates an inability to reach our fullest potential because we are allowing our unconscious selves to run the show. (More on this in Part I-Section 6.)

With astrology, we begin to pick away at our unconscious self, which, while being unearthed, exposes our self-destructive tendencies that have prevented us from achieving our highest life path. Studying your natal chart and the life events that surround your personal story helps you to comprehend and detect these unconscious forces. Astrology is a great system that can bring you toward the goal of self-understanding in a very matter of fact and objective way.

PRINCIPLE #2: Astrology is a working time-tracking system

Ease on Down the Road

The twenty-first century is a world of completely artificial time. We are permanently set and fixed into an artificial paradigm, with most people having no idea that there are real cosmic forces that govern our daily lives. The Gregorian calendar is highly cumbersome, especially when it is compared to a calendar based on the astrological year.[25] Following the hourly, daily, monthly, and yearly astrological calendar, you are no longer erroneously going against the current, but flowing with it instead.

When you start to align your life to the true nature and timing of our planet, you remove a lot of unnecessary obstacles and frustrations. This is because you are synchronizing your body and life to the true nature of our planet's journey around the Sun. In essence, you are riding the cosmic wave of life. You will learn how to interpret the astrological calendar in Part III of this book.

Principle #3: Forgiveness is required to evolve with astrology

Real Healing Happens

This principle is a substantial and crucial ideal within astrology. Some people want to continue to blame others for how their lives turned out. Others are

25   Brad Plumer, "We've Been Using the Gregorian Calendar for 434 Years. It's Still Bizarre," Vox News, archived October 5, 2016 at https://web.archive.org/web/20161005130206/https://www.vox.com/2016/10/4/13147306/434th-gregorian-calendar-anniversary-google-doogle; and Bob Enyart, "An Original 360 Day Year, Was There One?" 360 Day Year, archived January 20, 2018 at https://web.archive.org/web/20180120122832/http://360dayyear.com/.

holding on to so much pain and tension that it is tearing them apart inside. Healing is a natural part of the astrological journey, but it does not make it a fun or easy one.

An individual cannot go on their entire life without forgiving those that have hurt them in the past. Astrology teaches us about the patterns of cycles and with this understanding comes immense forgiveness. With this forgiveness comes untold healing from the release of psychological and emotional baggage. So carry nothing that would be a load.

Principle #4: Respect and adoration for the workings of nature

The Higher Intelligence within Astrology

When I was preparing for my astrology certification test, I had to learn how to compute astrological birth charts by hand like the ancients had done for thousands of years before the computer age. When I was teaching myself how to accomplish this, I came to an amazing revelation: natal charts are incredibly mathematically precise and so unique that there is no other explanation other than an overarching influence of a higher consciousness, or energy, involved in the making of one's life.

Again, astrology is not a belief system, so even if you don't believe in a higher power, which is perfectly fine, you still cannot not deny that there is some all-encompassing cosmic force at play. This is the same force that binds the entire universe; what some scientists call the *cosmic web*.[26]

Every life is special, and every life journey is just as special as it is unique. Coming to this realization, there grew inside of me a deep and profound adoration for the cosmic web of life, the workings of nature, and the life-plan that has been mapped out for every individual according to their own unique birth chart. When you work with astrology, you start to personally witness these complexities of the natural world and your place within.

---

26   Matt Davis, "What is the Cosmic Web?" Big Think, archived September 29, 2020 at https://web.archive.org/web/20200929020109/https://bigthink.com/surprising-science/cosmic-web?rebelltitem=5#rebelltitem5.

Principle #5: Astrology explains the multiple layers of our trauma

Sometimes, Life's Just Not Fair, But That's OK

The more you study astrology, the more you start to understand the patterns that govern the trauma of your parents, your family, and indeed all of humanity. People are not aware of this because they do not usually look back on their life experiences, those of their parents, their parents' parents, etc., etc. There will always be issues that we have inherited from the ones that have lived before us. Indeed, it is their own unconsciousness that has caused them to pass these issues onto their children in the first place, allowing for the cycles of trauma to continue.

Astrology helps us to break these cycles and heal them instead. As a natural consequence, you not only heal yourself but your family, your children, your nation, and truly, the entire world. If humanity understood this, we would create a reality of complete and total unconditional love for everyone on this planet. Pretty trippy, huh?

In her famous book, *Time to Remember*, astrologer Nancy Hastings famously says, "You can't blame your mother." In her statement, Ms. Hastings points to one of the biggest remedies that astrology can provide to an individual. Astrology removes blame, shame, guilt, and even vengefulness because it demonstrates that we are all here to grow; we are all here to constantly evolve and struggle within that evolution.

There cannot be growth without struggle. The butterfly cannot escape the chrysalis without force and will. The snake cannot shed its skin without first feeling uncomfortable. In this same light, we should not cower in the past and within our own misery. Instead, we should be thankful for the harder times and our lot in life because our experience brings us closer to our true self. If life were simple, easy, and worry-free, then what would be the point? The good news is: if you allow yourself to fight through the inner friction and conflict and arise out of studying astrology, you not only grow and evolve as an individual, but the entire world benefits from your hard work. As I have mentioned in the introduction, for the twenty-first century, this is the work that must be done.

SECTION 3—ASTROLOGY AND THE "IDEAL HUMAN"

Peeling the Layers

As previously mentioned, astrology is a journey to realize the true self. But what do we mean when we say this? Who we think we are is not who we truly are. Due to false impressions based upon our past experiences and future desires, we have created a persona that acts and reacts to these stimuli. The outcome is a person who we might think is us, but it is only a mask we use to operate in this world. This is called the ego. Egos have opinions, preferences, judgements, and trauma. Our ego becomes the mask and we start to lose say in our autonomy within ourselves.

That's great and all, but it still doesn't answer the question of the true self. That is for you to discover, with the help of astrology. As you begin to slowly peel away the layers of trauma, judgment, opinions, and faulty character traits, you will soon find a person of unconditional love and beauty. When you let go of your preconceived notions of the world and of yourself, you will begin to see the dark as darkness and nothing more. You will begin to see your enemies as yourself, and your hard life-lessons as the catalyst which awakens your true nature from within.

Our egos, even if we perceive them to be inherently good, are nonetheless subjective and based upon our attachments toward our thoughts, which stem from our past experiences and future desires. The ancient Chinese philosopher Laozi understood this universal truth in his incredibly succinct quote:

"Watch your thoughts, for they become your words; watch your words, for they become your actions; watch your actions, for they become your habits; watch your habits, for they become your character; watch your character, for it becomes your destiny."

Astrology is a window to the soul. It exposes to you the dust that covers this window, which is preventing the light from shining through. Slowly, one step at a time, with astrology, you begin to wipe away the dust of ignorance, allowing for your true nature to finally shine through. Nobody is perfect. Please understand I am not writing this from a place of "holier than thou." I am fully aware that I have my own shortcomings and imperfections. Just like you, I am only human, and to err is to be human. I am simply echoing what sages and wise people have understood about human nature for millennia. Sages like the Himalayan guru *Babaij* who once said, "There is no saint without a past, there is no sinner without a future."[27]

We all have within ourselves the capacity to let go of our own preconceived and artificial ideas of who we are for the higher ideal of the archetypal supreme human being. Astrology is the gateway to this understanding, and if we put forth the effort, we begin to truly evolve into our true self. Then and only then will the world around us begin to change, but this can only start from within through our own conscious desire to right the wrongs so that we may grow.

SECTION 4—ASTROLOGY AND KARMA

For Every Action, There is an Equal and Opposite Reaction

When I use the word *karma* in this setting, I am defining it in the simplest of terms: karma equals action. This is the same truism that is defined in Newton's Third Law of Motion: For every action, there is an equal and opposite reaction. Just as it is with the laws of motion in regard to matter, every action we perform has intended and unintended consequences.

In addition to action that you create in the present, astrology also argues that there are manifestations of action from the past. For example, some individuals could have good fortune and ease when it comes to their career, and others must deal with a harder struggle in life in order to achieve success. Some would say one person is lucky and the other is simply unlucky. But where does luck come from? And why do some people get a ton of luck and others no luck at all? Astrology says that these predetermined situations are fixed within the birth chart, that they stem from the actions of the past, which leads an individual to their specific life journey that they must presently experience.

27   James Braha, *How to Be a Great Astrologer: The Planetary Aspects Explained* (Hermetician Press, 1992), 10.

According to astrological theory, individuals with good luck or bad luck have unique lessons to learn so that they can evolve in their own way. The good news is, according to the wisdom of the past, both individuals are nevertheless headed toward the same goal of self understanding. It is simply up to the individual, by their own autonomous actions, how quickly or slowly it will take them to get there. Everyone is on this journey of self-discovery. Astrology simply accelerates this process by removing all of the guesswork and allows you to become aware of your unconscious tendencies.

SECTION 5—ASTROLOGY, FATE, AND FREE WILL

What Does Science Have to Say?

One hundred and twenty years after Albert Einstein postulated the Theory of Relativity, scientists have been attempting to further understand the mysterious principles that govern the fabric of time and space. One of the biggest unsolved mysteries in this regard includes the *Grandfather Paradox* when it comes to theoretical time travel. The paradox goes as such: if I were to travel back in time and murder my grandfather, would I no longer cease to exist? This similar quandary was the main basis for the timeless movie classic *Back to the Future*, along with other great films and stories in our culture.

As recently as 2020, new mathematical models have allowed scientists to further understand inconsistencies such as these, which sheds new light on the true workings of time and space. In a new revolutionary study, scientists have now deduced that time actually has the ability to re-adjust itself in order to avoid theoretical paradoxes like the Grandfather Paradox from even occurring.[28] In an online interview, astrophysicist Dr. Joe Pesce explains further:

Let's give an example here: I travel back in time to stop COVID-19 and I want to keep Patient Zero from being infected. So, I travel back in time and if I stop Patient Zero from being infected, then I stop the pandemic, then that eliminates my motivation for going into the past. That is the crux of the [Grandfather]

---

28   Germain Tobar and Fabio Costa, "Reversible dynamics with closed time-like curves and freedom of Choice," *Classical and Quantum Gravity*, vol. 37 no. 20. https://doi.org/10.1088/1361-6382/aba4bc.

Paradox. What researchers have now found within the mathematics is that the events would re-calibrate themselves. So maybe I go and I stop Patient Zero, but I then become Patient Zero and I start the infection. Or someone else becomes Patient Zero that is outside the realm of mine being able to manipulate. So, ultimately, the end point is still the same. There is still going to be a pandemic, but the particular events . . . change . . . The end point will be the same, we just might get to it in a different way.[29]

Could it be that there is some consciousness behind the fabric of time and space which is not only aware, but simultaneously co-creating and reacting to our autonomous decisions? Science has already proven the existence of implicit bias and how observations influence outcomes many times over.[30] Now, there are mathematical models to prove that these same rules function within time itself.

As Dr. Pesce described, it seems that there are some events that are indeed inevitable and unavoidable. However, if fate was the all-pervading force, then one could argue that people who perform evil works like murder had no real autonomy in doing so and could therefore not really be blamed for their actions. This is not the case either because it seems everyone still has the free will to behave and act as they wish within the logical confines of their own experience.

Do We Really Have Control?

Instead, astrological theory would argue that both fate and free will exist as a hybrid of sorts. We might not have the ability to prevent certain fated events, but we always have the free will to react to them as we see fit. Within the astrological context, the individual is going to have a certain life-event occur at a specific point in time no matter what. How prepared they are and how healthy their psychology is at the time of the event will determine their ability to handle the event, which, in turn, influences the outcome. Similarly, if the individual was being proactive and working on the themes that the life-event was going to

---

29   Joe Pesce, "Researchers PROVE Time Travel Mathematically Possible," *Rising with Krystal and Saagar* posted Nov. 26, 2020 on The Hill, Youtube, 5 min., 42 sec., https://www.youtube.com/watch?v=2G886HiSgWk&t=15s.

30   Weizmann Institute of Science, "Quantum Theory Demonstrated: Observation Affects Reality," ScienceDaily, February 27,1998. www.sciencedaily.com/releases/1998/02/980227055013.htm.

bring about, then it is also possible that the event "readjusts" and manifests in a less-impactful way.

For example, Pluto transits in astrology usually accompany a death or a severe ending of some kind like a marriage or a career. Let us say that the individual always had deeply seeded issues with their father throughout their entire life and never attempted to resolve them. Then, at the time of the Pluto transit, their father passes away and all the sudden, the pile of unconscious agony that they have been repressing finally emerges and reveals itself as a result. However, if the individual was in therapy for years prior to the event, they would have been more psychologically grounded and able to handle the event more maturely. The death of the father was inevitable, but the individual's freewill to tackle the issue prior to the event allowed for the event (and time) to re-adjust appropriately. As was mentioned in the introduction, it pays to be proactive in astrology.

Another example: let us say the individual has always had issues with eating unhealthily. They do nothing to fix the problem, and then Saturn conjoins their Sun, which causes them to have a severe heart-attack. They survive, but the experience makes them realize they need to fix their diet once and for all. Had they have gone to an astrologer prior to the event, they could have seen the Saturn conjunction ahead of time and could have warned the individual that they needed to be more mindful of their diet now before it is too late. If they take the astrologer's advice, then time, along with the event, would readjust to where the heart-attack is no longer needed for that individual to learn that lesson. Keep in mind, they will still have an intense and unavoidable life event, but it will be less drastic and intense. Perhaps this time, instead of a heart attack, they experience an event which emotionally triggers them back into their bad eating habits. In other words, instead of life throwing them a hard life lesson like a heart-attack, life instead tests their dedication toward a healthy lifestyle, allowing them to further understand why their bad eating habits existed in the first place. As these newer developments in physics have demonstrated, science now confirms that time does indeed operate in this fashion.

Another thing to keep in mind involves the perception of fated events. Fated events in our lives may only appear fated because we are operating within our unconscious motivations. In other words, a person could experience an intense life-event and go, "Wow, God must really hate me. This came out of the blue and I do not understand why life had to throw a wrench in my life which was working out so perfectly for me beforehand." The astrologer would counter, "Was your life really working perfectly, or were you just giving yourself a false sense of security while unknowingly manifesting events that led you to this outcome?" This philosophical quandary is part of our next topic where we observe the workings of the individual and global psychology through the lens of renowned psychologist Carl Jung.

SECTION 6—JUNGIAN ASTROLOGICAL THEORY

The Genius of Carl Jung

Jungian psychological theory is a foundational cornerstone within modern astrology. Concepts like archetypes, conscious and unconscious motivations, projection, and ancient mythology applying to our lives today integrate beautifully within astrology's context. Everything suddenly becomes a metaphor for real-life problems but also brings about real-life solutions. Jungian psychology encourages self-introspection and aligning our life story to the core personality types that exist in this world and have existed for eons.

THEORY #1: Our subconscious mind heavily influences our conscious actions. Therefore, it is important to understand our unconscious motivations in order to obtain greater freedom within our own lives.

Running on Autopilot

Without even knowing it, we are easily influenced by our unconscious mind. Astrology lays out these unconscious motivations with great transparency. If we understand these motivations, we can stop them in their tracks. This causes us to work less on autopilot even though we may think we are operating with complete lucidity.

For example, let us say an individual is highly introverted and abhors all types of confrontation, good and bad.

Maybe this was due to a childhood experience where they always witnessed their parents fighting and therefore assimilated conflict with feelings of anxiety and stress. These memories are so distant in the past that they do not realize their influence. They go on through life assuming that their introverted nature is just a part of who they are.

Now, that individual needs to find a job. Naturally, they consciously choose jobs that do not involve working with the public. They think this is a willful act, but in reality, their unconscious fears are driving them to find a career of this nature. However, as we will discover, the unconscious constantly strives to be unearthed, exposed, and understood. Therefore, the unconscious mind will manifest situations where these various phases can occur.

Back to our example: the individual works in a highly isolated job and has been doing well in this regard, but suddenly, the business goes belly up and they no longer have that safety net. When the individual tries to find a new job, they have no choice but to work with the public and face their fear of confrontation. Or, their job may be isolated, but they experience confrontation with their superior on a daily basis. In other words, your unconscious problems will always seek to find you so that you can address them. You then have the choice to either repress it further or confront the issues at hand. With astrology, you are shown where these unconscious motivations exist so that you can address them and become aware of their existence.

> **THEORY #2:**
> Psychological projection is the primary agent for unconscious motivations to be expressed.

Everything and Everyone is a Mirror

We experience psychological projection all the time within our lives, either as the person who is projecting our insecurities onto an individual or vice versa. In essence, everyone we encounter becomes a mirror where we are placing judgement onto that person, but really, we are judging ourselves through that individual because they possess a quality which we lack and therefore envy.

The good news is, if we are able to catch ourselves in the act, we obtain amazing insight into our own psychology. The next time you have an intense thought like this, stop yourself and ask, "Well, what does that say about me?" This ties back to Theory #1 because it is vitally important to understand where these *voices in our head* come from. They usually come from our unconscious self, expressing itself through psychological projection. When we place judgement, shame, guilt, and other intense emotions onto others, we are reflecting our own selves. The same goes for when other people project themselves onto us.

THEORY #3: Global consciousness and unconsciousness are directly related and proportional to the individual consciousness and unconsciousness.

Society and the Individual Are One

The positive and the negative aspects of our individual natures are similar to the positive and the negative aspects of our society at large. An example of this is the toxicity found within social media. Online platforms have allowed individuals to say really nasty things about each other, resulting in real life tragic consequences. We look at these problems as issues outside of ourselves and as someone else's trash to clean up. Even so, it is safe to say that everyone has contributed in one way or another to this noxious vat.

Jung postulates that conflicts within society equate to conflicts within ourselves. Unexpressed and unhealed shadows of our unconscious mind eventually become unearthed within our culture, which forces us to deal with these issues because they become part of our daily living. To our previous example, cyber bullying and the exploitation of influencers have now arrived at the forefront of society, where people are becoming more aware, and some are now even trying to advocate and heal the problem.

In this light, all positive contributions that have been uplifting for the world were due to personal inspiration and realization. The more we understand and heal ourselves, the more this world also heals and transforms.

> **THEORY #4:**
> Mythological archetypes, both ancient and modern, serve to comprehend and express the personal psychological condition.

Tale as Old as Time

In 2006, researchers at Texas A&M University performed an experiment to see if archetypal symbols could be matched to their respective universal word associations. For example, the subject would be shown a picture of a heart, which is associated with the word *charity*. The participant would then have to choose if the symbol matched with the proper word association. Some pictures and word associations were logical, while others were more abstract, like an image of the number seven representing *completion*. Furthermore, the study included bilingual Spanish-English speaking individuals in order to determine if the symbols were understood over linguistic and cultural barriers. From their data, they concluded that participants identified the correct image/word associations more often than an incorrect matching. They therefore deduced that the results ". . . provide further support for the Jungian concept of collective (archetypal) unconscious memory aid in recalling words that are matched with archetypal symbols."[31]

According to Carl Jung, "An archetype is like an old watercourse along which the water of life has flowed for centuries, digging a deep channel for itself. The longer it has flowed in this channel the more likely it is that sooner or later the water will return to its old bed."[32] This is why timeless classics are still relevant and experienced in today's world, either through the original source material or through a reinterpretation of the story and its morals, using modern characters and themes. These stories reflect universal truths of the human experience, which is why we identify so strongly with them, and why their place within the

---

31   Jeffrey M. Brown and Terence P. Hannigan, "An Empirical Test of Carl Jung's Collective Unconscious (Archetypal) Memory," *Journal of Border Educational Research*, vol. 5, (2006)119.

32   C.G. Jung, *Civilization in Transition, Second Edition,* (Princeton University Press, 1970), 189.

global society is just as prevalent as it is permanent. This concept explains why astrology's use of ancient archetypes works so effectively when it comes to an individual's psychological analysis.

Ancient archetypes are firmly grounded within the personal and global psyche simply because they have existed for thousands of years through multiple generations and societies. The natal chart becomes a functioning metaphor of these timeless archetypes. The astrologer simply explains these archetypes as a metaphor for the individual because these archetypes are literally embedded within our global society.

Jung Gives Astrology the Thumbs Up

Jung himself once had this to say about astrology, "Astrology, like the collective unconscious with which psychology is concerned, consists of symbolic configurations: The 'planets' are the gods, symbols of the powers of the unconscious."[33] The natal chart is incredibly objective, with no biases or hidden answers. The entire psychology of the individual is exposed for the world to see. All it takes is a trained eye to understand how to properly analyze its content.

Hopefully, by now you are starting to understand that astrology is indeed deeply rooted within legitimate psychological and scientific theories which have been confirmed by academic and scientific experimentation and exploration. Now that we have a firm fundamental understanding of these various theories, we are ready to learn more about astrology itself, but before we get there, we need to go over common pitfalls, rules, and strategies.

---

33   "Carl Jung and Astrology in Psychoanalysis," Exploring Your Mind, (2018), archived March 18, 2025 at https://web.archive.org/web/20250318044441/ https://exploringyourmind.com/carl-jung-astrology-psychoanalysis/.

SECTION 7—APPROACH, TIPS, TOOLS, AND RESOURCES

Blazing the Trail

This section is my version of astrological trailblazing, which I compiled by looking back at my personal studies over the past decade. Astrology requires a lot of self-study. Along the way, you discover your own guideposts, which require constant readjustment the further along you travel. I am most certain these insights will help to make your time with astrology less difficult and more efficient because you will have a better idea as to what to expect. To begin, I want to discuss eight basic tips that will help you as you embark on your astrological journey.

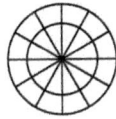

EIGHT TIPS FOR STUDYING ASTROLOGY

TIP #1: Do Not Panic!

Without a doubt, at first glance, astrology is incredibly overwhelming. You are not only trying to understand various archetypes and how they inter-act with one another, you are also trying to apply these energies toward your own psychology and the psychology of others. Always remember to take it easy, take your time, and if it gets to be too overbearing, take a step back and regroup.

TIP #2: It is Okay to Take Breaks

Astrology requires a good amount of mental capacity, fortitude, and hon-esty. When I began to study astrology, sometimes I would overwhelm my mind with too much information and analysis. I found that if I closed the book and stepped away for a few days, this gave my mind ample time to process and integrate the new information. After these break periods, my mind was able to reset and continue. If you need to take a break, by all means, take a break.

TIP #3: It is Okay to Be Wrong

When it comes to the skeptics of astrology, they always expect you to be 100 percent correct all of the time. If you are not, then they see that as a way to invalidate astrology altogether. This obsessive desire to prove astrology wrong is why astrologers always feel pressured to be completely accurate and right all of the time, but this expectation is absurd.

If a doctor misdiagnosed a patient, do they deserve to have their license to practice revoked? No, instead they learn heavily from their mistakes and improve. Hence why it is called a practice in the first place. Remember, it is not about being right, it is about trial and error. If you interpret a chart and you are completely off, at least you are trying. See what works, see what doesn't, and give yourself permission to be wrong.

TIP #4: Allow Time for Daily Introspection

When you begin to observe your personal transits and natal chart, you will inevitably begin to perform introspective analysis on a daily basis. This means you are utilizing astrology to the fullest. When working with astrology, take time every day to really dig deep inside yourself with openness and honesty. Slowly, over time, you begin to peel away the layers of your unconscious mind, which brings you closer to astrology's end goal of healing and realizing the true self.

TIP #5: Be Patient and Forgiving of Yourself and Others

As we discussed previously, letting go and learning to forgive your past is a substantial boon astrology provides us. The more you forgive and forget, the more you release unwanted baggage. If you begin to study astrology without a willingness to be forgiving, you are closing yourself off to one of the greater healing potentials of astrology.

It takes substantial courage and awareness to release the ego in this way, but you are showing a level of great maturity by pardoning your less-favored life choices, your upbringing, and the various people that have shaped your world perspective for the worse. It is up to all of us to learn the lessons they provide so that we can grow.

TIP #6: Be Prepared for Changes in Your Life

Studying astrology advances your character due to the vast amount of introspection you perform. Consequently, your true personality begins to shine forth because you begin to discern what aspects of your personality are not really a reflection of your true self. Therefore, you can expect to witness changes not only inside yourself, but with your associations, hobbies, interests, and perhaps even changes in profession, living situation, and life direction. You are shedding the skin of the false ego and begin to arise as your authentic self. You should trust that the changes that occur to you are for the betterment of your own existence, because you are becoming more aligned with your authentic nature. That which no longer serves you will naturally slip away.

TIP #7: Pay Attention to Astrology's Influence on Others

When you work with astrology, you will begin to understand that everyone is influenced by the celestial calendar, whether they know it or not. Paying attention to how other individuals work either with or against the tide gives you daily case studies that demonstrate astrology's validity. Additionally, if you find that people around you are planning events during inauspicious moments, you are then able to circumnavigate, because you are paying attention to the actual forces at play.

TIP #8: Astrology is Filled with Paradoxes

How can a planet like Saturn, which represents themes like tradition, obligation, and limitation rule the free-spirited sign of Aquarius? Look at Mars as another example. How can a planet that we associate with action, drive, and assertiveness rule the strategically introverted sign of Scorpio? (Both of these questions will be answered later.) Contradictions such as these are merely a reflection of the countless paradoxes that exist within human nature.

We are all filled with opposing forces that cancel and contradict one another, so it makes sense that astrology is similarly filled with contradicting data here and there. It is good to be aware of this to avoid accidentally reaching the conclusion that astrology itself is a made-up system with no logic involved. The good news is, I have found that the more you work through these inconsistencies, the greater your understanding of astrology becomes.

FIVE QUALITIES OF THE WELL-TO-DO ASTROLOGER

Before you begin your studies into astrology, there are five distinct character traits that would be best to cultivate within yourself in preparation. These qualities put you in the correct mindset.

QUALITY #1: Trust

Sometimes you must take a leap of faith with astrology. At moments when you want to act, astrology could be telling you to wait a day, a month, or even years, which begs the question: would you rather have your aspirations happen quickly, or to their fullest potential when the time is right? Timing is incredibly important in astrology. Indeed, one of astrology's primary functions is to track time. Using the celestial calendar requires trust because you must assume that astrology knows what is best for you, even more so than you do. This can be difficult because when it comes to your own life, it is hard to take a backseat. Nevertheless, once you learn the important lesson of releasing control and surrendering when it is needed, you will find astrology to be accurate and most helpful.

QUALITY #2: Introspection

In today's world, introspection is not a regular part of our daily living. Instead, we are encouraged to conquer others; not ourselves. We are pushed to achieve and attain material possessions and status instead of comprehending who we truly are on the inside. Looking deep into yourself raises your awareness into these matters.

QUALITY #3: Strength

Astrology requires perseverance and fortitude. Given the amount of objective truth you are receiving, it can become a challenge to continue. Therefore, maintaining a strong foundation into your personal character is essential to your success. Take whatever changes come your way and allow yourself to understand the truth. The rewards are worth the struggle.

QUALITY #4: Ethics

We will discuss this further in Book II, but for now, there are a few ethical rules to understand. For one, do not provide astrological information to anyone unless you have been given explicit approval to do so. When using astrology, it is important not to interfere with other people's problems or predicaments unless you have been personally asked to intercede. You do not want to cheat anyone out of any karmic lessons and take on their karma for yourself, which was not meant to be yours in the first place. Similarly, do not use astrology to trigger other people's pitfalls for your own personal gain. Having a high ethical standard leaves everyone, especially yourself, in a better predicament every time. Manipulating individuals, or attempting to help them without their permission, are sure ways to receive more complications and struggles in your own life, so don't even bother trying.

QUALITY #5: Patience

This is a big one when it comes to astrology. Life events can take years to experience, understand, and overcome, but knowing what to expect and when to expect it can allow for you to prepare your life for the storm that lies ahead. If we are about to experience a purge of unwanted and unneeded circumstances, then it is better to have our lives uncluttered with unnecessary activities, jobs, and people. The more time and space we allow for these bigger life events, the better the outcome can be because we are listening to the higher energies that are at work.

The modern world is incredibly goal-oriented, which pressures the individual to constantly strive toward something external and material. However, astrology will sometimes tell you that there is simply no energy behind your motivations, which means it is better to regroup and retreat than it is to push onwards. This is a very hard lesson for people in today's world to understand, but if you can surrender when astrology tells you to, you will be flowing through life with greater ease.

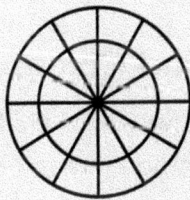

TOOLS

This section is a checklist of highly recommended tools and supplies you will need before you can apply astrology, and this book, to the fullest capacity.

☑ TOOL #1: Your Personal Birth Chart with Accurate Birth Data

Start by obtaining your birth certificate and make sure it has the time of birth. Do not go by the time your parents think you were born even if they have tremendously reliable memories. The only time that matters is when the Doctor that delivered you declared you alive as an individual on this planet. This is the only time that matters and should be located on your birth certificate. Refer back to Table INT-1 in order to obtain a free natal chart though astro.com.

☑ TOOL #2: An Ephemeris for the 21st Century Set to Midnight GMT/UTC or Your Current Time Zone

In Book II, we will explain further how to obtain an ephemeris online for free with your current time zone. Nevertheless, it is still advisable you purchase a twenty-first century ephemeris set to Midnight GMT/UTC (more on the details are found below in the annotated bibliography section.)

☑ TOOL #3: Basic Calculator

You will need to use a calculator in Book II of this book series. Any standard calculator will do.

☑ TOOL #4: Regular and Colored Pencils

It would be a good idea to have colored and regular pencils to help you better map out your thoughts and ideas on astrology.

☑ TOOL #5: Graph Paper, Index Cards, and a Ruler

Items to help you jot down your ideas and study astrology.

☑ **TOOL #6: An Astrologer's Calendar/Datebook**

There will be more details on this below in the annotated bibliography section. In order to properly use the skills learned in Part III of this book, you will need to purchase an astrologer's calendar that provides the void of course, moon periods, daily transits, moon phases, eclipses, and retrogrades. You will find my recommendation below.

☑ **TOOL #7: A Journal**

It helps to have a journal where you can write notes, ideas, and insights you have gathered along your journey. Have a journal handy and try to write in it daily.

Annotated Bibliography

The study of astrology does require an investment into a mini library of sorts. The books I have listed below are, in my opinion, a great place to start because they contain some of the most comprehensive, accurate, and easy-to-read information. I have also ranked them in order of difficulty so you can progressively work upward toward more advanced topics and books.

LEVEL: BEGINNER

- *Llewellyn's Daily Planetary Guide (for current year),* by Llewellyn Publications. As mentioned above, an astrological calendar is essential to study astrology. *Llewellyn's Planetary Guide* provides accurate and readable information with a good amount of blank space for you to add your own notes and personal calendar.

- *American Ephemeris Trans-Century Edition 1950-2050 Midnight*, by Niel F. Miechelsen and Rique Pottenger. This is the recommended Ephemeris for every beginning astrologer. It provides the latter half of the twentieth century and the first half of the twenty-first century, giving you a wide range of data from the recent past to the near future. Be sure to get *Midnight* and not *Noon*!

- *Alan Oken's Complete Astrology*, by Alan Oken. Astronomy, mythology, and spiritualism are beautifully intertwined in order to explain the various planets, signs, and houses found in astrology. This book is a good starting point in order to understand the stories, mythologies, and energies surrounding the various archetypes in astrology.

- *The Contemporary Astrologer's Handbook*, by Sue Tompkins. Similar to Mr. Oken's book, this book provides insightful paragraphs into aspects, planets, houses, and signs in astrology. Ms. Tompkins also delves into interpretation techniques with interesting case studies.

- *The Rulership Book*, by Rex E. Bills. You can take this book anywhere you go. The author has taken countless records from antiquity to modern times and has aligned planetary, sign, and house rulerships to all things animal, plant, and mineral. This is a good book to observe which astrological archetypes rule which objects. It is also a good tool if you want to quiz yourself by guessing what rules what before you look it up.

- *The Only Astrology Book You'll Ever Need*, by Joanna Martine Woolfolk. This book has become a modern-day classic. Similar to Mr. Oken and Ms. Tompkins, this book provides explanations of the planets, signs, and houses involved in astrology. Ms. Woolfolk pays close attention to ascendants and sun signs and does so in a language that is witty and light-hearted.

LEVEL: INTERMEDIATE

- *Relating: An Astrological Guide to Living with Others on a Small Planet*, by Liz Greene. Every starting astrologer should have this book. Although psychological in its approach, this book is easily understandable as astrologer Liz Greene explains the various elemental, planetary, and zodiacal archetypes, and how they interact with one another. Ms. Greene also discusses how one addresses the relationships inside oneself, and how this inner exchange between the personal feminine and masculine is reflected through the people that we attract into our lives.

- *The Gods of Change: Pain, Crises and the Transits of Uranus, Neptune and Pluto*, by Howard Sasportas. Outer planetary transits, which will be explained further in Book II, represent the big life events that we experience within our lifetimes. This book helps you to understand the energies and themes involved with the three most outer planets Uranus, Neptune, and Pluto. This is important because these planets (in addition to Saturn) create intense energies and situations within our lives.

- *How to be a Great Astrologer*, by James Braha. In all of his books, James Braha perfectly combines the knowledge and wisdom of western astrology and Jyotish (Indian) astrology. His book goes over natal planetary aspects as well as nodal house and sign placements. Throughout the book, there are profound quotes to live by along with angelic and inspirational pictures.

- *Astrology for the Soul*, by Jan Spiller. This is a very insightful book into the moon's nodes in astrology. By looking up your north node by sign and house, you are presented with common pitfalls and weakness associated with that placement. Ms. Spiller provides amazing diagnoses and remedies for such ailments, which help you align your life to the appropriate karmic path of this lifetime.

- *Planets in Youth*, by Robert Hand. This is the first book of what I like to call "The Robert Hand Collection." *Planets in Youth* provides an insightful look into your natal aspects and is written as if he was talking to your parents about you. This makes it easy to form a connection between your current psychological predicament and your childhood. There is also a great section where Mr. Hand discusses the astrological mother and father in the birth chart and their connection to one's life.

LEVEL: ADVANCED

- *Horoscope Symbols*, by Robert Hand. This is Mr. Hand's thesis on all symbols found in astrology (aspects, signs, planets, and houses). The reason this book is advanced is that it is highly psychological and requires a firm understanding in Jungian astrological theory.

- *Planets in Composite*, by Robert Hand. *Planets in Composite* is a great resource for when you are looking at composite charts (charts about relationships) in astrology. This is the best resource on the topic, and if you are interested in doing a lot of relationship/comparison charts within your studies, this is the book to get.

- *Planets in Transit*, by Robert Hand. Once you learn the techniques in Book II, this resource will become your most essential tool. *Planets in Transit* provides every combination of planetary transits and ingresses from the Sun to Pluto. Every time you experience a personal transit, this book gives you several paragraphs that explain what to expect and how to approach the given situation.

- *Astrology, Karma and Transformation*, by Steven Arroyo. Being a psychologist himself, Mr. Arroyo's insights are heavily grounded within Jungian theories as he covers themes that you have found in the previous sections. Mr. Arroyo's book simply adds a layer toward your understanding of astrological archetypes.

- *How to Predict Your Future: The Secrets of Eastern and Western Astrology*, by James Braha. This book has two parts. The first part of this book goes over the planetary transits and ingresses of the outer planets (Jupiter-Pluto) in a very fatalistic, yet accurate, way. Using this book in parallel with *The Gods of Change* and *Planets in Transit* is highly recommended. The second half of this book touches on the same life events but through the Jyotish system. Even if you only use this book for the first half, it is worth the purchase.

- *A History of Western Astrology Vol. 1 and 2*, by Nick Campion. Mr. Campion provides academic evidence in order to demonstrate the history of astrology within a historical context from antiquity to modern times. This two-volume series establishes a credible connection for astrology within the context of human history using academic integrity.

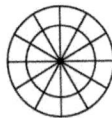

The trail has now been blazed, your supplies have been gathered, and you are now in the proper mindset to begin your astrological studies. Finally, it is time to discuss the various components of astrology.

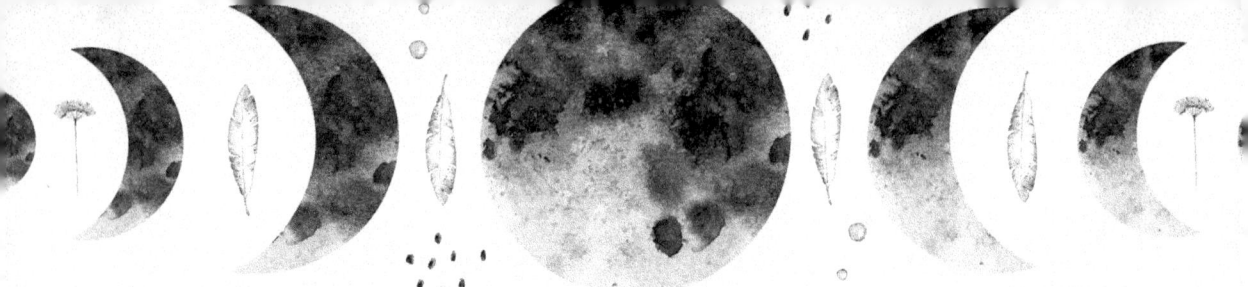

PART II

ASTROLOGICAL SYMBOLS AND ARCHETYPES

Astrology is the study of [an individual's] response to planetary stimuli. The stars have no conscious benevolence or animosity, they merely send forth positive and negative radiations. Of themselves, these do not help or harm humanity, but offer a lawful channel for the outward operation of cause-effect equilibriums which each [individual] has set into motion in the past ... all that we've done, we can undo.

—Swami Sri Yukteswar from *Autobiography of a Yogi*, Chapter 16

Chiseling Deeper Into Archetypes

Let us begin this section by further detailing the nature of an archetype and its use within astrology. One way to think of an archetype is to picture one of the numerous Greek god or goddess statues that still remains after thousands of years (Figure II-1).

FIGURE II-1. Statue of the Greek Sun God Apollo.[34]

Greek statues such as these all contain three vital qualities of an archetype: fixed, idealistic, and universal. Fixed in that their attributes and mythologies never change. Apollo will always be the god of light and truth, Athena, the goddess of war, etc., etc. Over time, the stories that surround these characters are simply a retranslation through the contextual lens of the culture and time that the interpretation took place. However, their core characteristics, themes, and stories never change.

Archetypes are idealistic because they represent qualities that we as humans strive to embody within our own lives. Christians, for example, try to imitate the values of Jesus, Hindus of *Krishna*, etc. Archetypes are perceived to be god-like because they do not possess the imperfections that we as humans possess — recall the timeless axiom, "to err is to be human." Due to this fact, humans constantly idolize archetypes that they consider to be personal heroes, which in turn motivate and drive them to achieve their goals.

Lastly, archetypes are universal because they cross cultural, linguistic, and religious barriers. To this point, it should be noted that the ancient sages of the Jyotish tradition attributed the same exact planetary archetypes as their

34   Dennis Jarvis, *Italy-3104 – Apollo*, October 22, 2010, photograph, https://www.flickr.com/photos/archer10/5378415112.

ancient Mesopotamia, Egyptian, and Greek counterparts within their own respective astrological traditions. Similarly, in today's world, movies and novels can be enjoyed by individuals from all walks of life because every culture has a hero's story, the story of a broken heart, and the story of the prodigal son. These tales are universal human experiences that are felt and understood by all.

The Archetypes in Our Chart Tell a Story

According to astrological theory, these various archetypes are expressed within ourselves in either a healthy or unhealthy way. How they are manifested within the individual depends on the coordination and condition of the various planets within the birth chart, which is the bulk of Book II of this book series. To this point, the birth chart shows us the personal hero and enemy archetypes that individuals embody, idolize, and strive toward, or cower away from, fear, and shun.

In this part of the book, we will establish a firm understanding of all the various archetypes that are found within astrology and how they are expressed in both a positive and negative light. Think of this section as a hermetically sealed version of astrology where every archetype will be individually explained. It is vital to have this strong foundation now because when we get to Book II, all of these archetypes will blend together, forming an individualized psychology. For now, we will take it one step and one archetypal symbol at a time, starting with the elements and modalities, and furthering our discussion into the signs, planets, houses, and cardinal points. To crystalize our understanding of these archetypes even further, we will also discuss traditional rulerships and rules which will help you to obtain an even greater understanding of the energies at play.

SECTION 1—THE ELEMENTS AND MODALITIES

Simplicity, Simplicity, Simplicity

What's great about the elements and modalities is that it's a simple way to look at astrology. Later down the road, when you need to combine all of the smaller pieces into a larger, more complex picture, you will be able to do this with ease.

The elements and modalities are a quick way to get an easy snapshot of the birth chart and determine if there are any deficiencies or an overabundance of energies within the chart. Although it will not provide you with the entire picture, you can learn a lot from this analysis. Typically, with a surplus of a modality or element, that person tends to overexpress said quality, and if they are lacking they tend to overcompensate. Let us now look at the elements and modalities a little closer and get a better idea as to what they entail.

THE FOUR ELEMENTS

AIR-OUR INTELLECT

Air is the element of our mental capacities. Gemini (II) represents our basic mental functions. It tells us how we take in information, how we store this information, and how we communicate this information to others. Libra ($\triangle$) is the exchange of these ideas to another person. It shows us how our ideas need compromise in order to provide harmony with one another, and how learning other people's viewpoints is important for us to understand our own. Aquarius ($\approx$) represents global consciousness. It shows us how thinking outside of the box and having an open mind can uplift and expand society so that we can evolve our personal outlook and create a brighter future.

When Air is balanced in the chart, there is a good mental outlook, an ability to learn things well, and an openness toward other people's ideas, perspectives, and thoughts. When Air is lacking in the chart, there could be learning disabilities, a lack of objectivism, narrow-mindedness, and an unwillingness to push oneself intellectually. If there is too much Air in the chart, there can be elitism, ungroundedness, use of the intellect to demean others, and a tendency to live in a sort of bubble where they do not consider other viewpoints because they consider theirs to be superior.

WATER-OUR EMOTIONS

Water is our inner emotional self. Cancer ($\mathfrak{S}$) represents our actual feelings. It shows us how we feel, how we process our feelings, how we attach to others, and how connected we are to our own inner self. Scorpio ($\mathfrak{M}$) represents how our emotions evolve over time. It shows us how we create strong bonds with others by becoming intimate, how our inner psychology changes through life experiences, and how we care for others and protect them. Pisces (♓) represents universal and unconditional love. It is our understanding of spirit, the concept of universal oneness, and our connectivity toward all living things, non-living things, and the creator of the universe.

When Water is balanced, they are well connected to their emotions and can express them properly, are able to harness unconditional love by being welcoming of others and of oneself, and do not feel the need to sacrifice the self for the sake of others. If Water is lacking, they can be cold and emotionally inept, unable to process their feelings and repressing them instead. There is an inability to relax around others and an inflexibility toward individuals and situations that befall them. If they have too much Water, they can be unreasonable, emotionally volatile, too subjective, possess too much guilt or put guilt onto others, and use emotional manipulation.

FIRE-OUR INTUITION

Fire is the element of action and going with our gut. Aries (♈) represents doing what we want to do when we want to do it. Aries goes without fear and with full confidence that the first choice is always the right choice. Leo (♌) represents the spark of our creativity. If we have an original idea, it comes from our own creative intuition, and Leo encourages us to go with that intuition and explore our ideas further. Sagittarius (♐) is the flame of righteousness and justice that maintains a well-ordered society. It shows us the higher truth of what is right and wrong so that our society can stay civilized and in harmony with one another.

If Fire is balanced, they are courageous, confident, non-judgmental, and fair. If Fire is lacking, they have a hard time believing in themself and getting things off the ground. They can second-guess themself and think that their self-expression is not important or worthy. They lack self-confidence and are introverted. If they have too much Fire, they are egotistical, judgmental, "shoot first, ask questions later," too energetic, and have a hard time being focused due to impatience.

EARTH-OUR FIVE SENSES

Earth is how we view the world by using our five senses (touch, taste, smell, vision, and hearing). Taurus (♉) represents our ability to be grounded and relaxed so that we may enjoy the moment and our surroundings. Virgo (♍) improves upon our five senses and shows us how we can make things even better and more enjoyable for ourselves. Capricorn (♑) works with the physical resources it has so that it can manifest what it wants by using discipline and concentration.

When Earth is balanced in the chart, they are frugal, practical, grounded, and focused. If Earth is lacking, they have a hard time with consistency, issues with money, unable to think logically, and have trouble with discipline and obtaining goals. If they have too much Earth, they are lazy, unmotivated, unambitious, expect things to come to them, closed-minded, and too self-critical.

THE THREE MODALITIES

CARDINAL-START OF THE SEASON

The cardinal signs Aries (♈), Cancer (♋), Libra (♎), and Capricorn (♑) bring forth the start of each season. This is the time of our solstices and equinoxes, which indicate important changes in our weather, the amount of daylight, and the overall temperament of the coming months.

Positive attributes of Cardinal energy are initiation, getting things off the ground, general optimism, strong self-identity, and confidence. Negative attributes are lack of follow-through, selfishness, and being overly ambitious.

FIXED-SEASON PROPER

Fixed signs Taurus (♉), Leo (♌), Scorpio (♏), and Aquarius (♒) occur when the season reaches its fullest expression and thus, all attributes related to that season are in full bloom. The fixed signs act as anchors and allow for permanence in state so that the seasons can reach their purest embodiment.

Positive attributes of fixed energy are seeing things through, sticking up for causes and beliefs, lasting impressions, and permanence. Negative attributes are stubbornness, elitism, selfishness, and being unable to let go/surrender.

MUTABLE-END OF THE SEASON

The Mutable signs Gemini (Ⅱ), Virgo (♍), Sagittarius (♐), and Pisces (♓) occur when the season begins to dissolve and reach their conclusions before entering the next season. Mutable signs remind us of the ever-changing state of things, and how the blending of one season into the next is all part of the organic process of life, death, and rebirth.

Positive attributes for mutable energy are the ability to compromise, consider different opinions and ideas fairly, and the ability to work as a group.

Negative attributes are a lack of autonomy, indecisiveness, constant changes in opinion, and low energy.

Alright All You Cool Cats and Kittens

Let us now apply the above knowledge and look at the birth chart of everyone's favorite crazy zookeeper from the documentary *Tiger King*: Mr. Joe Exotic himself (Fig. II-2A)

FIGURE II-2A. Birth Chart of Joe Exotic from Tiger King

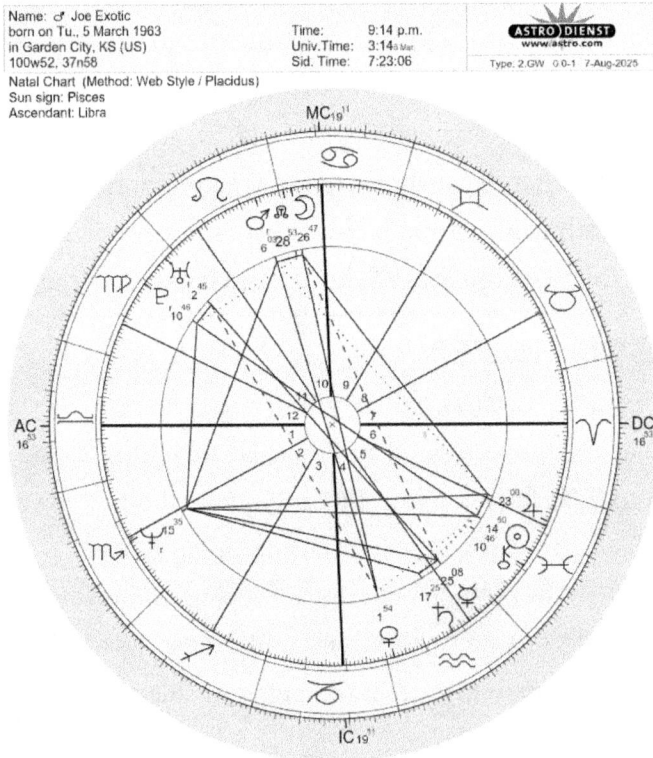

☉ Sun	14 Pis 49'51"	
☽ Moon	26 Can 47'20"	
☿ Mercury	25 Aqu 7'55"	
♀ Venus	1 Aqu 54'29"	
♂ Mars	6 Leo 2'38"r	
♃ Jupiter	22 Pis 59'51"	
♄ Saturn	17 Aqu 24'32"	
♅ Uranus	2 Vir 45'14"r	
♆ Neptune	15 Sco 34'34"r	
♇ Pluto	10 Vir 46'17"r	
☊ True Node	28 Can 53'25"d	
⚷ Chiron	10 Pis 45'34"	
AC: 16 Lib 53'15"	2: 14 Sco 30'	3: 15 Sag 40'
MC: 19 Can 11'20"	11: 22 Leo 11'	12: 21 Vir 48'

This birth chart has a Rodden Rating of "A" More on this in Book II) which means the birth time is fairly reliable. For now, we are only concerned with the element and modality grid located in the lower right-hand corner of the chart above. For the sake of convenience, let us zoom in to get a better look (Fig. II-2B).

FIGURE II-2B. Elemental and Modality Grid of Joe Exotic

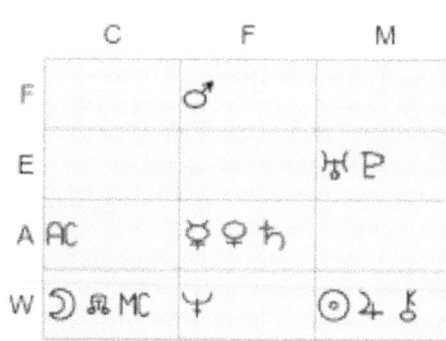

On the left side of the grid, we see the four elements Fire, Air, Earth, and Water, and on the top, we find the three modes Cardinal, Fixed, and Mutable. Without even knowing the astrology glyphs, it is easy to see which elements Joe Exotic has in abundance, and which ones he is lacking. In his case, he has an overabundance of water (Moon (☽), Midheaven (MC), Neptune(♆), Sun(☉), and Jupiter(♃), and is lacking Fire (Mars ♂).

At first, I was very surprised to discover this arrangement. Mr. Exotic is known for acting as though the entire world is a stage and is a pyromaniac who enjoys shooting guns and explosives. He also enjoys being in front of a camera and working with dangerous, exotic animals. All these things lead to a Fire personality. When I discovered that he was mostly Water, at first, it seemed confusing and contradictory, but remember, if someone is lacking an element, they tend to overcompensate.

Mr. Exotic's insatiable need for heat, attention, and firepower is him attempting to manifest the element that he is lacking within himself. Instead of trying to feed the fire within, he projects it outwardly through his various pyrotechnic antics and heavily ego-driven decision making. As you can see, without even looking at the birth chart, I already have an idea of Mr. Exotic's temperament and weaknesses.

When it comes to Mr. Exotic's modal placements, they are relatively balanced as he has three objects in Cardinal, five in Fixed, and four in Mutable. To get a better idea of an imbalanced modal arrangement, we now must look at Joe Exotic's sworn nemesis Carole Baskin.

Her chart has a Rodden rating of "X" which means the birth time is unknown, but we do know that she was born June 6, 1961, in San Antonio, TX. This is enough to get a picture of her modality and elemental grid. For the sake of convenience, let us simply look at her grid instead of the entire birth chart (Fig. II-3)

FIGURE II-3. Elemental and Modality Grid of Carole Baskin

	C	F	M
F		♂ ♅	
E	♄	♀	♇ ♏
A		♃	☉
W	☿	♆	☽ ⚷

Ms. Baskin has two planets in Cardinal, five in Fixed and three in Mutable. This means that she is lacking in Cardinal energy and has an overabundance in Fixed energy. One character trait Ms. Baskin is known for is her tenacity. She is a person who wants things to go her way and will even pay millions and wait years to do so.

This is shown by her surplus of Fixed energy, which makes her stubborn, opinionated, and unyielding. What is interesting is that she portrays herself to be a "go with the flow," flower-power kind of person who can sacrifice her own ego for the sake of something bigger. However, I would disagree with her self-assessment, and say this is her overcompensating for her lack of Cardinal energy, which can give someone a low self-esteem and self-image. Instead of working on her lack of self-esteem, she must put other people's egos in check by stating that it is the world that is the problem and never her. Ms. Baskin also has issues with initiation due to her lack of Cardinal energy and tends to react more than act.

The Starting Point

The elements and modes may not give you the entire picture, but they are a good place to start. If right off the bat you observe an imbalance in an element or modality, you can immediately give remedies. Or, when you start to learn more about who they are, it can remind you why they keep winding up in the same pitfalls. However, the elements and modalities are only the place to start, not the place to end. With that in mind, let us now dive even deeper into our exploration with the twelve signs of the zodiac.

SECTION 2—THE SIGNS OF THE ZODIAC

The Circular Band in Which All Planets Travel

If you were to lay out the entire sky map that surrounds our planet onto a two-dimensional sheet of paper, you will find this map to be cut into eighty-eight different pieces or constellations. To further the argument that mythological archetypes are universal, it should be noted that ancient Greek, Middle Eastern, Jyotish, and Egyptian civilizations came up with very similar mythologies and pictures for the same corresponding constellations.

Out of the eighty-eight constellations that create our entire sky map, all the planets in our Solar System, including the Sun and the Moon, run along the same band of twelve constellations, which we call the zodiac. This circular band of twelve constellations is also called the ecliptic when referring to the Sun's yearly pathway from Earth's perspective (Fig. II-4).

FIGURE II-4. The Ecliptic/Zodiacal Band with the Earth in the Center.[35]

The Zodiac is Mathematically Perfect

These twelve constellations perfectly fit into a 360° circular wheel, which is divided into twelve equal parts of 30° each with the Sun traveling approximately 1° per day on this pathway. This means that one celestial year is equal to three hundred sixty days every time, with no leap years. Due to the easily divisible nature of twelve by two, three, four, and six, the signs and planets therein interact with one another through various connections, which we call aspects. This will be covered more in Part II-Section 5.

35   Zeevveez, *Urania Zodiac Albrecht Durer*, September 30, 2008, photograph, archived August 7, 2020, at https://web.archive.org/web/20200807160624/https://www.flickr.com/photos/zeevveez/2900531631/.

Each of the twelve signs within the zodiac contain within them a specific modality, element, planetary ruler(s), time of the year, key phrase, and visual symbolism based upon the constellation itself. We will now discuss these various qualities along with three positive and three negative attributes for each sign.

ARIES ♈

"Be. Here. Now."

—Ram Dass, Aries

The Ram

Sheep have been an essential part of human history and tradition for thousands of years. For generations, we have used their wool for clothes, their grazing abilities to clear land, ate their meat, and drank their milk. In ancient Hebrew culture, *rabbis* would blow the ram's horn, or *shofar*, during important religious services such as *Rosh Hashanah* and *Yom Kippur*. The Celtic god Cernunnos was always depicted with a ram by his side, and the Egyptian god Khnum has the head of a ram. Even Jesus is considered to be "the good shepherd" by his followers.

Throughout many cultures, rams have been a symbol for power, drive, energy, virility, and fearlessness. Rams have no problem defending themselves by head-butting their opponents or by stomping their hooves into the ground as a warning. Goats also make the best mountain climbers and can scale a mountain with much ease. This parallels Aries in their ability to push forth and reach the top regardless of the obstacles before them. Aries always love a good challenge.

"I Am"

The key phrase for Aries is "I am," the ultimate statement of being present and accounted for. Aries individuals are not ashamed to feel important, nor do they feel unworthy when it comes to being noticed. It is the sign of personal identity and not being afraid to share that identity with the rest of the world. Aries people make themselves known and are the first ones to try anything.

They very much live in the moment and only worry about things if they need to be worried about presently. They do not bother themselves with hypotheticals or second-hand experiences. Instead, they would rather experience it personally and be the ones to share their experiences with others, as they tend to take pride in being the trailblazers of our society.

Cardinal Fire

Aries energy can be thought of as a match. That first ignition of the flame that sets the entire firepit ablaze. It is that initial spark of inspiration, that intrinsic motivation inside of us, that convinces us to get things accomplished. However, much like the match that represents them, eventually, that once explosive flame will die out quickly if it is not tended to properly.

Aries people need to learn to continue with their inspirations and see things to the end. They do a great job of going with their gut, but sometimes, they do not follow their gut in order to reach the end-goal. Instead, they usually get bored or interested in something else along the way. Regardless, cardinal fire is the inspiration that has initiated many changes, both globally and personally. It is when we finally decide to go on a diet, or when revolutionaries finally decide it is time to take up arms. When we experience cardinal fire, we feel motivated and ignited to get things done and to do things our way.

Planetary Ruler: Mars ♂

Mars is the planet of action and assertion. It tells us how we are driven, how well we stand up for ourselves, and the quality of our temperament. Aries embodies these qualities by always seeming to be the confident go-getter of the group. Aries waits for no one and does not feel the need to explain themselves to anyone. Just like a rocket being launched into space, Mars is the planet of focused direction and using our own personal will to steer in that direction toward whatever ends we desire.

Mars does not tend to consider the thoughts and opinions of others because he sees himself as his highest priority. Because Mars is aware of the self in this way, he can defend himself and knows the difference between the self and others. This provides a strong sense of self-identity, which Aries people tend to embody.

Spring Equinox

The start of Aries is a very important time for astrologers because it is the beginning of our astrological calendar. The spring equinox is the moment when the sunlight during the daytime on the Earth is equal to the dark of night. From this moment onward, the amount of sunlight will slowly grow in duration, causing the climate to become warmer and the days longer.

During this time, the snow from winter slowly melts away, preparing the Earth for spring and life to flourish once again. It is a time of great celebration, as ancient cultures knew it was the time to no longer be afraid because life was coming back to earth, which meant the soil would once again be able to harvest crops. In fact, usually before crops were planted in the spring, some farmers would conduct a controlled burn of the soil to eliminate the weeds and prepare the land for seeding. Here, again, we observe the fire motif of the Aries cardinal fire as farmers prepare their lands for the planting.

Positive Attribute #1—Heroic

Heroes tend to have a quality that goes beyond the self. They seem to be above their own human limitations, which allows them to easily strive for the unthinkable and obtain it with ease and fearlessness. In *The Odyssey*, for example, we witness Odysseus' determination to reunite with his wife after the Trojan War. Even when he is faced with every kind of obstacle imaginable, he pushes himself for the sake of love and honor. This sort of unyielding passion is what we look for within our own personal heroes. People that have pushed themselves in order to become something bigger than themself whether it is for glory, fame, personal dignity, or righteousness, inspire us to accomplish the unthinkable in ourselves.

Aries people always endeavor to be great in whatever they do. This drive motivates others around them to achieve their own goals because it makes others feel that if an Aries can do it, so can they. This is why Aries people make good personal trainers and motivational coaches. They lead by their own example, sending the message that you do not have to be special in order to achieve. You just have to possess the courage and drive to be yourself, and to believe that you are worth obtaining your own personal aims.

Positive Attribute #2—Defender

You can always count on Aries to stick up for themselves and for the ideas and people they care about because they view these things as an extension of who they are. One cannot help but feel protected around an Aries. Aries is the front line in a battle. The group of people that are sacrificing their own lives for the sake of defending whatever they feel deserves defending. You can guarantee that an Aries will stand up for their own ideas and opinions of the world because they come from direct experiences.

Aries knows what is best for them because they have experienced it first-hand and therefore they do not need to consider your opinion. However, because Aries is not fixed, it is possible to change their perspective if it is brought to them through a path of self-discovery. For example, if an Aries is unable to tap into their feelings, show them a movie that you know would evoke emotions within them. This helps the Aries to relate to themself through their own identification. Or, if you are in an argument with an Aries, it is important to put them inside your own shoes. Once they understand your perspective through their own experience, they are then able to empathize and relate.

Positive Attribute #3—Pushes Limits

Aries are highly self-motivated. They seek to improve and test their own plateaus frequently by seeing if they can just tip the scale a little bit more before giving up. This is why follow-through is very important for an Aries person to harness. If they are able to make their goals more long-term, they are able to improve over time quite well due to their endless supply of determination. Aries loves a challenge, and they love to challenge themselves even more.

This is why they have to make sure they pay attention to their actual limits, as they can physically hurt themselves in an accident. Still, Aries are keen to go one step further than what is expected, not to show others that they can, but to show themselves that they can. Having others be impressed by their abilities to endure is just an added bonus.

Negative Attribute #1—Forceful

Aries can sometimes become intimidating and too forceful when it comes to dealing with others. When this happens, it is usually the Mars energy that gets ignited and becomes out of control. This can put others into a corner where they are left to either fly or fight. Either way, the Aries wins.

The best way to handle this situation is to diffuse the energy immediately. When the Aries fire becomes too hot to handle, you do not want to feed it with more energy, but sizzle it out by breaking the fourth wall, and bringing their behavior to their direct attention. Sometimes Aries people are simply not aware that they are being too forceful on an issue. Bringing that to their attention helps them to take a step back and evaluate a bit more.

Negative Attribute #2—Shoot Now, Ask Questions Later

Aries people are risk takers, but they are not calculated risk takers, as this is more of a Capricorn trait. This is because they can become so enthralled in the present moment, that they do not think too far enough ahead in order to consider the consequences of their actions. Similarly, Aries people can become so obsessed with the need for instant movement and gratification that they rarely question their actions beforehand.

Aries need to think about the pros and cons before making important and risky decisions. This will safeguard them for the better and will prevent them from getting out of sticky situations. Not that the Aries should doubt their choices or hesitate on their choices; they simply need to ponder to see if their choice is the best option at that moment. This will also help Aries individuals with a better sense of strategy and planning.

Negative Attribute #3—Bully/Bossy

When Aries' energy is out of control, it becomes that of the bully. Ruled by Mars, Aries can create a world full of power struggles. Aries can sometimes feel that they should be the boss without question. They achieve this by asserting fear, dominance, and power over others. When this occurs, they need to seriously consider therapy because it is usually a projection of them not feeling secure inside their own body. Consequently, they feel that they need to make others feel inferior. When Aries children are showing these traits, parents should take care to nurture their feelings better and figure out the root causes of these frustrations.

Cunning and Brave

We start out the gates running to begin the new year and the zodiac story with independent and courageous Aries. Their ability to live in the present moment is how they gain respect and admiration. Instead of dwelling, pondering, or regretting, the Aries moves forth without hesitation. Rules by Mars, Aries has stamina, attraction, and a sense of adventure. However, it is within the Aries nature to also be pushy, aggressive, and intimidating, if it is not operating functionally.

TAURUS ♉

"You are unique, and if that is not fulfilled, then something has been lost."

—Martha Graham, Taurus

The Bull

The cow has been a staple part of the human experience for millennia. Not only do we consume the cow's milk and meat, but bulls have also been used to plow the land in preparation for the seeding of crops. In countries like India, cows are heavily revered and honored for their service to humanity.

Cows are also highly intelligent animals that can remember things for a long time. In fact, animal behaviorists have found that cows interact in socially complex ways, developing friendships over time, and even holding grudges against other cows that have treated them badly; very Taurian indeed. Although their stature is robust, cows can be surprisingly agile and playful. However, they can be just as stubborn, not wanting to leave a spot or moving only if they so desire.

"I Own"

The key phrase for Taurus is "I own" which makes these individuals attribute their personal qualities to the things that surround them. A Taurus feels the clothes they wear, the decorations in their house, and even the cars they drive make a statement toward their own personality and as an extension of themself.

Tauruses can have trouble sharing their valuables with others because they are afraid that if they do not get the item back, a part of themself is also lost. You will rarely see a Taurus disheveled or looking drab. In fact, if you see a Taurus looking this way, this is a sign that they are not feeling in tip-top shape. Wanting better valuables and surrounding themselves with nicer things are big motivators for Tauruses. Similarly, as their personality evolves and changes, so does their wardrobe and valuables.

Fixed Earth

Although our own planet is not considered in astrology, Taurus is the sign that best represents Mother Earth. Fixed earth is how we are able to create a foundation, support ourselves, and beautify our spaces. Just like the bull, fixed earth is not going anywhere and in doing so, creates a secure space for us to plant our goals, our things, and our relationships.

Being fixed earth, Tauruses are literally the physical anchors on this planet. They maintain stability, keep situations pleasant, and allow for others to simply relax and enjoy comforts. Fixed earth reminds us to stop and smell the roses. A Taurus conceptualizes that we are put on this earth to enjoy life and need to remember to take breaks from the rat race so that we can recharge our batteries and admire the fruits of our labors.

Planetary Ruler: Venus ♀

As mentioned above, the element earth functions through the five senses. Venus, as the ruler of Taurus, is a literal manifestation of our five senses and the enjoyment of using these senses to understand and experience the world around us. Venus is the planet of luxury, aesthetics, pleasure, and enjoyment; all of which are embodied within Taurus. For a visual example, the empress card within the tarot deck is an archetypal representation of Taurus and Venus. Here, we see the empress reclining on her couch, surrounded by a forest and wheat with her symmetrical crown and heart shield with the Venus symbol engraved on the front. Venus and Taurus remind us of the beautiful works of art that humanity has created over the years, and Taurus certainly knows how to enjoy these pleasures.

Spring Proper

During the month of Taurus, the flowers are in full bloom, the birds are singing their songs, and the weather is perfectly mild and pleasant for a nice picnic and other outdoor activities. Once the frost of winter is finally gone, thanks to the onset of spring brought on by Aries, it is now time to seed the harvest into the fertile soil. This explains why the astrological calendar was important to our ancestors because it told them when the timing was right to plant the crops for a year's harvest. Indeed, much of our vegetation is planted during this time.

POSITIVE ATTRIBUTE #1—Arts Curator

Tauruses appreciate all of the arts and tend to become patrons by purchasing works of art, attending concerts, and visiting museums. The arts are a vital part of human history, and thanks to Tauruses, the arts are preserved, honored, and valued. Tauruses act as a great litmus test to see if certain styles are going to catch on or not (famous *Vogue* editor Anna Wintour is a Taurus). They usually surround themselves with paintings and statues, and even their clothing is an art piece in itself. Thanks to their admiration of the creative, the arts are able to continue within our culture.

POSITIVE ATTRIBUTE #2—Femininity

Tauruses, both male and female, carry with them the positive attributes that society usually associates with femininity. Qualities like grace, poise, culture, and being well-presented, with a lightness to their movements, speech, and attitude. However, this is not to say that Tauruses should be expected to act inferior to masculinity.

Over the course of history, there has been a firm definition as to which character traits constitute femininity and which ones are more masculine. Today, we live in a world where these qualities are no longer divided by the sexes. Nor is a woman expected to act feminine, or a man masculine. Furthermore, we live in a society that encourages, and should encourage, a lack of labels and categorizations.

However, the fact that Tauruses contain these positive feminine characteristics is meant to be a compliment because they possess all of the favorable qualities society traditionally associates with femininity. If a Taurus is invited to a gala, you can guarantee that they will be the best dressed, elegantly received, properly groomed, and thoroughly admired for their social graces.

POSITIVE ATTRIBUTE #3—Connection to Mother Earth

As previously mentioned, Tauruses are strongly connected to Mother Earth. Taurus people, if they so desire, can create an easy link to the spirit of Earth and communicate with her along with fairies, nature devas, and gnomes. Tauruses have a natural green thumb and can create robust and lush gardens. They also have big hearts when it comes to environmentalism, animal cruelty, and conservationism. The Venus quality of Taurus makes them lovers of peace, and Tauruses wish for world peace between humanity and nature.

NEGATIVE ATTRIBUTE #1—Vanilla

Taurus people know what they like and tend to not push themselves outside of their comfort zones, making them predictable and unadventurous. It is very hard to convince a Taurus to try a new food or a new activity that is unfamiliar. Nor do they appreciate spontaneity and not having a plan.

Taurus people need to learn to push themselves out of routines and monotony so that they can experience more of what this world has to offer. The issue is, when it comes to the fixed signs, in most cases, stubbornness tends to be the biggest downfall. Taurus needs to be more flexible when it comes to trying new things, meeting new people, and just going with the flow.

NEGATIVE ATTRIBUTE #2—Unmotivated

Tauruses can have a very hard time getting motivated in everything from working out, to diets, to personal projects. The fixed earth quality hinders their ability to become inspired and stay inspired, as they usually tend to enjoy the inspiration of others. Taurus people need to find whatever it is that encourages them to become a better person and to pursue their vision.

Sometimes, it is easy for Taurus to become too complacent and not really care about grand schemes or big dreams. This is where the Taurus is doing a discredit to their own self because they are, in fact, immensely talented if they can focus their energy toward a goal. Having some sort of thought-out plan prior by laying out their goals into smaller pieces will help them to stay motivated and realize that they can accomplish anything.

NEGATIVE ATTRIBUTE #3—Fairy Tale Expectations

Due to the pleasant nature of "Happily Ever After," it is easy for Taurus people to fall into the trap of unreal expectations when it comes to love. This is complicated by the fact that Tauruses tend to be more of the romantic type of the zodiac, preferring candle-lit dinners and massages to more risqué activities. If you are dating a Taurus and forget your anniversary or Valentine's day, it is probably better that you do not show up at home at all.

Taurus people need to release expectations of these fictional ideas of romance when it comes to their own relationships by remembering that people are not perfect, and that there will always be some discord when it comes to their partner. It is also important to remember that although they may be romantic, sometimes their partner may not be as mushy as they would like, but this does not mean they love them less.

Glamorous and Artful

Taurus is the bed we lay on, and the bed that the entire world rests upon. They bring stability and relaxation, but they can also bring predictability and complacency. Ruled by Venus, they have style and love the arts. They also have a great eye for aesthetics, colors, and living spaces. This is the time of the year when Spring has sprung and the breath of life has been brought back onto this planet in one big inhale and exhale. Be that as it may, a Taurus should not base their life too much in a world of fantasy, and remember that goals and accomplishments of their own are just as important and achievable as anyone else's.

GEMINI ♊

"We must never forget that the highest appreciation is not to utter words, but to live by them."

—John F. Kennedy, Gemini

The Twins

Twins are two people that have identical experiences but view these experiences differently due to their differences in personality. They have the same mother, father, and upbringing, but somehow, their psychology is incredibly unique and special.

For Geminis, there are two sides to every story. Like their fellow air sign Libra, they are concerned with weighing options and the variances of opinions. The difference is: Libra tries to take both sides of the argument and come to a compromise, where Gemini literally experiences both sides of the argument at the same time.

This ties into Gemini's mutability. Sometimes, it can be very hard for them to make a decision because they see both decisions as valid. Either way, the twins represent an exchange of information from two different sides of the argument at hand.

Another theme that we see in twins is the sibling association. Even if the Gemini does not have any siblings, they associate with their friends and the like as if they were their own brothers and sisters. This creates a very informal, yet intimate, connection with the ones they care about. Geminis are always looking for their other twin, a person with whom they can experience the same events together, and then share their differences in opinion. However, we must also remember that the term "sibling rivalry" exists for a reason, and that Geminis can become unreasonably argumentative and hostile toward those close to them.

"I Communicate"

For Geminis, communication is key, as they are very curious individuals, wanting to ask other people their thoughts, opinions, and knowledge. Not only do they enjoy the exchange of communicating, they are very good at adjusting their own speech in order to keep conversations going.

Geminis are always asking the "what and how" of things. Just like Scorpios, they are inquisitive people. The difference is: Scorpios ask questions to get to the bottom of the situation, and Geminis are simply curious, and want to ask people what they think just for the sake of asking and understanding.

Mutable Air

When it comes to mutable air, just think about the air in which we inhale and exhale. One moment, we are inhaling oxygen, which travels into our bodies though our lungs, and then, we exhale carbon dioxide back out into the world.

Indeed, it is breathing that allows for us to communicate in the first place because we use this air to vibrate our vocal cords.

Mutable air literally goes where the wind takes it. They are free-flowing and unconcerned with where things are going. It is more about the journey than the destination. Because mutable air is adaptable, Geminis can talk about anything because they are interested in learning about anything with anyone. They enjoy going with the flow of the people and the surrounding situations.

When it comes to participating in various activities, Geminis are not as concerned with the activity itself as long as they can participate in the activity with their intellect and speech. For example, a trip to an art museum might not be as fun to a Gemini as it would be for a Taurus, but if the Gemini is able to discuss the artwork and read up on the descriptions, they will have a fun time. However, if it is a strictly no talking affair, they will not have much fun, and may in fact become a little mischievous in the process in order to protest.

Planetary Ruler: Mercury ☿

Mercury (or Hermes) was the messenger of the gods in Roman and Greek mythology. Not only was he a fast traveler, he was also a fast thinker, able to come up with workable schemes at the quickest moment. In the natal chart, Mercury not only tells us how we communicate, but also how we think and process information.

Geminis, being ruled by Mercury, are quick on their feet, quick in their thoughts, and quick with their ideas. They have a pace about them that makes it hard to catch up sometimes. They can take in information rapidly and exchange ideas just as quickly. Geminis are naturals when it comes to anything related to technology and the internet.

End of Spring

Toward the end of spring, we are wrapping up the academic school year with students graduating, saying their goodbyes, and tying up friendships they would like to continue throughout summer and beyond. Many pictures are taken, many speeches are given, and many yearbooks are signed.

This is a very active time when people are starting to conclude their work calendars and prepare for their summer vacations. Similarly, in nature, now that the warmth of the Sun is in full swing, animals and people tend to be more relaxed as the fear of winter is no longer apparent and the intense heat of summer is on the way. Thus, people tend to be in lighter moods and are able to enjoy their friendships and families once again because not only is the weather more agreeable, but children are now on their vacations.

Positive Attribute #1—Social Chameleon

If you put a Gemini into any social setting, they will be able to get along with anyone, regardless of how different they are. Gemini people know what to say and how to say it, depending on the social circumstances in which they find themselves. This makes them very relatable people, as anyone can feel as though they can talk to them.

This comes in handy when a situation needs to be diffused. Mutable signs have a talent for calming down heated arguments or tensions, and Geminis do this best by simply knowing what to say and when to say it. They usually do not have to think about it beforehand as they have a natural talent to have the most appropriate phrase simply roll off the tongue.

Positive Attribute #2—Brotherly and Sisterly Love

If you are living with a Gemini or have a Gemini friend or partner, they try to make you feel as though you are one of their siblings. This makes the environment intimate, yet lighthearted. Even if you are meeting a Gemini for the first time, they try to create this association up front, making you feel at ease, as if they have known you their entire life.

Geminis are fun, loving, playful, and enjoy good humor and a carefree attitude. Geminis want you to feel as though you can trust them, and the casual feeling they bring to their relationships make it easy for others to approach them. Not only for comfort, but also for fun and enjoyment. You can guarantee that the Gemini is up for anything and enjoys outings and get-togethers.

Positive Attribute #3—Good with Technology

When it comes to anything involving technology or the internet, Geminis are the masters in this department. Highly skilled in social networking and internet searching, they make great media experts. Their speed, matched with their ability to understand the technological process, allows for them to compute, create, and find whatever they need on the internet with ease and speed.

This also makes them talented in creating spreadsheets, computing data, working with digital financial books, word documents, and fast responses when it comes to emails and texting. Geminis are also great at troubleshooting technology as well as buying the latest technological products such as smartphones, laptops, and smart cars.

Negative Attribute #1—Instigator

Sometimes for a Gemini, any communication is good communication. It can be very hard for a Gemini to be still and silent, which causes them to demand a perpetual dialogue, even though the other person does not want to engage with them. The Gemini frankly does not care. In order to keep the conversation going, they encourage conflict so that the other person will talk to them, even though it is argumentative.

Geminis really know how to push buttons. They tend to do this by riling up the other person, getting them flustered, and when the other person voices their frustrations, the Gemini makes it seem as if it was you that caused yourself to feel that way instead of the Gemini.

When Geminis are acting in this way, they need to learn the art of silence. Sometimes we need to rest, and not converse. This is not a bad thing, nor does it indicate that something is wrong. Simply, if everyone were to spend every moment in conversation, eventually we would run out of things to talk about, and the quality of the dialogue would dwindle with each passing moment.

Negative Attribute #2—Compulsive Fibbers

As mentioned above, Geminis have the ability to keep others engaged without thinking twice. That, mixed with their ability to say things in the right tone, allows for them to easily lie and have the other person believe them with much ease.

Unlike water signs, who can use emotional manipulation to get what they want, Geminis get what they want by having you foolishly believe that they are right because they sound so sure. If you come across this issue and something does not register within your own deductive logic, counter the Gemini by having them explain what they mean by asking for further details. Even Geminis have a hard time building up lies on top of lies.

Negative Attribute #3—Short—Term Focus

Just like Aries, Geminis tend to live in the moment and can have trouble seeing the bigger picture and working toward long-term objectives, as their critical thinking can sometimes be a little too much on the surface.

They need to do as Virgos do and ask themselves, "What is the function of the thing I am trying to understand?" This allows for them to go more in depth because they are attempting to comprehend the why and how in addition to what.

Inquisitive and Communicative

Gemini are great conversationalists and are genuinely curious to hear what you have to say. They are fast-paced, on the go, and very social. Being naturals at social media, they always know the latest trends and can keep tabs on many people and situations all at once. The end of spring is the time when energy starts to ramp up on the planet. Vacations start to be planned, celebrations are had, and the Gemini social butterfly can't get enough. Mercury as their planetary rule gives them the ability to say the right thing at the right moment, and skills to understand things quickly. However, Geminis need to work on being short-sighted, and mustn't instigate trouble just because they can. Either way, Geminis are great to be around and are masters of fun.

CANCER ♋

"Could a greater miracle take place than for us to look through each other's eyes for an instant?"

—Henry David Thoreau, Cancer

The Crab

Crabs are in tune with the tides of the ocean because they live under the sand where the land and water meet. Not only do they need to know when the water is approaching for breathing purposes, the low and high tides tell them when it is safe to emerge.

When crabs have gotten too big for their shell, they need to leave their outer casing in order to search for a bigger one, making them incredibly vulnerable until they have found a new shell that properly fits. However, when they do come across their new shell, they once again become impenetrable and protected from predators.

Crabs are known as bottom feeders because they feed on the smaller sea creatures and organisms that live on the seabed. The crab's pincers are used primarily for finding food, but if a crab feels threatened, they quickly become a dangerous tool for defense.

Cancers similarly possess identical attributes to the animal that represents their sign. Being ruled by the Moon, they are very much in sync with the ebb and flow of life just as crabs are in tune with the ebb and flow of the ocean. They also contain a strong intuition that tells them if the circumstance is a safe one or a dangerous one.

Cancers have a hard time coming out of their shell because they do not like to feel threatened or vulnerable. Still, if they take the leap of faith and put themselves out there, they find that they grow and indeed become stronger.

Cancers know what they need in order to be nourished, usually going about their lives peacefully, but are very much able to stand their ground if they feel threatened and confident enough.

"I Feel"

The keyword for Cancer is "I feel." Cancers are connected to their feeling function and operate on this level in everything they do. All water signs approach life through their emotions, but in Cancer's case, they are emotions incarnate.

When you talk to a Cancer, they understand the meaning behind what it is you are saying. They are able to tell if you are sincere or artificial not by what you are saying, but by the emotional content underneath what it is you are saying. They are gentle, delicate, and very loving toward the ones they care about.

Cardinal Water

With Aries, which was cardinal fire, we saw the initial intuitive reaction of going with our gut. With Cancer, which is cardinal water, we see the primary responses of our emotions. Our feelings sometimes have no logic. We can be angry, sad, or happy, with no real rhyme or reason. If we are in touch with our inner feelings, like Cancer, we experience our first emotional response fully, immediately, and genuinely, just as Aries is when it comes to their desire to act.

A lot of people tend to repress their emotions or negate their existence altogether. This is seen in the more traditional way men are brought up in this world by being taught to "suck it up" and that "crying is for babies." With Cancer, there is no hiding what it is they are feeling because, just like Aries, their responses are instantaneous.

Planetary Ruler: The Moon ☽

Put simply, the Moon represents our inner self. It shows us our capacity for emotions, how we handle our emotions, and whether we take our emotions seriously or not. If we are emotionally self-sufficient, we experience a kind of confidence where no matter what we do, we feel secure because we are grounded in who we are as a person on the inside. If we are not in touch with our inner self, we can become volatile or dependent on others because we do not feel that sense of inner security. Cancers should take care in paying attention to the moon phases because, although we are all affected by the moon's monthly nature, this is even more true for Cancers.

Summer Solstice

The summer solstice is the halfway point between the spring and fall. From now until the fall equinox, the days will get slightly shorter, but the temperature will stay warmer. It is hard to understand why a water sign ushers in the hot season of summer, but we must remember that during this time, the air is very humid and sticky, which is thanks to the added moisture and heat in the air.

Now that children are out of school during this time, families get together and celebrate traditional holidays like Independence Day in the United States, and Canada Day in Canada. Also, now that it is officially summer, people begin to visit the beach in addition to other tropical destinations. Watery fruits like oranges, watermelons, mangos, and coconuts are enjoyed during this time to cool ourselves off from the humid climate.

Positive Attribute #1—Good Listener

Cancers are very caring individuals who sincerely want to listen to your problems because they enjoy being there for the ones they care about. They can detect how you are feeling and are able to cool down frustrations quite easily if they are not angered themselves. Cancers have this unique ability to transmute your emotions while you are speaking to them because you are both cooperatively processing them, with their help, without you even realizing.

Positive Attribute #2—Builder

Like their opposition Capricorn, Cancers know how to work from the ground up. Not only are Cancers good at nurturing feelings, they are also great at nurturing projects and relationships. They understand the value of baby steps and building something significant slowly over time. Cancers take relationships very seriously. They invest their entire being toward whomever it is they care about and are thus willing to stick it out through thick and thin. This ability gives Cancers a great threshold for patience because they know that Rome was not built in a day, and that taking great care creates some of the most majestic, secure, and profitable outcomes.

Positive Attribute #3—Intimate

Cancers can create an environment that makes you feel secure and loved. It is very easy to become personable and close to them because you do not feel threatened. Cancers are non-judgmental people and are very connected to their empathy. Indeed, all elements have the capability to demonstrate some facet of unconditional love in their own unique ways.

With fire, you experience the love of experiencing life. Air is the love of conversing ideas and thoughts with others. Earth is the love of enjoyment. Water, however, is literally the purest essence of what we mean when we say love as the polar opposite to fear.

Cancers, without saying anything, send out a message that says, "It is okay to feel whatever it is that is inside of you. It is okay to cry, and it is okay to be scared. I am here for you." Because of this, Cancers create a bubble of emotional security where people can let their guard down and express whatever it is on the inside that needs to be expressed.

Negative Attribute #1—Irritable

When people are feeling moody or touchy, it is no wonder we call them crabby. Cancers can easily be at the mercy of daily moon energies, which makes it very easy for them to feel uncomfortable and irritable. They need to make sure to use objective reasoning when their emotions become irrational, so they do not lash out toward others. The best way to handle illogical outbursts is by thinking through the situation. Cancers should ask themselves if they have just cause for feeling the way they do, or if it is due to waking up on the wrong side of the bed. If it is the latter, they can put themselves in a better mood by engaging in activities that always make them calm and happy.

Negative Attribute #2—Dependent

Cancers have a reputation for being clingy. Similar to Libra, they become so focused on the other person that they can lose themselves in the process. Both signs love and desire to feel needed. The difference is: Libra is concerned about maintaining the relationship in the literal sense, and Cancer is concerned about maintaining their sense of security.

This comes from Cancer's love for memories and past experiences. If a relationship was positive and loving at first, the Cancer wants to keep these memories alive, even if it is no longer the case. Cancers need to make sure they can release relationships and situations when they have passed their expiration date, and to have the confidence to stand on their own two feet.

Negative Attribute #3—Irrational

Water, as our emotional function, does not use reasoning or logic in their processes like Air. Therefore, Cancers can have a reputation for coming up with bizarre conclusions that have no real findings within reality. This is especially true when they are riled up and allow for their emotions and mood get the better of them.

Although they make good listeners, Cancers need to be able to do some of the talking themselves. If they discuss their conclusions with others who are more objective, this will help them to realize the holes within their reasoning. However, if Cancers decide to bottle it up and create actions based upon their irrationalities, they find themselves unconsciously manifesting their paranoia.

For example, if a Cancer thinks that their partner is cheating on them with no real evidence, they might start to treat the relationship as if their partner was cheating on them, which causes unneeded tension and disharmony. Eventually, that partner will leave due to the unjustified anger Cancer is emanating toward them. But instead of understanding that this was due to the Cancer's own self-undoing, they might instead say "See?! I knew you were going to leave me," further perpetuating the irrationality that got them there in the first place. Cancers should strive to balance emotions with rationality to alleviate this common pitfall.

Caring and Careful

Cancers are emotionally nurturing and pragmatic. They are great with taking baby steps to one day manifest into something grand. You feel warmth and calmness around Cancers, and their sense of nostalgia is incredibly comforting. This time of year marks the start of summer family gatherings and vacations where bonds are forged stronger for each passing year. Being ruled by the Moon, Cancers feel and base their entire reality and motivations on their feelings, which can sometimes be too subjective and irrational if they're not careful. Cancers should also push their limits and try new things. If they do, they might surprise themselves.

LEO ♌

"Love yourself first and everything else falls into line. You really have to love yourself to get anything done in this world."

—Lucille Ball, Leo

The Lion

The power, majesty, and glory surrounding Leo is paralleled to the multitude of stories and regal representations of the lion that we observe within history and mythology. For example, King Richard I of England was known as "The Lionheart" due to his military prowess and bravery. Strangely enough, the heart is the body part that is ruled by Leo.

A Leo does not require a literal kingdom because whomever they are and wherever they are, they will build up a monarch-like following in which they are constantly admired. Similar to the Sun that rules their sign, Leos have a natural gravitational pull about them where others cannot help but be tugged into their orbit. This is because Leos, without even realizing it, project an aura of confidence, poise, and an all-encompassing ability to be present. If you have the Leo's attention, you will have all of their attention, which is one of the reasons people are so attracted to their energy. The catch is, of course, that you need to be able to keep the Leo's attention, else they slip away looking for their next form of entertainment.

The allure that Lions have is almost indescribable. People tend to respect and admire their beauty along with their ability to harm if they so choose. Just like lions, people are incredibly curious around Leos. They possess within them the ability to exist so well in the moment that people are amazed by their ability to possess that spark of originality which comes from a purely genuine individual. What you see is what you get with Leos and if you dislike it, the Leo does not consider it to be their problem but yours. The lesson people learn from a Leo is to be yourself and to not care about what the world thinks.

Leos walk the fine line between mercy and tyranny. They can either understand the value of paying it forward and that good deeds come back to you, much like the fable of the Lion and the Mouse. Or they can act like King John of England, who was cruel and vindictive just because he simply could. When Leos balance power with perspective, in other words, if they can put themselves in other people's shoes while in their positions of authority, then their truly regal nature shines forth because they are balancing personal agency with control and restraint.

"I Create"

Leos are immensely talented within the arts. This is because the act of creating involves imprinting your own self and your own expression onto a medium. Leos, like their fellow fire sign Aries, do not question their motives and simply do. Leos do not need or ask for approval, nor do they question or second-guess their creative output. This intuitive approach, mixed with Leo's confidence, allows for them to blossom wonderfully artistic expressions out of nothing and be honored for their work.

Furthermore, Leos are able to create just for the sake of creating. There does not have to be a message or some sort of pervasive theme. The simple fact that it came from within is itself a genuine enough reason for their creation to exist. Even if the Leo does not work in the arts, they are imaginative, inspirational, and are able to think up original ideas in whatever profession they chose.

Fixed Fire

Fixed fire is that of the eternal flame. The all-pervasive, unceasing, omnipresent light of the soul that exists within all of us. Leos stand as a reminder of this fire, which is simply spirit shining forth as a unique expression of the energy that manifested this universe. People are attracted to Leos: they see their souls on full display and people crave that ability to be as true and genuine to themselves.

Fixed fire burns away and purges all of the sorrows on Earth. It reminds us of the happiness and light-heartedness of our experience that makes life worth living in the first place. Within our souls, there is no suffering, agony, or duality, but only light and love. Leos take away our pain with their cheerful and carefree attitude, and we thank and honor them as kings and queens for keeping this flame alive within our tumultuous world.

Planetary Ruler: The Sun ☉

The Sun is unceasing in its light and warmth. It loves us so much and has so much love to give that not only is our planet pulled in by its gravitational force, but all other planets in our solar system are as well. Indeed, without the Sun, there would be no life on this planet.

Stars within our universe are born out of nebulas, which contain the chemicals needed for life. It is a scientific fact that all organic life, including ourselves, is composed of this star-stuff. Naturally, the Sun represents all parts of us that we have in common, but the difference is that Leos act more individualistically because they appreciate that their unique life was meant to be lived. Leos, being ruled by the Sun, emanate light and joy.

Just how ancient cultures honored the Moon as the mother and provider, the Sun was also worshiped. Indeed, our entire celestial calendar's primary function was to tell ancient cultures when the seasons would change due to the Sun's apparent path around the zodiac.

Just like the Sun, Leos tend to give off a warmth that helps others burn away their own darkness and fears. The Sun does not fear. On the contrary, as the giver of light, it sizzles out fear and darkness. Light from the Sun makes the crops grow, gives us warmth, and keeps the earth in orbit. If a comet, which could destroy our planet, gets pulled into the Sun's gravity, it dissolves into nothingness as it approaches the Sun's rays and surface.

All planets in our solar system are loyal to our Sun and the Sun is similarly loyal to its planetary subjects. As such, Leos are very loyal creatures. If you have been swept into their sphere of influence, it is because they truly care about you and want to provide for you in the same way that our own Sun provides for every living thing on this planet.

Summer Proper

Leo occurs during the heart of summer, when people have the most freedom from their obligations. This is the time for enjoyment and doing what it is you want to do because of the agreeable weather and open schedule. This is also the time where "summer bodies" are shown off and admired, as people tend to wear fewer layers. Themes involving children are also observed because this is a time when children tend to go to summer camp, theme parks, and zoos so that they may enjoy their carefree existence.

Positive Attribute #1—The Child Outlook

In Eastern philosophy, the goal of having a "child's eye" is one many people aspire toward. This Buddhist concept means you approach everything in life with innocence, non-judgmentalism, curiosity, and unconditional love just as a child would, with no comprehension of fear or dread. As children, we start off life without care and worry; it is only the world of adults that slowly corrupts the mind to think a certain way, which causes the child to eventually lose touch with their once carefree mentality.

Leos very much embody the child's outlook by approaching life with gusto and confidence, not being concerned with the opinions of others, and with an excitement about life. They are naturally curious individuals who simply observe more than they analyze. Instead, Leos are present in the moment and are open to whatever experiences come their way.

Positive Attribute #2—Loyalty

Leos are very loyal creatures, not only in relationships and friendships but also toward their ideals and objectives, because they are very true to themselves. You can expect a Leo to defend what they believe in, protect who they care about, and finish their endeavors to the end.

This is because Leos have an innate understanding of the self. To them, there is no question or doubt about who they are as a person. It is their fixed fire quality, their lack of second-guessing, that allows for them to stand up for their opinions. Leos are very good at expressing themselves through action. What you see is what you get because they are so sure of their understanding and therefore see it as truth.

Positive Attribute #3—Social

Leos are very much social butterflies. They make great hosts and hostesses and guests at parties. Their liveliness mixed with their interesting personality makes them a great addition to any social gathering. Leos are able to create large social circles around them with admirers and professional associations.

Leos always feel that they are on a stage performing for those who are watching (and not watching). This makes them entertaining and energetic creatures in whatever social situation they are placed. Their curiosity makes them interested in other people, even though they tend to always turn it back toward their own knowledge and experiences. For example, if you are conversing with a Leo and you mention astrology, the Leo will then take that opportunity to dive into everything they know about astrology and might even neglect to ask you about your opinion. Still, people find Leos fascinating and interesting because they seem to have an opinion on any topic.

Negative Attribute #1—Self-Absorbed

Leos can sometimes forget that there are other people in a room. They can become so obsessed with their self-importance that they assume everyone around them is simply an audience member for their own one-woman or one-man show. Leos need to remember that, although they have strong opinions, they are not the only person with opinions and thoughts.

Leos need to make sure that they do not become too self-centered to a point where they flat out ignore other people in their lives. This ties back to their dedication toward their own objectives and ideas. They can sometimes forget the need for collaboration for the sake of the group. This is where Leo stubbornness can become their worst enemy because not only are they unwilling to budge in their opinions, they have this attitude that their opinion is the only one that matters, which can put them in a bad light.

Negative Attribute #2—Gets Away with It

When you are trying to discipline a child, sometimes they can become so endearing, so adorable, that you cannot even fathom punishing them. Leos can captivate this charm readily to where they easily slip out of consequences. This is particularly dangerous if you are in a relationship with a Leo, or if they are your employee within a professional setting.

Even when Leos are 100 percent in the wrong, giving them a free pass only encourages their bad behavior and keeps others in toxic environments. The Leo then has free range to do as they please while the others have to suffer and obey the rules. Leos are not unintelligent and know when they are in the wrong. Meaning, they should be more honest with themselves and own up to their wrong doings instead of manipulating those around them with their smile and charisma.

Negative Attribute #3—Tyrannical

If a Leo is in a position of authority, they need to make sure that they lead by example and not by "do as I say, not as I do." When they are the ones with the power, they then have the approval to boss others around due to the power structure that is in place.

Although the Leo can get what they want, they are leaving space for feelings of bitterness, anger, and resentment toward them, if forcing others do as they command is solely due to the division of power. Consequently, when that division of power disappears and the Leo is then put on the same level as the ones they once terrorized, this can make them prone to feeling alone, isolated, and in their eyes, disrespected. Leos should remember that throughout history, there are many examples of dethroned kings and queens who took their power a little too far. To this point, a great example is King Charles I of England who was so obstinate with parliament's decisions, he eventually decided to dissolve the parliament, which subsequently led to a civil war and his execution for high treason. The Leo must never forget that their crown is only as secure as the people's trust that put them there in the first place.

Individualistic and Charming

A Leo's nature is a very bright and captivating one. Others are drawn in like a moth to the flame and are dazzled by the Leo's brilliance, confidence, and uniqueness. They're creative, attention-getting, and joyful. The time of Leo is the climax of Summer, where kids have the freedom to be kids, and everyone is able to let their hair down, filling their schedules with recreation and relaxation. Ruled by the Sun, Leos burn away fear and darkness and attract others with their jovial nature. Still, Leos need to be mindful of using their charm for nefarious purposes and giving others the same freedom and expression they themselves enjoy.

VIRGO ♍

"Talent is cheaper than table salt. What separates the talented individual from the successful one is a lot of hard work."

—Stephen King, Virgo

The Virgin

The archetype of the Virgin is one that has been honored for thousands of generations. In Rome, Vestal Virgins were keepers of the temple of the goddess Vesta and were revered as the maintainers of Roman society. In Christian mythology, the Virgin Mary is likewise honored as a symbol of temperance, good deeds, duty, and morality.

In many religions, leaders are asked to take vows of chastity. In the Hindu faith, for example, the reasoning behind this is to preserve their sexual energy stored in the lower chakras so that it may be used to awaken the kundalini.

Being chaste not only requires discipline, it requires the sacrifice of one's animal instincts of procreation for the sake of something higher like that of spiritual evolution, the preservation of a culture, or simply our own goals and ambitions. However, in our society today, we do not honor the choice of abstaining. On the contrary, those that decide to save their more intimate encounters for either someone special or for a greater cause are chastised and criticized within our culture.

To this point, academia has noted a contemporary phenomenon known as "the Virgin/Whore dichotomy," which tends to affect women more than men. Put simply, if a woman decides to not be sexually active, they are thought of as a prude. However, if a woman is decisively sexually active, they are thought of as a whore. Men also experience this dichotomy because if they decide to be abstinent, they can be teased for not being a "real man." However, men are less likely to experience the whore label of this dichotomy because men are very much encouraged to be sexual creatures within our society.

Patience, discipline, and saving your most sacred part for the person or situation that you feel is worthy are some of the great gifts that Virgo offers. The problem is, because we are no longer a culture of the land where we cultivate crops and pay homage to our harvest gods and goddesses, Virgos can feel shunned, dishonored, and rejected because their energies are not considered valuable within our modern-day culture.

Virgos teach us to be patient when we are taught to want things immediately. Virgos preserve their energy for the most sacred of experiences. Virgos improve because they have a higher standard and value quality over quantity.

"I Analyze"

Virgos seek to understand and attempt to comprehend everything from the ground up. This makes them superb learners and teachers because they understand the function of things in addition to the thing itself. Where Gemini is the actual data, Virgo takes the data and looks for trends, patterns, and inconsistencies.

This gives Virgos a good critical eye and a talent to improve upon matters because they can easily discover flaws, not for the sake of criticizing, but for the sake of improvement. Virgos like to ask, "What is the meaning?" behind the circumstances. They feel as though there is always a lesson to be learned and that one can discover the truth if they simply analyze their observations.

Mutable Earth

Mutable earth is the loose soil that we use to grow our crops. If the soil is rich enough and in the proper climate, it is able to grow just about anything we so desire. Once the crops have been harvested, the soil is then replaced, replenished, and the cycle starts again.

Moss, which is considered the earliest plant life, is highly adaptable to its surroundings. It simply plants little roots into where it wants to grow, and its seeds then fly away and attach themselves to trees or stones. Moss does not require a lot to grow and is able to work with what it has in order to live.

Virgos, in this light, can stay planted within short-term situations and easily move their ideas and processes toward whatever the situation calls for.

Planetary Ruler: Mercury ☿

In our discussion, we have now come to the point where we find one planet ruling two signs. In this case, it is the planet Mercury ruling both Gemini and Virgo. When it comes to Mercury ruling Virgo, we see the furthering of data that

Gemini has brought about. Mercury, in regard to Virgo, improves upon communication by having an extensive vocabulary as well as the ability to break things down into smaller pieces and filter information to its most essential essence.

Mercury ruling Virgo also represents the health aspect of the planet. The staff held by Mercury, the caduceus, is used as our symbol for the health sciences in our society. Similarly, the image of the two snakes intertwining around a pole imitates the idea of kundalini energy rising up and down the spine, which can be thought of as the purest form of spiritual health.

Mercury ruling Virgo is where we get puns, poetry, novels, editors, and critics. We simply see a more refined way of looking at communication. Virgos choose their words carefully and understand that sometimes, less is more.

End of Summer

The time of Virgo is the time of the harvest where the seeds that were planted during Taurus are now ready for the picking. The harvest moon allows for bright light to occur even during the nighttime, as our ancient cultures would work around the clock harvesting their crops in preparation for the upcoming fall and winter.

This is where we get the phrase "separating the chaff amongst the wheat," as the time during Virgo is all about trying to identify what part of the harvest was usable and which parts were not. Again, this emphasizes their sense of quality and having high tastes and standards. In our modern times, this is the conclusion of summer vacation as students mentally prepare for the start of school and the academics that lie ahead.

Positive Attribute #1—Hard Worker

Regardless of their profession, Virgos take pride in their work and hold themselves to do the best job they can. Employers of Virgos do not need to tell them how they can be doing better because they are most likely doing the best job out of all of their employees.

Virgos understand the value of using discipline now in order to get the reward later. This makes them good at focusing on smaller steps with amazing precision. Just like Geminis, Virgos have a good amount of endurance and stamina and use it to work until the job gets done.

Positive Attribute #2—High Attention to Details

Virgos make sure nothing gets past them. They are very good at leaving no stone unturned, and they even constantly consider the stones that others might have missed. This makes them natural double-checkers, making them highly prepared for any situation. If you are working on a group project, you want a Virgo on your team because they will make sure all parts of the project are completed and that everyone does what needs to get done.

This talent is also helpful when the Virgo needs to observe a lot of information all at once. They are able to correlate evidence well and detect patterns in statistical and correlative analysis. This is also helpful in the health sciences because they are calculating, caring, and comprehensive. If you go to a Virgo doctor with issues involving your kidney, rest assured that they will also consider your liver, your stomach, and everything in-between.

Positive Attribute #3—Teacher

The art of teaching is the ability to understand a topic so comprehensively and thoroughly that you are not only able to grasp the information yourself, you are also able to relay this information to your student in an adaptable way. Virgos are able to explain the same topic in many different ways, making them excellent teachers. They also have a good sense of patience and understanding, allowing for the student to learn at their own pace without pressure.

Teaching also involves taking a larger curriculum and breaking it down into smaller lessons and sections. Virgo's organizational skills make it easy for them to break larger plans and concepts into smaller and more modest chunks so that students do not become overwhelmed.

Negative Attribute #1—Debbie Downer

Virgos can fall into the habit of thinking that everything could be better. When this happens, they criticize everything just to belittle others which can make them unpleasant people to be around. If the atmosphere is happy and joyous, the Virgo could say something rather depressing or awkward, causing the entire mood to shift.

They need to remember that although perfection is a noble pursuit, to err is to be human, and there is no such thing as a perfect anything. Everything simply is as it should be, and Virgos should admire whatever circumstances and people they encounter.

Negative Attribute #2—Workaholic

Virgos are hard workers, but they can become obsessed over their work to a point where it becomes their life's focus. Virgos need to make sure they listen to their bodies and take breaks from working or else they can become immensely run down and unhealthy. With any addiction, the person tends to sacrifice all other aspects of life for the thing that they are addicted to. To prevent this, when it comes to Virgos and their jobs, they need to balance their professional life with their personal life, and remind themselves that sometimes the overtime is just not worth it.

Negative Attribute #3—Wound Up

Virgos can have a hard time relaxing and simply enjoying the situation. This makes them stiff and unable to relax because they are constantly seeing how things could change and improve. To safeguard this, Virgos should learn from Leos and understand that sometimes in life, you just have to let loose and enjoy yourself. Like Capricorns, Virgos can have a very somber and serious attitude and they need to remember that although there is a time and place for professionalism, there is also a time and place for fun, games, and enjoying the fruits of your labor.

Detailed, Oriented, and Efficient

Virgos analyze, prioritize, and scrutinize. They are great when it comes to analysis, understanding processes, and how to improve things. Nerdy and admirable, these are the worker bees who are of service to society such as teachers, therapists, and nurses. Virgo is the conclusion of Summer when harvesting the crops has been a timeless human endeavor in preparation for survival of the upcoming colder months. Virgo is ruled by the analyzing, medical, and clever side of Mercury, where Virgos are great at explaining, healing, and wordsmithing. Still, Virgos need to let their hair down and not get consumed in their work, and be mindful of tension and being too hard on themselves.

LIBRA ♎

"The truth is rarely pure and never simple."

—Oscar Wilde, Libra

The Scales

One of the greatest ancient stories around the scales of judgement has to do with "The Judgment of Osiris" in Egyptian mythology. According to ancient Egyptian lore, when a soul passed into the afterlife, they were met with Osiris, the god of the dead, who then tested the soul's purity to see if it was worthy enough to enter into the blissful field of reeds. If the soul was not pure and good, it was cast into the great void of nonexistence.

The measurement of the soul's purity was determined by Osiris placing the heart on one side of the scale, and the white feather of truth onto the other. If the heart was lighter than the feather, this meant they lived a pure and morally sound life. If it was heavier than the feather, the crocodile-faced god Amenti devoured the heart, and they were then cast into the void.

This idea of righteousness translates into the archetype Justice, who appears on top of our courts, usually blindfolded and holding scales that are equally balanced.

To a Libra, each side of an argument is equally valid. The key is to have these two ideas coexist in harmony because all ideas are true depending on the person who perceives that truth. For example, creationism to one person is just as valid as atheism is to another. For the Libra, both are right because they are true for that individual and every person is entitled to an opinion and to seek their own truth.

"I Balance"

Moderation, equilibrium, and the middle road are all important to a Libra. In a world full of extremes and polarity, Libras strive to work and live in harmony by finding commonality. At the end of the day, we are all human, which is very much an Air message. Libras attempt to bridge this gap by having two sides come together and listen to one another for the sake of understanding, coexistence, and empathy. Moderation is so important to a Libra that they understand the crucial importance of spending an equal amount of time working, relaxing, eating, and so forth. They try to live life with a balanced agenda and divvy up their time appropriately.

Cardinal Air

When we find ourselves in a disagreement and have stopped talking with another person, it takes cardinal air to break the silence in order to mend the gaps. This is why Libras are very talented with diplomacy and world affairs. They are able to let both sides know that they are being listened to equally.

Libras are the first to inquire about anything. They are interested in hearing other people's opinions, which encourages people to open up and share their own thoughts. Geminis tend to communicate about anything and everything, but Libras want to talk about your perspective on things. Another difference is with Geminis, conversations usually revolve around two people but for Libra, it usually involves three: the two people on opposite sides of the argument with the Libra standing in-between.

Planetary Ruler: Venus ♀

Once again, we see a planet ruling two signs, as Venus rules both Taurus and Libra. Venus ruling Taurus represents the relaxation and enjoyment of the senses, but Venus ruling Libra represents the harmony between one another, humanity, and nature. Venus embodies peace and tranquility. Both Taurus and Libra strive toward these goals. Taurus does this through means of luxury and the enjoyment of life, and Libra through personal relationships and through a balance within oneself.

Just like Taurus, Libras are a calming influence that tend to relax the atmosphere wherever they may be. They both have a talent for making you feel comfortable and at ease because, unlike Mars, Venus does not enjoy conflict. Instead, Venus strives for serenity on all fronts.

Fall Equinox

During the time of Libra, we have reached the fall equinox, where the daytime and nighttime are again equal, just as it was during the spring equinox. Only this time, the days will get shorter, and the weather will start to become colder.

It is no coincidence that the fall equinox happens during Libra because the daytime and nighttime are both 50/50 in duration. Now that the school year has started, relationships between teachers and students emerge along with interactions between employers and employees and politicians toward the public if it is an election year.

It is vital for humans to cozy up to one another during this time, in preparation for the colder months ahead. Due to this fact, this is a time to find like-minded individuals and to also mend any conflicts from the past because pretty soon, everyone will be huddled up in a hut somewhere around a fire and will need to get along for the sake of survival.

Positive Attribute #1—Diffuser

Libras have an amazing talent for neutralizing any conflict and tension within a situation. Their Venus influence allows for a calming demeanor, and their love for harmony superimposes any anger felt between two parties. Libras are amazing moderators in this way because they see what the other person cannot and therefore they do a great job at diagnosing where the misunderstandings are stemming from.

Positive Attribute #2—Fair

If a Libra parent has two children, you can guarantee that both children will be treated with fairness and equality. Libras strive to make things right through fairness. If something does not sound fair, they will usually speak up to make sure that the punishment fits the crime.

Libras understand the sacrifice of the self for the sake of equality. Even if they were offered a bigger slice of the pie than someone else, they are more than willing to speak up and make sure everyone gets an equal share. Even if that means less for them. This explains why Libras are in harmony with their fellow air sign, Aquarius, as both strive for social justice of some kind.

Positive Attribute #3—Pleasant

Libras have a calming and pleasant aurora about them. They are great to talk to and make excellent company. Again, we see the influence of Venus at work. This calming demeanor makes people trust them, which allows for Libras to be talented social workers, professional mediators, and counselors.

Similar to Taurus, Libras know how to enjoy themselves when others are in their presence. One cannot help but feel relaxed and cared for because the Libra's energy is naturally soothing.

Negative Attribute #1—No Personal Opinions

Libras spend a lot of their time trying to understand the thoughts and opinions of others. The issue is, if you were to ask a Libra what they thought, they would probably draw a blank. Libras need to ask themselves the same question they ask others: what do they think?

This is where the Libra can learn a lot from its opposition, Aries, who is full of personal opinions and ideas. One of the reasons why Libras feel as though they cannot have any opinions is because they feel that it might interfere with their objectivity and neutrality. However, the truth is, you can be both. There is simply a time to be opinionated, and a time to hear the opinions of others.

Negative Attribute #2—Indecisive

That old story of asking your partner where they want to go for dinner, and your partner replies with "I don't know, where do you want to go?" is the typical Libra response. It is very hard for a Libra to make a firm decision on anything because they try to weigh in all the options by simultaneously observing the pros and cons to each one within their head.

Sometimes, a Libra just needs to make a decision and go with it. It does not matter if it is the right one or the wrong one. All that matters is that the Libra decided on one direction over the other, automatically making it the right choice. By doing this, the Libra starts to learn the thrill of spontaneity and how going with your first thought is usually your best thought.

Negative Attribute #3—Self—Doubt

Because Libras are so concerned with others, they sometimes forget to create a persona around themselves. Consequently, they are not able to make decisions because they genuinely do not know how they would respond in the first place. They are not familiar with their own character.

It is important for Libras to ask themselves these questions and figure out what they like and dislike, in addition to what they would do or not do within situations. Libras need to remember that they themselves are also human beings with opinions and a life of their own.

Amicable and Intelligent

Libras are very interested in each other, and others appreciate their interest. They want others to coexist in harmony with everyone's rights not being impeded upon. They help to humble the ego when they make us realize that there's always a side to a story that you're not seeing. As the start of the fall, Libra is a time of enjoying the company of others and cozying up as the temperature starts its ongoing decline until winter. Venus, as their ruler, brings about the harmony of fairness and justice and of global relations. However, Libras need to be more self-assertive, possess opinions of their own, and not rely on the other for a sense of self.

SCORPIO ♏

"Nothing in life is to be feared, it is only to be understood. Now is the time to understand more, so that we may fear less."

—Marie Curie, Scorpio

The Scorpion

Scorpions representing Scorpios is a little misleading because there are in fact three animals that are associated with this sign: the scorpion, the eagle, and the phoenix. Each one of these animals represents the three stages of evolution and transformation.

With the scorpion, we see our most basic instinct of flight or fight. Just by their appearance alone, scorpions are terrifying. However, their personality is a lot like the bee in that they only attack you for self-defense and not just for the sake of it.

Scorpions do not want to harm you unless you give them a reason. Similarly, Scorpios can seem very intimidating just by appearances alone, as they tend to have a very stern and dominating stature. But what you are experiencing is the same phenomenon one experiences when dealing with the other water sign, Pisces. Namely, you are simply looking at yourself through them, and what you fear is really the exposure of the darker side of your own personality. Indeed, it can seem that Scorpios can see right through you at times.

You feel vulnerable around a Scorpio because you are not sound within your own self. This is where we find the stages of evolutionary transformation to be of importance. When we do not feel at ease within our own skin, it is because there are parts of our personality that are outdated and thus desire to be eliminated.

When the Scorpio sheds their skin of worn-out behaviors, they evolve onto the next stage and become the eagle. Eagles are very majestic and respected creatures. Chiefs of many Native American tribes wear eagle feathers as part of their regalia. Although eagles are predators, we honor them and admire them for their ability to use their sharp vision in order to attack their prey.

Transformation comes in three stages: the old, the limbo where the old is dying and the new is trying to obtain a solid footing, and the new. This explains why transformation is difficult for individuals because the middle stage, where you have one foot in the old and one foot in the new, can bring about a lot of chaos and frustration. Anyone with addictive tendencies can attest to the difficulty of rehabilitation and the upheaval of emotional suppression contained therein. Once the middle stage of limbo is surmounted, however, the next and final stage is that of the phoenix.

The phoenix is a mythological creature thought to possess the highest form of magic and majesty. Indeed, when we release our old self so that our true self can come about, it is quite a magical experience because we have struggled where many people have failed, usually because their vices eventually get the better of them.

Scorpios remind us that who we are is not who we really are, and that is why we sometimes feel uncomfortable around Scorpios. Their ability to pierce through the layers of B.S. and see the truth of the matter is very hard for artificial people to handle. In this light, Scorpios have a hard time being social because they feel that they are the ones making other people feel uncomfortable.

"I Desire"

Desire is usually a trait that is seen as a sin. Desire is having a want so intensely that you become blindly focused in achieving that desire. We are taught that desire is bad because it implies a lack of self-discipline and contempt for society and others.

But desire is one of the reasons Mars traditionally rules Scorpio. Desire is a self-motivator that seems to have a vigilant bend. The Scorpio asks, "why is pursuing our desires a bad thing?" After all, desire is not that far from passion. The only difference seems to be that passion is more of an exterior feeling, something you are passionate about, and desire is an internal feeling, something you embody or become.

Desire shows you what your body and mind truly want even if it is bad for you. If we have desires that, even in the long run, would do us harm, we still feel the need to experience these desires because we have a need to learn from them. In fact, it was Carl Jung himself who once said, "[Someone] who has not passed through the inferno of [their] passions has never overcome them." Scorpios are heavily driven individuals because of their desires. This makes them honest in who they are because, like all fixed signs, they do not deny any part of themselves.

Whether we want to admit it or not, we all have desires, and this ties back to the three layers of transformation. Desires are basic and animalistic. Before we can transform to higher states of being, we must look into our desires and learn how much they lead to our downfall. The biggest challenge is to not become swept up within our desires while we explore them, for it is too easy to get stuck into the abyss of our animal nature, and therefore become stagnant within that negativity, for a very long time.

Desire shows us what we unconsciously need to purge out from ourselves. If we do not acknowledge this, we experience repression, which only exacerbates the issue. Conversely, the moment we address our desires, experience them, and learn from them, we evolve.

Fixed Water

Fixed water is that of the river. The contours of the river tell the water where to go, and the flowing current continues until it reaches its destination: the ocean. In our culture, we talk about the metaphors of *going with the current* or *fighting up stream*. When we need to experience change, we can either fight or surrender. The power of Scorpio, and Pluto, for that matter, is inevitable and beyond our control. That is why we must listen and adhere to what we are being told to change about ourselves.

Planetary Rulers: Mars ♂ (Traditional)/Pluto ♇ (Modern)

Ruled by Mars, Scorpio people are forceful and determined. Their fixed quality allows for them to maintain discipline, and the courage that Mars gives them allows for them to be confident in who they are. Scorpios also have very potent sexual energies that can be channeled through intimacy or through spiritual and magical endeavors.

Pluto is the god of the underworld, and with Scorpio, we see a lot of parallels to the unconscious underworld inside ourselves. Pluto exposes the hidden forces of our psyche. When these forces appear out in the open, we can experience chaos because we do not understand or acknowledge what we are feeling and why we are feeling it. Pluto is the awakening of the unseen shadow self that influences our decisions without us even knowing. Scorpios, by embodying Pluto, have a great ability to get to the bottom of situations and people. They have the gift of penetrating laser vision that directly addresses the heart of any matter.

Fall Proper

During this time of the fall season, we start to notice the death of our planet as leaves begin to change, animals prepare for winter hibernation, birds prepare to fly south toward warmer climates, and ancient cultures began to store their crops in order to prepare for the coming winter. One of the metaphysical lessons we learn during fall is that although it appears that the Earth is dying, it is only eliminating that which is not needed in order to survive the winter, until life inevitably returns to the planet in the springtime.

Positive Attribute #1—Healer

Scorpio's ability to figure people out allows them to be great healers because they can aid others through psychological transformations. Their connection to the unconscious mind allows them to see what people cannot see inside themselves. This makes Scorpios a guide of sorts toward an individual's journey of self-discovery. Not only do Scorpios possess psychological healing, but they also embody magical healing, like that of the shaman.

Positive Attribute #2—Guardian of the Strange

Scorpios love all things violent, bizarre, abnormal, and taboo. These topics are very much subjective, and what society considers strange is simply an opinion of the times and the society therein. Scorpios remind us that it is okay to be an outlier and not accepted by society. As long as you are true to yourself, that is all that matters.

Scorpios are fans of horror movies, gore, anti-social crowds, occult teachings, and anything else shunned by the mainstream. They keep these darker aspects of our culture alive to remind us that they are, yet again, the hidden part of our culture's personality. Remember in Part I-Section 6, the individual unconsciousness is directly proportional to society's unconsciousness. Scorpios are here to remind us of this universal truism.

Positive Attribute #3—Protective

Scorpios are highly protective over the people they care about. They see them as their own kin and are willing to do whatever they can to make sure they are safe. Scorpio parents are not afraid to stick up for their kids if they are bullied in school by calling out the bully's parents on their poor parenting. Like their fellow water sign, Cancer, Scorpios have a lot of love to give, and they express this love by showing that they can shield their loved ones from danger. This is the effect of Mars ruling Scorpio.

Negative Attribute #1—Self—Destructive

When Scorpios are not in control of their energies, they can do more harm than good, as they tend to push the limits of people or situations a little too far. If a Scorpio is just starting to get on their feet from a time of turmoil, they might purposely self-sabotage themself so that they can fall right back into misery. This is also due to the fact that Scorpios can sometimes become too obsessed with negative emotions, situations, and people. They can become so comfortable around the darker side of life that they surround themselves with the wrong kind of people and circumstances. Instead of breaking free, a sort of self-masochism occurs where they love inflicting pain onto themselves. It is true that "misery loves company," but the Scorpio should learn not to thrive within this predicament.

Negative Attribute #2—Vengeful

"All is fair in love and war" was most likely said by a Scorpio. To them, revenge and backstabbing is fair game if the ends justify the means. Scorpios need to watch out for questionable tendencies they can use to get their way or to make others feel pain. They need to remember that, although they help others transmute their karma, they themselves are not the bringers of karma.

One of the reasons Scorpios feel justified in being vengeful is because they want others to feel as much pain as they have felt. Instead, they should take their own advice and ask themselves to see what the pain they are feeling says about their own life choices.

Negative Attribute #3—Complacent

Much like their opposition, Taurus, Scorpios can have a tendency to become stagnant. It takes a lot to motivate a Scorpio because they must become motivated with every fiber of their being. If not, they are more than likely to just stand around, wait for things to happen, or not happen. It is a balancing act where the Scorpio needs to be an agent of change within their own lives, but not in the form of self-destruction and implosion.

Magical and Meaningful

Scorpios contain immense power within themselves that could transmute the world. They know how to heal, and if others are trusting enough, they can get incredibly vulnerable around them. Scorpios understand the beauty within the hidden and misunderstood, and with this comes knowledge from our elders. This time of fall is when we see the leaves wilt and detach, acting as the great metaphor for the cycle of life and death which Scorpio embodies. Ruled by Mars, traditionally, and Pluto, Scorpio contains hidden knowledge and a knack for strategy. Scorpios need to be mindful of their self-destructive tendencies and their sense of morality when it comes to vengeance.

SAGITTARIUS ♐

"If you tell the truth, you don't have to remember anything."

—Mark Twain, Sagittarius

The Centaur Archer

Sagittarius contains a lot of symbols within its depiction. Sagittarius, as the archer, possesses focus, calmness, and an unwavering path toward their goals. The centaur is always depicted with a bow in the aim position, as if he were ready to shoot the arrow at any given moment. All they need to do is to find their target and release.

In most cases, the archer is not aiming at a target in front of him, but behind, as if he were in motion, galloping away from someone or something. Shooting a target in this pose is not only harder, but it also requires some reliance on intuition because it is hard to keep your hands steady. In other words, it is not only the aim of the Sagittarian that gets them to their target; it is their trust that everything will work out as it should because that is the law of nature. They inherently feel that connection because that are ruled by the ultimate planet of manifestation: Jupiter.

In other words, Sagittarians are lucky because they are highly con-nected to the power of manifestation and have the mentality of life being full of abundance. Therefore, they deserve this abundance because, after all, they are one of nature's creatures, and all nature wants to do is provide for their children.

Sagittarians are inherently lucky, not because luck is some sort of God-given blessing, but because they believe in the power of abundance and manifestation even on an unconscious level. Within our society, our main thesis of economics is that all supplies are in limitation, but if a Sagittarian oversaw our economy, there would be no limitation for one's basic needs.

The idea of the centaur (half man, half horse) represents the higher intellect of humanity having control over their more animal self. This explains why Sagittarius represents institutions, ethics, morality, and philosophy. They emanate a higher intelligence that demonstrates an elevated thinking that has been obtained from a command over the grosser self through the exploration of human academics.

"I Understand"

Sagittarians are able to comprehend ideas rather quickly. They usually do not have to rely on repetition or meaningless drills in order to grasp an idea. Instead, they have a natural ability to study just about anything with a strong appetite to learn.

Sagittarians also have high ethical standards. They understand that all are entitled to the innate rights of humanity, which enable us to live in a civilized society. Sagittarians hope to maintain these principles so that our human institutions are functioning for the greater good of humanity.

Mutable Fire

The mutability of Sagittarius allows for their ideologies to adapt and change over time. If the courts still followed laws from the sixteenth century, people would still be burned at the stake for bogus crimes. Similar to Libra, Sagittarius allows for everyone to share their own ideals when it comes to creating some sort of doctrine or democracy. In this way, Sagittarius heavily relies on the morality of the current culture so that the rules can parallel the current step on the human evolutionary ladder. They plainly accept humanity for what it is and therefore accept whatever institutional ideals arise out of their respective societies. In other words, they respect the process of societal evolution and understand that this is directly related to the contemporary views and ideals of the time in which they live. According to the Sagittarian, institutions of power should uphold these doctrines, whatever they may be, because the integrity of these institutions (i.e. democratic, academic, or religious) is just as important as the doctrine itself.

Planetary Ruler: Jupiter ♃

In Roman mythology, Jupiter was the king of the gods. Similarly, Sagittarians receive a lot of their good fortune from Jupiter because he is revered as the god of gods. In traditional astrology, Jupiter is said to be the "great benefic," making Jupiter's influence, for the most part, highly favorable and auspicious. Being ruled by the great benefic, Sagittarians have an overall jovial mentality and content demeanor. Like Leo, this brightness emanates outwardly, and others cannot help but feel great around them.

End of Fall

It is a little strange that the bright, optimistic sign of Sagittarius occurs during the time of the year when fall is coming to a close and the colder season of winter quickly approaches. Even within this context, this is still a time of celebration and joy because it is the last hurrah before winter. The holiday Thanksgiving in the United States not only celebrates family but also togetherness and brotherhood, with the hopes that one day, all cultures will come together at the dinner table and feast as brothers and sisters. University applications become due, and first-year college students are similarly getting their first taste of freedom while continuing into their fall semesters. This is a time of looking back, observing where you have come from, and seeing where you are going. With the optimistic outlook of Sagittarius, to them, the only direction they are headed is up.

Positive Attribute #1—Generous

Sagittarians want to share their abundance with others. They are immensely generous with their resources and love. Even on an energetic plane, the Sagittarian loves to share their energy, and you cannot help but feel brighter in their presence. The idea behind this generosity is that when all people have what they require, people tend to be more civil, as they do not see any reason to covet. Sagittarians tend to embody this ideal, which is why they are always willing to pay it forward. They also find great joy in giving people chances and opportunities in life and will seek to open doors for others. For the Sagittarian, when anyone succeeds, everyone succeeds.

Positive Attribute #2—High on Life

Sagittarians do not spend a moment of their time in self-pity or depression. They are genuinely happy to be alive, and this joy keeps sad and depressing energies from invading their personal bubble due to their higher vibrational thinking. When Sagittarians feel frustrated, it is mostly due to the negative people around them trying to bring them down. This is not because Sagittarians live in blissful ignorance or that they repress their sadness, it is because, like Aquarians, they seek to understand a more spiritually elevated way of living where the denser emotions tend to no longer exist.

Positive Attribute #3—Believes in People and in Society

Sagittarians make the greatest utopians and motivators because they believe in the power of uplifting and encouraging others. Sagittarians never run out of their optimism and love to aid others in surmounting their negativity by encouraging them to find the brighter side to things. They have tremendous trust that people will eventually do the right thing.

   These feelings of trust and hope translate into society at-large. Sagittarians believe that humanity is inherently good, and that genuine human nature is to be loving and caring, not evil and selfish. The Sagittarian philosophy on this subject can be found within the preamble of the US constitution where it promises to ". . . establish justice, ensure domestic tranquility. . .promote the general welfare, and secure the blessings of liberty to ourselves and our posterity. . . ." These lofty goals, Sagittarius believes, are already understood by all of humanity, and they trust that one day every person will enact these ideals for the betterment and evolution of society.

Negative Attribute #1—Too Philosophical

Sometimes, Sagittarians can live in a hermetically sealed utopia without considering the reality of people or situations. They know how things should be handled and how people should act in theory, but do not realize that this is not how things truly operate in practice. This can make them quite naïve and too trusting of people they should be more cautious around. They need to remember that although they treat others with respect and kindness, others have yet to learn those lessons. Therefore, they should not give their energy so freely toward people who would not return the favor.

Negative Attribute #2—Overindulgent

Sagittarians can sometimes take the expansive quality of Jupiter a little too literally and neglect their health because they always feel protected by Jupiter. They can easily gain weight or perform other unhealthy habits because they do not think it will cause them harm. Sagittarians need to remember that bad habits are bad habits any way you slice them, and that they are never worth the risk because, even with Jupiter on your side, sometimes your luck does eventually run out.

Negative Attribute #3—Blind Sighted

Sagittarians are such big thinkers that they can have a hard time with the details. They have difficulty pondering the specifics of theocratics and tend to base their decisions on their own personal outlook, sometimes neglecting their own two eyes when the truth of a person or a situation is right in front of them. Sagittarians would do best to think things out a bit more and put a little bit more rationality into their inherent trust.

Lighthearted and Brilliant

Sagittarians make you believe that everything will be all right at the end of the day. They have a great enjoyment for life and want everyone around them to have just as much enjoyment. They have a natural ease of things going their way, but their high moral code gives them maturity to understand the humility of their opportunities. This is during the time when fall is dwindling into winter, where your positive outlook is going to be sorely needed in the tougher days ahead. They have great intuition and see the best in people. They love intellectual debates and their application in various institutions of our society. Be that as it may, Sagittarius needs to not push their luck and take in figuring out the finer details of their overarching plans.

CAPRICORN ♑

"Intelligence is the ability to adapt to change."

—Stephen Hawking, Capricorn

The Sea Goat

The sea goat is quite an awkward animal to say the least. Half of the animal is supposed to live on land, and the other half is supposed to live in the water. Both cannot accommodate for the other, which parallels Capricorn's attitude of working with what you have, as there is no use in complaining about what you cannot change.

Similarly, the humorous idea of watching a goat with a fish's tail trying to scale a mountain or trying to breathe underwater matches Capricorn's capacity for humor and comedy. Capricorns are known for their gifts in comedy because they are very familiar with Murphy's law. However, instead of taking this as a negative, they tend to flip it around and laugh at their misfortunes. Remember, it was Paramahansa Yogananda, a Capricorn, who once said that the first stage in overcoming the world's sufferings is to learn how to laugh at the suffering outright.

"I Use"

Capricorns are the masters at building something out of nothing. They are calculating, resourceful, and follow the principle of "waste not, want not." Where Taurus represents actual resources, Capricorns know how to use their resources in order to achieve their goals. Unlike the ram of Aries, the sea goat is not able to climb the mountain on their own, which is why they heavily rely on teamwork and are very appreciative when others help them toward their objectives. However, the Capricorn will never explicitly ask for help because they abhor dependence almost to a fault. They will be the last to ask their friends for money or ask for help in school. Instead, they will use whatever tools they can first in order to accomplish their goals and almost always prefer to do it alone. From a young age, Capricorns learn to become self-reliant and find much pride in being able to say, "Back in my day. . . ."

Cardinal Earth

Capricorns are highly motivated people, even though they may not seem like the most exuberant. If Taurus is the earth and Virgo is the soil, Capricorn is the big oak tree that stands tall and proud so that others can marvel at its accomplishments. Just as a tree takes many years to become strong and sturdy, Capricorns consider patience to be one of their biggest virtues.

Their cardinal nature makes them stubborn up to a point in that the Capricorn usually feels that they know what is best for them until they are proven otherwise. It can take a long time for a Capricorn to change their strategy or opinion because they usually only trust themselves. Therefore, before a Capricorn will shift their perspective, they first need to be shown that their thinking needs adjustment. Until that time, like the mountains that represent them, they will continue to be steadfast and immobile until they are ready to move.

Planetary Ruler: Saturn ♄

In the simplest of terms, Saturn is karma. Saturn represents limitations, discipline, obligations, structure, and dealing with the cards that were handed to you. Just how Sagittarians inherently possess Jupiterian qualities of abundance and joy, it is common for Capricorns to always face some sort of adversity in their lives because they are ruled by Saturn, the "great malefic."

Nothing comes easy for the Capricorn, and their struggles can sometimes outweigh the easier times. Again, it is their humor that sees their misfortunes as a satire to their own lives, which keeps them from falling into a deep depression. Capricorns understand that there are circumstances that you simply cannot control, so there is no use in focusing on these issues because it is rather pointless. If Capricorns continue to strive and surmount their obstacles, they are some of the most successful and wisest people of the zodiac.

Winter Solstice

Capricorn ushers in the cold season of winter, which is where we witness Capricorn's sense of discipline. All of the resources that our agricultural ancestors saved up during the fall are now ready to be used in order to get them through the harsh winter. However, as abundant as their supplies may seem, and as tempting as it is to use a lot of their resources now that the days are getting colder and shorter, it is best to conserve during the time of Capricorn because colder months still lie ahead. Similarly, in our modern world, saving one's money is important because when the holidays approach during the time of Capricorn, we can use our savings to buy presents for the ones we care about.

Positive Attribute #1—Fatherly Wisdom

Capricorns are great people to turn to if you need guidance and wisdom in your life because they understand the concepts of suffering and striving. They are incredibly practical, realistic, and well in touch with reality, which diffuses other people's illusions within their own situations. It may be tough love, but it is love nonetheless. Even if you do not realize it at that moment, you eventually become thankful.

Positive Attribute #2—Disciplined/Frugal

Capricorns know how to stay focused and concentrated on any goal they decide to achieve. They can save and conserve money and energy easily because they understand that not spending money now is worth the ambitions they have for their future. This all has to do with Capricorn's great ability to appreciate the art of sacrifice. Similarly, Capricorns will not spread themselves too thin and will only make promises they can keep.

Capricorns can become masters in whatever they choose. For example, if a Capricorn partakes in martial arts, they can easily become black belts over their long journey because they maintain the concentration and steadiness that is required in order to master anything. Indeed, this is why we call them "disciplines" in the first place.

Positive Attribute #3—Calculating

When a Capricorn takes a risk, it usually works out in their favor because they are always calculated risks. Unlike Aries, Capricorns do not just jump into things headfirst. They consider the pros and cons and are great at making executive decisions. This sharp eye is how they observe *move A* affects *move Z* down the road.

This provides stability and success in whatever they do because they are able to positively manipulate events toward their goals without doing much of the manipulation themselves. It is interesting to see how, although Capricorn is concerned with creating and developing, which are active activities, they do it in a very passive way by having others make the first move. Then, they work with what they have and allow for the circumstance to unfold naturally without too much personal influence.

Negative Attribute #1—Old-Fashioned

Capricorns can sometimes be too conservative both in lifestyle and mentality. As we further our society into the progressive Age of Aquarius, some Capricorns can have trouble as they tend to enjoy traditional gender, familial, marital, and societal roles.

Similarly, Capricorns are not ones to be personally expressive or flamboyant. Like their fellow earth sign, Virgo, they can be a little uptight and unwilling to let their hair down. This has to do with the pervasive seriousness that seems to always surround the Capricorn. They can have very somber and mundane attitudes which can make them, as my astrology teacher likes to say, "meat and potatoes" kinds of people. In other words, they can sometimes be bland, boring, and not really motivated to try new things.

Negative Attribute #2—Unimaginative

You would not want to go to a Capricorn for new ideas or creativity. Capricorns are funny, but their humor comes from their observations of the world, not necessarily from creating an imaginative world of whimsy. Capricorns can be quite predictable and not the best at thinking outside of the box. They rely more on the tested and true ways of doing things adhering to the saying, "if it ain't broke, don't fix it."

Negative Attribute #3—Conceited

This character trait is a little bizarre as we tend to not think of Capricorns as egotistical. Nevertheless, sometimes they take their accomplishments and hard work as badges of honor and can develop an "I know better than you" mentality. This can make them opinionated, holier-then-thou, and always giving you their advice even though you did not ask for it. This is a different kind of self-centeredness, where Capricorns feel they should be appreciated and honored by those around them, not through their creativity or talents, but through their accomplishments and struggles. Capricorns should take their life experiences to help guide others, but not out of a sense of self-importance.

Disciplined and Decisive

Capricorns are survivors. They roll with the punches and don't get dragged down into the struggle of life, but instead overcome. Their accomplishments amount to great accomplishments, and their stories of how they got there are admirable and inspirational. This is the time at the start of winter when conservation of resources and discipline is required for the colder days ahead. They are ruled by Saturn, which gives them focus, sobriety, and a comedic outlook, but this planet also gives limitations, karma, and struggle. The Capricorn should not be afraid of letting people into their emotional side, and finding trust when people genuinely want to help.

AQUARIUS ♒

"If there must be trouble, let it be in my day, that my child may have peace."

—Thomas Paine, Aquarius

The Water Bearer

Aquarius is readily mistaken for a water sign, but one must remember that Aquarius is not the water inside the jar, they are the bearer of that water. Aquarius is the archetype of the angel, who is depicted to be a conduit between humanity and god—benevolent beings that have the job of aiding humanity toward goodness, oneness, and enlightenment, as the water contained within the jar is the spiritual and unconditional love that Pisces represents and embodies.

Aquarius and Pisces are the only signs of the zodiac whose mythologies merge together in this way. It seems that Aquarian optimism and empathy comes from an underlining current or understanding that is surprisingly spiritual and Piscean in nature.

The problem is, a lot of Aquarians eventually lose this spiritual part of themselves and become immensely jaded due to their acute observations of humanity's sufferings and mistreatments. This parallels the way they have been treated within their own lives by being marked as bizarre, strange, and different, according to others. We will discuss traditional rulers in Part II-Section 4, but for now, we need to know that the Sun is in Detriment in Aquarius. Because of this, Aquarians automatically become shunned by society, which makes it difficult for them to express themselves.

Aquarian minds are so open, and their empathy so grand, that the grosser levels of human nature are incomprehensible to them. Aquarians do not understand why humans seek to destroy, and as a consequence, they become orphans within this denser world of duality. Just as Scorpios have taken on the burden of reminding society of its darker side, Aquarians have taken on the burden of keeping society awake and aware of the injustices that exist within this world, even if that means they themselves must suffer from this knowledge. Although ignorance is bliss, the Aquarian believes that the truth, as painful as it might be, does indeed set you free, and the embodiment of freedom is Aquarius.

Aquarians are friendly and likable because they look at their fellow humans without judgment. They believe that all humans are victims of circumstance brought on by society's rules, judgments, and autocracy. They want you to be just as true and free from your own insecurities and from these limitations brought on by societal structures as they are. They understand that it is our present-day culture's expectations and presumptions that prevent our true individualistic nature from shining forth. This naturally makes others feel respected around an Aquarius, simply because they are treated as a fellow human being with equanimity. Aquarians tend to put everyone on this equal plane regardless of who they are.

"I Know"

Aquarians have a sharp sense of intuition. They can gauge people and circumstances rather quickly, and most of their insights come through like a flash of lightning. The Aquarian brain works very fast, and they are able to process multiple layers of meaning within a single moment. This allows them to conceptualize reality through multiple dimensions and angles.

When Aquarians say, "I know," they truly do. The more negative side to this ability is that they can use this as a weapon to demean others. The more positive side, however, is that Aquarians have developed an inherent knowing of truth, empathy, and justice. Aquarians conceptualize their idea of society vividly and see it as an obtainable future within the pillars of egalitarianism, non-judgment, and the right to self-expression and freedom to be the cornerstones of a just society, which would create a world of peace and abundance. Clearly, this is why Aquarians can be thought of as daydreamers, never having a solid footing in reality. They simply do not live in the harsher world of the present. Instead, they live in the reality of the future realm of what could be, or, more importantly, what should be.

Fixed Air

Fixed air is a little bit of an oxymoron, but if you think about breathing, fixed air is that zero point where the inhale and exhale are in flux. During that moment, you're placed in between the paradoxical realm of inhale and exhale, of non-existence and existence. Aquarius, in this respect, is the medium of two worlds: the spiritual and the human.

They want to introduce higher ideals into society. Thankfully, Aquarians honor democracy and typically do not have a reputation for tyranny. However, a lot of Aquarians think that if they could be king or queen of the universe, a whole lot of good would get done rather quickly. Permanence is characteristic of the fixed signs and with Aquarians; their fixed nature says this is the way life ought to be, this is the way society should be, and my requisites are not negotiable.

Planetary Rulers: Saturn ♄ (Traditional) and Uranus ♅ (Modern)

It can be a little confusing to see that Saturn, the planet of authority and conservatism, rules the avant-garde and nonconforming sign of Aquarius. To remedy this, we must remember that in order to rebel (Uranus), we must first have something to rebel against (Saturn). Like Capricorns, Aquarians strive toward their goals and can be quite successful if they overcome their personal obstacles. Also, similar to Capricorns, the Aquarian's life is simply a little more difficult than it would be for others.

Uranus is the aching need for rebellion against the old that lies within every one of us. When it comes to revolutions within history, the symptoms have typically been a group of people that have reached their personal threshold of mistreatment. In this respect, Uranus reminds us to constantly rebel against ourselves because the only true constant in this world is change.

Winter Proper

During the dead of winter, hope for the future is all you have. Our ancient ancestors had to remind themselves that the world would eventually get warmer once again. All it will take is time and patience. During this time of the year, early human tribes were huddled up inside housing to escape from the cold. Thus, strong bonds of brotherhood and sisterhood were formed.

Positive Attribute #1—Free Thinkers

Aquarians are not susceptible to propaganda or toward other individual's baseless ideas. They are creators of their own mentality and view every argument with the discernment of Occam's razor. They are objective and not easily convinced. People admire their ability to not be held down by any sort of dogma or tradition. Aquarians tend to question the validity and truth in everything and if it proves to not pass their litmus test, they easily and quickly discard it. Either way, they are still willing to give everything a fair chance, but will always come to their own conclusion.

Positive Attribute #2—Genius

Aquarians truly are the geniuses of the zodiac. They can think outside of the box and are able to understand concepts through many layers of comprehension. The work that they produce in this world has been known to change and influence society and people's lives through invention, art, and ideas. FDR, Mozart, Darwin, Galileo, Rockwell, Lincoln, and Edison were all Aquarians. In fact, according to a statistical study, there have been more Aquarian presidents of the United States than any other sign of the zodiac (20% or 1 in 5).[36]

---

36   Dr. Eric Ostermeier, "Presidents Day Special: The Astrological Signs of the Presidents," Smart Politics, (2010), Archived November 1, 2020 at https://web.archive.org/web/20201101065750/https://smartpolitics.lib.umn.edu/2010/02/15/presidents-day-special-the-ast/.

Positive Attribute #3—Empathy

Aquarians are thought to be emotionally detached and cold to a fault, but it is not that they are emotionally aloof, it is that being ruled by Saturn. They understand that karma is karma and do not enjoy it when people expect their sympathy. However, when it comes to empathy, the ability to put yourself into another person's shoes, Aquarians are the best at this. This is why they make good and honest humanitarians. They truly feel and understand the pain and suffering of others. Indeed, it is this empathy that makes them rebel against society because they refuse to live a life through rose-tinted glasses just to become another peg in an unjust system.

Negative Attribute #1—Anarchy

If the Aquarian feels shunned enough by society or if they feel powerless to face the injustice in the world, they can easily turn into an anarchist with a desire for chaos in order to seek change. Aquarians believe in the full independence of a person both internally and externally and anarchy parallels this message.

The problem is, when it comes to anarchy, there is an assumption that people are civilized enough to maintain order. However, human nature does not operate this way yet, and the lack of social order causes severe atrocities to occur for the sake of the apparent freedom. Aquarians with this mindset need to remember Ghandi's famous quote: "an eye for an eye makes the whole world blind."

Negative Attribute #2—Demeaning

Aquarians are always going to be five steps ahead of you when it comes to intellectual discussions and debates. Having this kind of power can make it tempting for the Aquarian to belittle the people around them by mocking their perspectives, proving their inconstancies for fun, or correcting people on facts and figures. This is one way for the Aquarian to lose a lot of friends and allies quickly. The irony here is that Aquarians need the people they are alienating because they are incredibly people-oriented individuals. Aquarians need to remember that not everyone thinks as openly and quickly as they do. This does not mean that they are intellectually inferior.

Negative Attribute #3—Flighty

Aquarians are all about the new and fresh. If you cannot keep their attention, they will most likely leave without any remorse or regret. This is one of the keys to dating an Aquarius. The more freedom you give them, the better off the relationship will be. Aquarians can have such a carefree and *c'est la vie* attitude, that you will be quite surprised to see how easy it is for them to just drop everything and go. Aquarians should learn the value of investing in people, relationships, and projects, and should not back away from commitment in order to fulfill an artificial sense of autonomy and independence.

Intelligent and Compassionate

Aquarians have a mind and an intellect that is unmatched. They consume much knowledge and try to make the world a better place based on what they learn. Although they can be slightly awkward at times, they always mean well and want everyone to evolve and prosper together. Aquarius is the time of winter when things might seem at their bleakest, but the Aquarian knows deep down that the darkness is not real, and days will always be brighter. Ruled by Saturn and Uranus, Aquarius both takes on the wisdom of the past without its dogma, and adjusts the knowledge to be relatable in the times they are living. Still, Aquarians need to make sure they don't come off as know-it-alls or entertain chaotic ideologies that can make them unnecessarily rebellious.

Pisces ♓

"Said I'm a Pisces, Zika deka del, Well well I'm raising hell, People always tryin' to find the world I'm in, I'm the envy of the women and I rule the men, Two fish, one swimmin' up stream, One swimmin' down livin' in a dream, But when she loves she tends to cling."

—Erykah Badu, Pisces

Two Fish Tied Together

When it comes to the imagery of the two Piscean fish, we sometimes forget that they are both tied together at the fin. This is because if Pisceans were given free range, their spirits would probably float away from Earth as quickly as possible, never to return. The rope attached to the fin reminds Pisceans of their karma here on earth, which is hard to understand sometimes because Pisceans are the embodiment of spirit, or spirit incarnate.

Fish have been essential to many people's diets, and the fish symbolism within Christianity echoes Pisces as the sign of religion. The two fish represent the constant force of yin and yang, the continual cosmic motor that creates relentless change in our world, and therefore, Pisces rules realms such as yoga, surrender, and ego denial.

However, these two fish also have a downside. As with all mutable signs, there are two forces at work that are trying to cohabitate. In the case of Pisces, we see the ultimate feminine trying to blend and mix with the ultimate masculine, making Pisceans a vortex of high spiritual energy that people pick up on and want to consume psychically. Due to this fact, Pisceans are highly susceptible to psychic vampires and need to make sure they are not influenced by the emotions of those around them. It is vital they keep themselves psychically guarded.

"I Believe"

Faith and trust are important parts to the Piscean nature because this is what is required to connect to spirit. However, before you can connect to spirit, you need to have faith that spirit is on the other end to receive you. This is why Pisces squares Sagittarius because Sagittarius thinks that seeing is believing, and Pisces thinks that you must first believe so that you can truly see. Pisces effortlessly takes leaps of faith, trusting that it will all work itself out in the end. The Pisces individual might have a strange way of getting to where they want to go, but they still get there, nonetheless.

Mutable Water

Mutable water is the vast ocean that covers most of our planet. Our entire rain cycle depends upon the evaporation of water. Similarly, countless life forms rely on the ocean for life and food. The ocean is all one body, but at the same time, you can put your hand in it and separate a portion.

Similarly, Pisces is the sign of ultimate surrender and assimilation. They are able to go where their life path and spirit takes them. Pisces encourages you to listen to your heart, not your head, and to approach all peoples and circumstances in your life with non-judgment, non-attachment, and gratitude.

Planetary Rulers: Jupiter ♃ (Traditional) and Neptune ♆ (Modern)

The expansive nature of Jupiter is seen in the all-encompassing love of Pisces and their trust in the universe. Just like Sagittarius, which is also ruled by Jupiter, Pisces innately feel that the cosmos has their back and will always protect them. The difference is, Sagittarius is better able to focus this energy into tangible goals, and Pisces interprets this abundance to be the hand of God, guiding them toward the goal of realization.

This mindset of trusting in the universe fully without question is simply amplified with the modern ruler of Neptune. Neptune is the god of the ocean and Pisces is likewise the sign of the cosmic ocean that combines all living and nonliving things on this planet and beyond. Neptune allows for Pisces to let go of ego drives and motivations so that they can quietly hear what the universe wants them to achieve. Neptune is also where Pisces get their big heart for unconditional love and non-judgement.

End of Winter

During the time of Pisces, it is the time of ultimate endings. Just how the spirit leaves this world at the time of death, so does the cycle of the yearly celestial calendar conclude as energies fade completely before starting once again. This is a time where the world has a strange quiet to it because there does not seem to be a lot of action externally. Instead, this is a time for meditation and contemplation.

One of the biggest morals of this story is that endings are never permanent, but simply a necessary step for a new beginning. As such, after the end of winter, we enter the new fresh start of spring with the celestial calendar at the start of Aries. When this happens, the seasonal year simply starts anew and will ceaselessly continue with its cycle of birth, growth, death, repeat.

Positive Attribute #1—Psychic

Because Pisceans are connected to the spiritual realm with much ease, they are highly psychic and can tap into the hidden angelic and spiritual worlds around us. They are very good at gauging what is going on with someone internally and can help them by communicating messages that their spirit needs to hear.

Positive Attribute #2—Unconditional Love

Pisceans embody the idea of unconditional love and non-judgment. They have the ability to ignore the other person's ego and look straight into the soul. This makes them inherently realize that we are all the same. Thus, people around them feel supported and loved simply by the fact that the Piscean communicates these feelings of being welcomed on an unconscious level.

Positive Attribute #3—Transparent

There is little guesswork when it comes to Pisceans. They are honest creatures, and this helps others to pick up on their frustrations in order to help them out. Like their fellow water sign, Cancer, Pisceans are uncensored and embody their emotions fully. This helps others to see their problems more readily and gives the Piscean a flexible body and mentality due to the fluidity of their thoughts and emotions.

Negative Attribute #1—Needy

Pisceans crave the merging of their soul with the soul of others. However, this can turn into emotional neediness, which can lead to drug addiction or staying in poor relationships for the sake of emotional security. Pisceans need to learn more independence and that their feelings of instability come from them not being grounded enough.

Negative Attribute #2—Unfocused

Because Neptune is so ethereal and foggy, it is hard for the Piscean to buckle down and come up with a coherent plan. This is more of a talent of their opposition, Virgo. Pisceans can live in a world of illusion and confusion. Thus, they sometimes have trouble remembering what is real. They need to keep both feet in this world before they can dive into the world of the unseen.

Negative Attribute #3—Emotional Punching Bag

Pisceans can act like a mirror for others. When someone is being harsh or cruel to a Piscean, they are actually projecting the things about themself that they do not like onto the Pisces individual. Sadly, Pisceans are so open and forgiving that they usually take the abuse. Pisceans need to learn when to put their foot down, and when to tell others to stop. This is a very hard thing for a Piscean to do. Still, the healthier their borders are around people, the better off their own health will be because they will be less prone to picking up the negativity of others.

Spiritual and Flexible

Pisces have such a depth to them which comes from their association to the deepest of wells of spirituality. As such, they are psychic, open, and nonjudgmental. They love to love and want to get to know people on an open and honest level. This time of the year marks the end of winter and the celestial calendar, which parallels the illusion of endings because every winter is followed by the start of spring since the dawn of time. They are ruled by Jupiter and Neptune, which gives them trust in the universe and trust in others. They are spiritual, relaxed, and honest, but need to be careful of becoming a victim and lacking a cohesive plan.

Coming Around Full Circle

The mythologies and symbolism within the twelve signs of the zodiac have been imprinted into the human psyche with each passing generation and society that has come before us. They tie us to the natural tug and pull of our yearly calendar and toward the other planets within our solar system due to planetary rulerships. Now, we will observe the ten planets within astrology because without the planets, the signs have no way of expressing themselves within the astrology chart. Indeed, it is the planets that bring out each sign's positive and negative traits within a birth chart; therefore, through the planets, the unique psychological makeup is born.

SECTION 3—THE PLANETS

Intergalactic Planetary, Planetary Intergalactic

The planets in astrology represent the mythological archetypes of the primordial gods and goddesses of our human culture. All planets up to Saturn can be seen by the naked eye, which has caused all of the human race to look up, ponder, and establish elaborate stories of these celestial rulers. Without the planets, the zodiac is nothing. The planets—their unceasing journey around the ecliptic, is how the zodiac is able to manifest itself. What I mean is, there are times when no planets are in a sign, and therefore that sign's energy is not expressed. However, the planets are always participating in the chart's manifestation one way or another.

Okay, Smartie Pants, Calm Down

Just to get this out of the way, of course astrologers don't consider the Sun or the Moon as a real planet in the astronomical sense. We know that the Sun is a Star and the Moon is a satellite of Earth. We simply call them planets for the sake of simplicity and to categorize them in the same equal category as their planetary counterparts.

Each Planet Has a Natural and Unique Character

By their very nature, some planets are focused on applying their will onto others, and others have that will placed upon them. Astrology has used a lot of linguistic combinations to explain this temperament: positive or negative, yin or yang, masculine or feminine, to name a few. For the sake of simplicity and semantic impartiality, I will use the following terms: active, passive, and neutral.

When it comes to the traditional planets in astrology (Sun, Moon, and Mercury through Saturn) these temperaments have been determined by ancient astrological systems. The modern planets (Uranus, Neptune, and Pluto) are placed within their respective positions based upon my own personal experience (Table II-1).

TABLE II-1. Natural Planetary Temperaments

ACTIVE		NEUTRAL		PASSIVE	
SUN	☉	MERCURY	☿	MOON	☽
MARS	♂			VENUS	♀
JUPITER	♃	URANUS	♅	SATURN	♄
PLUTO	♇			NEPTUNE	♆

Active planets are agents of doing. They cause events to happen and function as an outlet for our personal expression and motivations. Extroversion, movement, and manifestation are all due to the active planets.

Passive planets are receptive toward the actions of the active planets. They react rather than act and demonstrate how we function internally. Introversion, receptivity, and emotional states are derived from the passive planets.

Neutral planets derive their nature and motivations depending on how they are situated relative to the other planets within the birth chart. These planets react when they need to react and initiate when they need to initiate. However, because they are incredibly versatile, they can be easily influenced by the active and passive planets around them. This will be easier to comprehend when we cover aspects in Part II-Section 5, and chart analysis in Book II.

Planets with an Attitude

Another factor to consider is the natural temperament of the planets. Some planets are naturally pleasant and nice, and others are a bit more grumpy. This concept stems from traditional astrology, which means I will only be discussing the planets up to Saturn. Basically, the ancient astrologers created planets as benefic (beneficial) or malefic (unfavorable). They considered Venus and Jupiter to be the benefics (Venus as the lesser and Jupiter as the greater), Mars and Saturn to be the malefics (Mars as the less and Saturn as the greater), and Mercury as neutral. The temperament of the Sun and Moon depended on other factors such as their dignities and debilities, which we will discuss in the next section of this book. For now, it's interesting to consider that planets have their own individual attitudes.

Now, let us examine each planet individually and explore key concepts, major realms of rulership, and what happens when the planet is working harmoniously and inharmoniously.

SUN ☉—OUR INDIVIDUALITY

KEY CONCEPTS

The Sun represents our ego-expression and self-confidence. It is how we portray our personality out into the world, and how we individualize ourselves when compared to others around us. The Sun shows how we influence others by the impressions we make, and how we express our individuality by demonstrating our own uniqueness.

The Sun shows if we enjoy being chosen out of a crowd, and how much we desire or despise attention. It demonstrates our charisma and whether we are skillful at sacrificing our ego-drives for the sake of the group, or if we act more self-centered. The Sun shows how we tell the world who we are along with our comfortability as an individual within the world.

The Sun is like your fingerprint. There is only one individualized pattern throughout all of humanity. In this same light, the Sun manifests your own individualized mark on this world. Even within our own solar system, there are numerous planets but only one Sun. Similarly, there will only be one of you and anybody who came before or after you will not share your unique personalized individuality.

REALMS OF RULE

Creativity, charisma, ego-drive, self-esteem, leadership, self-awareness, ambition, extroversion, individuality, confidence, how we fit within social circles, the aura we project and how others are attracted to that aura, our interests and hobbies, and how we express our personal opinions, outlooks, and judgments.

IF FUNCTIONING HARMONIOUSLY

The individual is incredibly self-confident, but not egotistical. They are creative and know when to stand in and out of the spotlight. They are bright and cheerful, and others gravitate to them because of this. They stand out in a crowd and are well-liked, with few enemies. They are great with children and their confidence is contagious and inspirational to others. They make effective leaders because not only do people look up to them, people are willing to work for them.

IF FUNCTIONING INHARMONIOUSLY

The individual can either be a narcissist or incredibly introverted to a point of anti-social. They only consider their own priorities and do not care about the feelings and opinions of others. They have too much pride and cannot admit when they are wrong, and either crave too much attention or will avoid any kind of attention. Their opinions can get them into trouble and their ego-drives can come into direct conflict with others.

MOON ☽—OUR EMOTIONAL SELF

KEY CONCEPTS

The Moon represents our innermost emotional nature. It shows us how secure we are within our feelings and if we are good at nurturing the feelings of others. The Moon shows how we express our empathy and sympathy, and whether we are good at processing our feelings into healthy or unhealthy emotional responses.

The Moon demonstrates our inner comfortability and whether we are confident within our inner wellbeing, overly sensitive, or emotionally inept. It represents the meaning behind our words and actions and whether we are in tune enough to interpret these more subtle forces behind our own active tendencies and those of others. It shows if we are caring and supportive or if we are cold and callous.

The Moon signifies our unconscious side and where we hide our vulnerabilities. It determines if we are emotionally shallow or deep, and if we are consequently emotionally shut off or too open toward others. Our upbringing is reflected in the Moon and therefore demonstrates how we were comforted as children, and if we interpret the world around us as a scary or safe place.

REALMS OF RULE

Inner emotional wellbeing, comfortability within our own self and within the world at large, our sympathy, our ability to comprehend the subtleties behind language and action, ability to nurture ourselves and others, dependencies, our unconscious and more vulnerable side, and the mother or the mother figure within our lives.

IF FUNCTIONING HARMONIOUSLY

The individual is emotionally strong and can be supportive in this strength for others. They are not offended easily and can take a joke rather well. They are able to be easily vulnerable due to their emotional confidence. They can quash down frustrations and they are slow to anger or any other intense emotion. They do not get jealous easily and do not rely on others for emotional support and guidance. Instead, others come to them for those things.

IF FUNCTIONING INHARMONIOUSLY

They are either too emotionally volatile or not in tune with their emotional functions, making them cold toward the feelings of others. They can easily take offence, especially if they are teased over something that they are not confident about. They have a hard time putting themselves in new predicaments and do not enjoy going out of their routine, meeting new people, or going to new places.

MERCURY ☿—OUR MENTAL AND PHYSICAL PROCESSES

KEY CONCEPTS

Mercury represents our mental functions and capabilities along with how we communicate, conceptualize, analyze, and process ideas and information. It shows how well we can explain and develop intellectual concepts along with our own thoughts, and how receptive we are to the thoughts and opinions of others. It shows our desire for learning and our kinesthetic skills.

Mercury is where we get our discourse abilities, along with our talents in presenting in large crowds, and our skills in technology, typing, essays, and research. It shows how we can think outside of the box and how well we can teach others. Although Mercury is not where we get our sense of humor, Mercury shows us if we have any sense of comedic timing or any sort of linguistic emphasis in the way we speak, along with the overall quality of our lexicon.

Mercury shows how persuasive and convincing we can be. It also displays our approach and philosophy toward health and exercise. Our individualized metabolism comes from Mercury along with various processes of the body such as digestion, nutritional absorption, circulation, and breathing.

REALMS OF RULE

Mental capacity, learning and conversational abilities, general health and our approach toward health and exercise, our skills as a conversationalist, teacher, researcher, and writing abilities. Various ways we can approach mental quandaries, our desire for intellectual expansion and education, our analytical capacities, our vocabularies, and speech patterns.

IF FUNCTIONING HARMONIOUSLY

The individual is able to converse well with others and express their ideas clearly. There is generally good health and a proactive mindset in these endeavors. The person can think logically and is effective at explaining. They can self-teach and enjoy reading and obtaining knowledge. They have a voice that is easy to listen to with an extensive vocabulary and knowledge base. They are health conscious and do not have typical issues with their bodies.

IF FUNCTIONING INHARMONIOUSLY

The individual can have learning disabilities and be socially awkward in the way they speak or with what they speak about. They can use their words to demean others and are prone to arguments and instigating unhealthy interactions. They have a hard time saying what the mind is thinking and can have poor hand/eye coordination, which can make driving, writing, and sports difficult. There could be physical ailments and an overall poor outlook toward their health.

VENUS ♀—OUR AESTHETICS AND RELATIONS

KEY CONCEPTS

Venus indicates our ability to get along with others so that we can work cooperatively and live harmoniously with other individuals. It shows how we listen to the opinions and thoughts of others, how we share our ideas back to them, and the appropriate understandings that come out of that discourse. Indeed, Venus is the ultimate planet for finding common ground and dissolving conflict.

Venus is also the planet of style, aesthetics, and tastes in art. Our living environment and the types of clothes we wear are all ruled by Venus. She rules our ability to make others feel comfortable and relaxed, and whether we can feel the same way in other people's spaces.

Venus is where we get our appreciation for the arts along with our various preferences in music, visual art, home décor, and design. This is because, in many ways, the arts are universal in that all cultures have their own styles of artistic expression, although people from different cultures can come together based within the collective language that the arts possess.

REALMS OF RULE

Our ability to compromise and hear differences of opinion, our sense of style and artistic preferences, how well we can relax and be grounded within the environments we are placed within, artistic talents along with the type of art we enjoy, and the ability to sacrifice our ego for the sake of collective coexistence.

IF FUNCTIONING HARMONIOUSLY

The individual has a pleasing and symmetrical face and body and an acute sense of style and tastes. They have artistic abilities and/or an aptitude for spotting that talent in others. They have very few enemies because they easily meet people halfway. Their home environments are calm and grounded, and they can feel the same regardless of where they are located. They have a gentle, unthreatening demeanor. Their romantic relationships are typically healthy and fruitful.

IF FUNCTIONING INHARMONIOUSLY

The individual is prone to unresolved conflict, typically due to their inability to let go of their points of view and pride. They can have issues with hygiene and overall appearances. They cannot find solace in artistic expression and enjoyment. They dislike house cleaning or any kind of required upkeep. They also withhold information and feelings in relationships so that other people do not have to compromise on their behalf, which leads to resentment.

MARS ♂—OUR WILL AND POWER

KEY CONCEPTS

Mars is where we get our drive, ambition, and tenacity. It shows how well we initiate our personal goals and projects along with our willingness to see them through to the end. It is where we find our courage and willingness to face potentially dangerous situations. To this point, Mars shows if we are risk seeking or more prone to risk aversion.

Our confidence is highly tied into Mars because if we do not feel confident in who we are and in what we are doing, then our drive is likewise hampered by our lack of personal determination. Mars acts without thinking or hesitation and therefore is tied to our "go with the gut" intuition we find within ourselves.

Mars is also the planet of desire and sexual virility. It shows our various ranges of aggressiveness, forcefulness, and how much our sense of longing drives our motivations. Similarly, our athletic abilities and physical prowess are also determined by the condition of Mars within the birth chart.

REALMS OF RULE

Our sense of self-confidence not only in who we are but in what we are doing. The ability to react on instinct but also know when it is strategic to hold back or to push forward, our passions and motivations which fuel our ambitions and personal goals. Our sexual libido and desires, muscle tone and growth, physical stamina, and overall physical attractiveness.

IF FUNCTIONING HARMONIOUSLY

The individual is admired for their poise as they find it easy to simply be who they are and act upon these personal impressions. They are courageous and others see them as inspirational. They are athletic, toned, and people find them sexually attractive. Additionally, these individuals also know when it is a good time to act, and when is a good time to react. This is especially true in terms of intimacy because although they are heavily ego-driven, they can still make themselves vulnerable because they do not judge themselves.

IF FUNCTIONING INHARMONIOUSLY

The individual has a hard time with initiation and finding motivation to accomplish their goals. They can therefore be lazy and not really committed to self-help and self-improvement. There can either be sexual dysfunction or they could be too aggressive with their sexual desires. They are too prideful and readily seek conflict because they are absorbed with their sense of self. This makes it hard for them to be well received by others due to this intensity.

JUPITER ♃—OUR EVOLUTION AND OPENNESS

KEY CONCEPTS

Jupiter is the planet of mental and spiritual expansion. It shows our philosophical outlook and how our view of the world manifests due to this outlook. Therefore, Jupiter is also the planet that represents our judgments and opinions that are not necessarily based upon our actual experiences, but through our theoretical idealism found within our minds.

Fortune, speculation, and abundance all stem from Jupiter. Consequently, the powers of manifestation and optimism are determined by him. For example, if our personal outlook is consciously or subconsciously pessimistic, then we naturally shut off opportunities that could have come our way if we were only more open-minded and trusting.

Jupiter shows how we, as a society, function and rule. All our higher institutions (academic, governmental, religious, and vocational) stem from Jupiter because these are realms where we can apply our intellectual and spiritual ideas into practice within the real world. Similarly, Jupiter represents the universality of human nature, which either leads to acceptance or prejudice.

REALMS OF RULE

Our moral compass and ethical codes. Our opinions and thoughts toward individuals, cultures, and nations. Our ability to believe that the universe will provide everything we require. Our political and philosophical viewpoints and how these are reflected by the various organizations we associate with due to these preferences, and our sense of abundance and fortune.

IF FUNCTIONING HARMONIOUSLY

The individual easily obtains security and aid from the universe because they are open to such abundance. They are immensely positive individuals but not to a point of hopeless optimism. Due to this fact, others are attracted to their buoyant and generous nature, which they gladly extend outwards because they inherently know that they are paying it forward. They are nonjudgmental and very understanding when it comes to the errors of human nature.

IF FUNCTIONING INHARMONIOUSLY

These individuals gamble and speculate incorrectly because they think that their big break is right around the corner. This can breed a jaded and cynical outlook, which can consequently corrupt ethical principles. They have bad timing when it comes to obtaining their goals and typically need to work harder than those around them. They can have an over-inflated sense of superiority, which leads to bias and assumptions that get them into trouble.

SATURN ♄—OUR LIMITATIONS AND OBLIGATIONS

KEY CONCEPTS

Saturn is the planet of discipline and sacrifice because he understands the need to give up pleasures for today for the sake of tomorrow's achievements. It is the planet of slow and steady progress, especially toward career goals. Saturn believes that nothing comes easy and that everything worth obtaining requires the pushing of our own weaknesses so that we can grow from them. In this light, he believes that it is our own internal flaws that forbid us from reaching our fullest potential in the first place.

Limitations and the struggles that emerge out of our weaknesses are also represented by Saturn. He teaches you to work with what you have, and that restrictions are a way to help you maintain focus. Indeed, Saturn is the ultimate life-teacher whose lessons we may not enjoy, but they nevertheless give us great transformative powers if we are able to learn from those lessons.

Obligations and dedication also stem from Saturn. There are some parts of our life that simply hold us down because we have promised ourselves to see it through, such as a marriage, having children, or fulfilling contractual agreements. As such, Saturn is where we get our sense of integrity and reputation.

REALMS OF RULE

Our areas of personal weaknesses and restrictions. Areas in which we are inherently lacking and therefore need to overcome, not overcompensate. Our ability to be self-controlled and organized to see things to the end. Frugality and our sense of commitment. How truthful we are toward ourselves and toward others in this regard, and the father or the father figure.

IF FUNCTIONING HARMONIOUSLY

The individual is well-grounded and highly successful due to their own output. They have a good sense of humor and can provide insights and wisdom into your personal dilemmas. They make great parents and partners (romantic and business) because they are people of their word and will see it through thick and thin. They have no problem seeing and admitting their own faults for the sake of improvement.

IF FUNCTIONING INHARMONIOUSLY

These individuals have issues with authority and hearing the advice of others. They have a hard time with sacrifice and therefore their addictive and less-favored tendencies can get the better of them. They blame the world for their problems instead of admitting fault when it is needed. They can cut corners and try to follow the easier path instead of the path that must be taken.

URANUS ♅—OUR REBELLIOUS NATURE

KEY CONCEPTS

Uranus is the planet of freedom and peace when it comes to our persona and personal outlook. He reminds us that the only constant in the universe is change. Therefore, we need to be constantly ready to adapt and adjust our opinions and personality as we, and society, grow and evolve. He reminds us that an open mind and heart are the best way to approach life.

Uranus is where we get unconventionality and trendsetting because he can see into the future by examining the present and past. This is because he has a keen sense of human nature and therefore can see where everything is going years ahead. Uranus knows that societal norms and taboos are only subjective and impermanent due to the inevitable sands of time.

Uranus is highly intelligent and inventive because he can observe the issues within the current society and desires to help improve upon the condition. His open mind allows him to accept varying theories and outlooks that he then discerns within his own impartial filtration system. This allows him to take the personal out of the professional as he can simply see things as they truly are.

REALMS OF RULE

Scientific exploration, observation, and invention. Adaptability and open-mindedness with the ability to adjust based upon our observations. Fringe societal groups and unorthodox ways of thinking and lifestyles. Shocking and possibly disruptive events that take us out of our fixed mindsets. Unconventional wisdom, unpredictability, and going against the grain.

IF FUNCTIONING HARMONIOUSLY

The individual is highly intelligent and uses their intelligence to help humanity instead for selfish gains. They are open to all walks of life and lifestyles and do not judge individuals who follow a different path. They are not tied to familial or societal traditions and can therefore see how we can reform these realms for the better. They have a strong social net with deep and loyal friendships.

IF FUNCTIONING INHARMONIOUSLY

The individual is shocking and outrageous for their own sake. They are too extreme in their thinking to a point of being dogmatic. They are elitist and tend to demean others due to their over-inflated sense of intellectual superiority. They will take unpopular views and opinions just to cause a stir. They can be antisocial or a social recluse because they perceive the world to be the problem instead of themselves. They therefore expect the world to change to their unreasonable standards.

NEPTUNE Ψ—OUR SPIRITUALITY

KEY CONCEPTS

Neptune is the planet of human spiritualism that connects all religious ideals, but at the same time supersedes the ego-driven judgements found within religion. He understands that all souls come and go, and that everyone is on the same journey toward self-realization. Therefore, Neptune is filled with immense acceptance and understanding of all types of individuals.

Surrender and ego-denial naturally come as a consequence to accepting these Neptunian ideals because we need to not only let go of our own prejudices and judgments in order to see others as equal, we need to let go of our sense of self so that we may experience these universal truths within the nonphysical and meditative planes of existence.

Neptune represents worlds of reality other than our own, along with the unexplainable. Faith and trust are needed in order to "cross over" to the other side of the spiritual world, and Neptune shows us how this is accomplished so that we can attain higher states of consciousness and understanding.

REALMS OF RULE

Religion and the universal standards of acceptance and forgiveness that are found within. Meditation, yoga, and other spiritual disciplines. The ability to release our personal identity for the sake of connecting to our souls. Personal sacrifice so that we can unconditionally give to others. Universal love and acceptance that only comes from seeing others and the world as one.

IF FUNCTIONING HARMONIOUSLY

The individual has good psychic abilities and possesses faith in spirit and God. They approach others with ultimate unconditional love and forgiveness, and truly see others from a lens of non-judgment. They make great energy healers and therapists because they sympathize and understand the struggles of others. They can easily swallow their pride but at the same time stand their ground when it is required.

IF FUNCTIONING INHARMONIOUSLY

The individual can experience unhealthy victim/savior relationships where they are either too dependent or too giving toward their partners. They can have issues with drug addictions and can get swallowed up in the fog of confusion this creates within their personal outlook. They have a hard time connecting and believing in the existence of a soul or a universal creator. They also have a hard time relaxing due to their lack of trust in the universe.

PLUTO ♇—OUR HIDDEN WISDOM

KEY CONCEPTS

Pluto is the agent of change. Individuals, societies, and even humanity itself are in a constant cycle of birth, stability, and then destruction. However, Pluto does not destroy just for the sake of chaos, he simply terminates the unwanted and unneeded for the sake of improvement. Pluto removes the superfluous parameters that are holding us down, but we have allowed to remain due to a false sense of security that these useless structures provide.

Pluto reminds us that there is no such thing as an ultimate ending, for all endings always lead to a new beginning. As the axiom goes, "When a door closes, a window opens." Such is the nature of Pluto in that he simply concludes the current chapter so that you can move on to the next part of the story.

There comes immense wisdom with Pluto if we can understand and release our fear of change and fear itself. Pluto ensures that we never get stuck in a rut for too long so that we can always evolve and improve, the way we were destined to in this lifetime.

REALMS OF RULE

Power structures and power dynamics, such as institutions of law and justice, in addition to boss/employee relationships. Conclusions and completions of cycles whether this be toward relationships, life paths, or the ultimate conclusion: physical death. Therefore, Pluto rules our deepest, most unconscious fears and phobias that make us inflexible to the inevitabilities and universal truths of endings that Pluto represents.

IF FUNCTIONING HARMONIOUSLY

The individual has a healthy outlook on death and always seeks to improve the self. They are able to get to the bottom of situations, which makes them great detectives, doctors, and psychologists. They have a keen awareness into their unconscious motivations and can easily access more occult knowledge. They are emotionally open and willing to divulge their secrets to those they trust, and those they trust find it incredibly easy to do the same.

IF FUNCTIONING INHARMONIOUSLY

The individual is riddled with irrational fears and phobias that prevent them from being open to what they cannot control. Therefore, they can obsessively attempt to control whatever they can however they can. They find themselves trapped within power struggles and can either abuse power or be the one that is abused. They can be vindictive and have shoddy morals when it comes to treating others equally or when it comes to obtaining their goals, which causes many enemies to emerge.

Now We're Cookin'

At this point, you are starting to get a better understanding into the similarities between planets and signs. The overlap between energies is due to the planets and the signs that they rule. For example, you might have noticed themes around Venus also involve themes around Taurus and Libra, the two signs that are ruled by Venus, and so on. Indeed, planetary sign placements within the birth chart can drastically alter the natural temperament of a planet because there are some signs that give planets more power, and other signs that give planets less power. This is the main topic of the next section, and another layer where you can begin to see how planets change and adjust from birth chart to birth chart.

SECTION 4—PLANETARY DIGNITIES AND DEBILITIES

Planets Have Preferences

Now that you have a firm understanding of the twelve signs and the ten planets within Astrology, the next step is to mold the two together. When you analyze a birth chart, you will not just see Saturn ♄ or Venus ♀ but you will witness these planets within a sign of the zodiac, such as Saturn in Gemini (♄Ⅱ)or Venus in Pisces (♀♓). If you remember in the previous section, planets have a natural attitude and temperament that gives them a basis for their personality. Additionally, if they are placed in specific signs, this can either help or hinder their already natural state. For example, a Mars in Aries(♂♈) functions a lot more differently than a Mars in Taurus (♂♉).

Thankfully, ancient astrologers have devised a working table that helps to determine this adjustment, which we call the *table of planetary dignities and debilities*. The table is named as such because certain signs "dignify" a certain planet, which makes it more harmonious in its function. Or a sign can "debilitate" a planet and make it function inharmoniously.

This table stems from a collection of ancient knowledge that was first compiled by the Greek astrologer and astronomer Ptolemy in his book, *Tetrabiblos*, Second Century AD. As mentioned in Part I-Section 1, *Tetrabiblos* is thought to be the first astrological treatise to be written on the western astrological tradition. If you recall, western astrology is a cohesive mixture of Egyptian (rising signs), Mediterranean (planetary exaltations/triplicates, and wisdom of eclipses), Greek (system of planetary gods and their archetypes, dividing the zodiacal into equal parts) and Jyotish (the lunar nodes) astrological systems. *Tetrabiblos* was the first successful attempt to combine and consolidate this information into one reliable source.

Later, in seventeenth-century England, astrologer William Lilly finely tuned Ptolemy's initial findings and improved upon them in his books *An Introduction to Astrology* and *Christian Astrology*. Mr. Lilly demonstrated the practical application of planetary dignities and debilities within the context of horary astrology. This easy to understand and use system helps the astrologer to determine which planets are emphasized in a chart, if they are weakened or strengthened, and if they function to do us harm or good. In other words, dignities and debilities show us that in a natal chart, not all planets are created equal.

A Villa for Some, a Log Cabin for Others

Put simply, there are signs where planets love to reside, and signs where planets hate to reside. When they are in an accommodating sign, the planets are strong, healthy, and exist to support the person. However, if the sign is not as welcoming, planets can feel irritable, malignant, and inefficient.

The table of dignities and debilities does not incorporate the modern planets, Uranus, Neptune, and Pluto, because these planets were yet to be discovered. Modern astrologers have attempted to fit these planets into the table. However, in my opinion, I do not consider these placements for two main reasons: (1) there is too much debate and not enough consensus as to where these planets go and (2) because these planets move so slowly, it is insignificant what sign they are in because people born years before and after the individual in question will possess the same sign placement, regardless. With the outer planets, house placements and aspect configurations are significantly more important than sign placement. Therefore, in this section, we will only be observing the traditional rules and rulerships of the traditional seven planets, which begins with the Sun and ends with Saturn (Table II-2).

TABLE II-2. Abridged Table of Planetary Dignities and Debilities according to Ptolemy

SIGN	RULER	EXALTATION	DETRIMENT	FALL
ARIES ♈	MARS ♂	SUN ☉	VENUS ♀	SATURN ♄
TAURUS ♉	VENUS ♀	MOON ☽	MARS ♂	**NONE**
GEMINI ♊	MERCURY ☿	**NONE**	JUPITER ♃	**NONE**
CANCER ♋	MOON ☽	JUPITER ♃	SATURN ♄	MARS ♂

SIGN	RULER	EXALTATION	DETRIMENT	FALL
LEO ♌	SUN ☉	**NONE**	SATURN ♄	**NONE**
VIRGO ♍	MERCURY ☿	MERCURY ☿	JUPITER ♃	VENUS ♀
LIBRA ♎	VENUS ♀	SATURN ♄	MARS ♂	SUN ☉
SCORPIO ♏	MARS ♂	**NONE**	VENUS ♀	SUN ☉
SAGITTARIUS ♐	JUPITER ♃	**NONE**	VENUS ♀	**NONE**
CAPRICORN ♑	SATURN ♄	MARS ♂	MOON ☽	JUPITER ♃
AQUARIUS ♒	SATURN ♄	**NONE**	SUN ☉	**NONE**
PISCES ♓	JUPITER ♃	VENUS ♀	MERCURY ☿	MERCURY ☿

As you read over this table, you will notice new terms have emerged: Exaltation, Detriment, and Fall. We will cover these new terms more specifically in a bit, but before we do, I want to review and reintegrate the dual nature of some of the paradoxes found within the rulership column. That way, we firmly understand planetary rulerships before we get into further specifics.

Planetary Paradoxes

If you recall from Part I-Section 7, the study of astrology is riddled with paradoxes. As you can see in the table above and in Part II-Section 2, there are some signs that are ruled by the same planet. This is typically not an issue, but in some cases, the two signs that are ruled by the same planet make no sense because of the contradictory nature of the signs involved. I want to further discuss these apparent contradictions with the hope of clarifying and showing that, in reality, there are more similarities than incongruities. After that, we will further discuss Exaltation, Detriment, and Fall, and how they add another layer of analysis.

Contradiction #1: Gemini and Virgo are Ruled by Mercury but Square Each Other

We have yet to discuss aspects, but for now know that squares are the most difficult placement that planets and signs can find themselves. How is it that these two signs, Gemini and Virgo, are ruled by Mercury even though these two signs square one another at a 90° angle? One of the biggest factors that causes Gemini and Virgo to not understand one another is the way they both process and handle information; a Mercurial function.

Gemini is the data gatherer. They know how to obtain the information they need, say what they need to say, and take in whatever information they wish to gather. In essence, Gemini becomes a big storage facility of facts, figures, and information. The issue is, unlike their Virgo counterparts, Geminis hardly ever process the information given to them. This frustrates Virgo because they are all about the function of things. Virgo asks the Gemini why they are not doing anything with the information provided, and Gemini cannot understand why Virgo cannot respect communicating and gathering information just for the sake of mental exploration and expression.

Virgo wants to take information one step further via application and analysis, thus creating the efficiency and attention to detail that Virgos are well known for. However, Virgo needs Gemini because they are the best at obtaining the raw data that Virgo uses. Virgos are not known for their social charm, unlike Gemini, so both are needed in order to fully express the abilities of Mercury.

Gathering information (Gemini) and processing information (Virgo) are both important qualities that create the planet Mercury. So, again, the question remains: why the square? It simply has to do with the two specific stages of childhood development that an individual encounters. The Gemini experience occurs around the toddler years, and this is when you get your first understanding of the world around you. When we approach our Virgo experience, we are now in elementary school where our formal education officially begins. Now that we are acquiring new knowledge, our past Gemini experiences are improved upon, but first, a conflict occurs because you need to comprehend, blend, and adjust your previous thinking with your newly gathered information.

So, the conflict (square) occurs simply because of the stages of life that happen during the Gemini and Virgo phases within a person's life (this will be covered more in Part II-Section 6). Both experiences are required in order to understand the full extent of the planet Mercury. Virgo is, in some ways, the next evolutionary step to Gemini. Mercury "upgrades" into a more complex form of thinking and analyzing. This is not to say that Geminis are simpletons or less evolved, quite the opposite. Gemini is a required experience that needs to happen first before the Virgo experience can take place. However, when it is time for your Virgo stage in life (elementary school) you are adjusting your previous knowledge (toddler years) toward your growing and developing mental capacities.

Contradiction #2: Pisces and Sagittarius are Ruled by Jupiter but Square Each Other

Pisces and Sagittarius both involve ideas of expansion, but the difference comes from their respective elements. Sagittarius, a fire element, sees expansion through ideas, higher education, and institutions of truth and knowledge such as religion, government, and university. Pisces, a water sign, is all about the expansiveness of the cosmos and of spirit. Pisces is the most unconditional of all the signs, which makes people feel comfortable and at ease around them. Pisces subconsciously says, "I do not judge, I am a soul just like you," which causes Pisces to experience people and situations from all walks of life; a very Jupitarian theme.

Sagittarius also believes in spiritually expansive ideas such as human togetherness and equality, but through the vessels of societal institutions and community. Sagittarius understands Pisces' ability to live within the spiritual abundance of life, but cannot understand how they have no guidance or borders around themselves, their goals, or with others.

Sagittarius believes in the same principles as Pisces but believes that these ideas are obtainable through society at large. This is where the confusion with Pisces toward Sagittarius lies. Pisces, like their neighbor Aquarius, understands the imperfections of human error and thus believes that human connection is best done outside of corrupt institutions through a one-on-one, person-to-person basis or through spiritual techniques, such as meditation and yoga.

Again, just as it was with Mercury, you can start to see how both signs are still aspects of the same planetary themes of their ruler, Jupiter. Jupiter is welcoming of all ideas and situations and wants to give all it can to its earthly children. The difference is: Sagittarius sees this abundance and love through the evolution of the human experience, and Pisces through spiritual evolution.

Similar to Gemini and Virgo, Pisces is the next evolved step to Sagittarius. Sagittarius is when we experience our college years and our minds expand even further to understand and accept human ideas, cultures, and perspectives that are different from our own, giving us our first examples of "we are all one." This realization first comes through the Sagittarian mechanism of institutional academics. With Sagittarius, these ideas are more philosophical, but with Pisces, these ideas are then put into practice as Pisces literally lives out the ideas of love, kindness, and non-judgment, transforming the theoretical into the actual. Again, both are required for the individual to progress.

Contradiction #3: The Progressive Sign Aquarius is Ruled by the Obstinate Planet Saturn

Aquarius ruled by Saturn is the last paradox to observe. This planetary/sign combination is very confusing indeed, as Saturn is the ruler of Capricorn, a sign very much opposite to the ideals of Aquarius. Capricorn is about structure, stability, the status quo, corporate ladders, and the tested, tried, and true. Aquarius, on the other hand, represents the tearing down of structures, anti-establishment, anti-societal norms, the avant-garde, and individualism.

Put another way, at its most extreme, Capricorn can be viewed as capitalism and Aquarius as communism.

If this is the case, then how can a planet like Saturn possibly rule a sign like Aquarius, which is basically everything that Capricorn stands against? The answer is strangely within this inherent contradiction. You cannot have the protester (Uranus) if you do not have the thing to protest (Saturn). Similarly, you cannot improve upon the human condition (Uranus) if there are no institutional structures in the first place (Saturn). Uranus is simply the reaction to Saturn, but Saturn is needed so that Uranian futuristic ideas can come out of the initial struggle brought on by Saturn.

A great example that demonstrates Saturn's rulership of Aquarius and Capricorn can be found in both signs' ability for humor. Capricorns and Aquarians are known for an acute sense of humor. Capricorn is a common sign for comedians, and the court jester is an Aquarian archetype. The difference is: Capricorn humor is dry and sarcastic, whereas Aquarian humor is witty and outlandish. Still, both signs are equipped with a sense of humor because both understand the realities of the human condition. Capricorn sees the humor behind life's concept of Murphy's law, and Aquarius sees humor in the absurdities of life. These two different types of humor come from the same source of understanding of what it means to be a human being living and experiencing life on planet Earth.

Exaltation, Detriment, and Fall

Now that we have covered more extensively these contradictions found within the Rulership column, we can continue to discuss the other three columns: Exaltation, Detriment, and Fall.

According to Table II-2, there are four possible categories that will change the natural temperament of the various planets. These four categories differ in quality and strength and are described below:

EXALTATION: The planet revels in this sign and therefore their planetary energies are positively exemplified and powerful.

RULER: The planet is in the sign it rules and therefore it is comfortable, beneficial, and functions properly.

NEUTRAL: The planet is in a sign that does not affect it negatively or positively.

DETRIMENT: These are the signs in opposition to the planetary ruler and therefore, the planet's energies are thwarted and not well expressed.

> **FALL:** The planet feels incredibly agitated in this sign and therefore their planetary energies are destructive and need to be addressed.

Now, let us go into further detail as we will take each dignity and debility and explain why the planets and signs work harmoniously or inharmoniously. Again, we will only be observing the seven traditional planets excluding Uranus, Neptune, and Pluto.

Sun ☉

EXALTATION—ARIES ♈, Action Meets Drive

The Sun enjoys ego expression and Aries expresses themselves fully in the present. Here, the Sun is confident, engaged, and values the individual self.

DETRIMENT—AQUARIUS ♒, The Black Sheep

Aquarius is the sign of all of humanity, whereas the Sun wants to feel special and unique. Here, the Sun is shunned by society, does not think their uniqueness is worth exploring, and can be humble to a fault.

FALL—LIBRA ♎, The Need to Self-Sacrifice

The Sun hates having to compromise and only wants to do as it dictates, regardless of those around them, and Libra is the sign of compromise. Here, the Sun is lacking in self-identity, experiences indecisiveness, and is conflicted as to how to express their individuality out into the world.

Moon ☽

EXALTATION—TAURUS ♉, The Healthy Garden

Similar to the Taurus/Cancer sextile, the Moon loves the conformability that Taurus provides. Here, the Moon is nurturing, emotionally secure, and joyous.

DETRIMENT—CAPRICORN ♑, Peter Pan Syndrome

The Moon does not want to grow up, and Capricorn is all about growing up. Here, the Moon is a child in adult's clothing, emotionally callous, and unsympathetic.

FALL—SCORPIO ♏, Emotional Turmoil

The Moon wants to remain in one place while Scorpio is constantly in a state of change. Here, the Moon is self-destructive, unable to relax, and paranoid.

Mercury ☿

EXALTATION—VIRGO ♍, Double Power

Mercury is doubly powered in Virgo and works at its highest functionality in this sign. Here, Mercury is constantly moving and focused, possesses high energy and vitality, is intelligent, and has a talent with words and writing.

DETRIMENT No. 1—SAGITTARIUS ♐, Blind-Sighted

Mercury is about the day-to-day while Sagittarius is concerned with philosophy and the big picture. Here, Mercury is unable to see all angles, gets lost in the details, and can miss opportunities that are right in front of them.

DETRIMENT No. 2 and FALL—PISCES ♓, Making Sense out of Nonsense

Mercury wants to analyze and correlate while Pisces is nothing but ethereal and unexplainable. Here, Mercury is confused, has trouble communicating, and cannot stay grounded.

Venus ♀

EXALTATION—PISCES ♓, Unconditional Love

Venus is about love and harmony and Pisces is the higher octave of universal love. Here, Venus is highly psychic, unconditional, and nonjudgmental toward others.

DETRIMENT No. 1—SCORPIO ♏, Bringer of Bad News

Scorpio wants to get to the darker points while Venus wants to keep things light-hearted and pleasant. Here, Venus is irritated, unable to be calm, and seeks to put others down.

DETRIMENT No. 2—ARIES ♈, Fast and Furious

Venus wants to take it easy while Aries wants to go, go, go. Here, Venus is angered easily, has trouble thinking of their partner in relationships, and can be shallow.

FALL—VIRGO ♍, Cannot Relax

Virgo is the sign of constant understanding and analyzing while Venus is about luxury and leisure. Here, Venus is too critical, doubtful of others, and only sees the glass half empty.

Mars ♂

EXALTATION—CAPRICORN ♑, Productive Success

Mars' drive is geared toward the right direction thanks to the help of Capricorn. Here, Mars is successful, unafraid to take responsibilities, and enjoys physical challenges.

DETRIMENT No. 1—LIBRA ♎, Lack of Self

Mars wants to do what it wants to do, and Libra is about sacrificing the self. Here, Mars is unable to act on instinct, puts himself too much into other people's shoes, and lacks identity.

DETRIMENT No. 2—TAURUS ♉, Unmotivated

Taurus wants to relax and approach life in a calm and collected manner, whereas Mars wants to bolt out the door running. Here, Mars is a sloth, has a hard time staying active, and requires extra effort to get things done.

FALL—CANCER ♋, The Wanderer

Cancer is feeling oriented and Mars rules on instinct, not intuition. Here, Mars is insecure, unable to find direction, and lacks virility.

Jupiter ♃

EXALTATION—CANCER ♋, Connected to Spiritual Love

Jupiter wants everything to be all right in the end and Cancer wants to make everything all right in the end. Here, Jupiter is caring, supportive, and a provider.

DETRIMENT No. 1—GEMINI ♊, Lack of Focus

Gemini is about quick information in small doses, while Jupiter is too grand for those kinds of details. Here, Jupiter is unable to focus, has a hard time approaching conclusions, and cannot understand both large and small concepts simultaneously.

DETRIMENT No. 2—VIRGO ♍, Halted by the What-Ifs

Virgo is constantly criticizing, while Jupiter hates thinking in terms of limitations. Here, Jupiter is cynical, bitter, and unable to trust in his own power of manifestation.

FALL—CAPRICORN ♑, The Land of Plenty vs. The Land of Drought

Jupiter is about abundance and Capricorn is about limitations. Here, Jupiter is unable to stay optimistic, does not believe in his own power, and cannot bring forth opportunities.

Saturn ♄

EXALTATION—LIBRA ♎, Let's Work Together

Libra is about teamwork, and Saturn enjoys the help of others to achieve a goal. Here, Saturn is proud of their output, responsible, and collaborative.

DETRIMENT No. 1—LEO ♌, Son Versus Dad

Leo wants to do what Leo wants to do, and Saturn pushes Leo into a box. Here, Saturn hates to spoil itself, does not take things lightly, and does not like children.

DETRIMENT No. 2—CANCER ♋, Dad Versus Mom

Cancer is loving, while Saturn is about tough love. Here, Saturn is emotionally stunted, cannot open up to others, and can be irritable and grumpy.

FALL—ARIES ♈, Over Before it Began

Aries is about the here and now, and Saturn is about building up slowly over time. Here, Saturn is unable to see things through, easily angered, and can have patterns of ignorance and bigotry.

Old Knowledge That's Still Useful

Although this is not an extensive list of how every planet interacts within every sign of the zodiac, this is a great first step into understanding how signs and planets operate with one other. Already, you are getting a better understanding about how signs and planets operate, and the various dignities and debilities help to conceptualize this. Dignities and debilities have been a part of astrology for centuries and their ideas shouldn't be ignored.

SECTION 5—ASPECTS

Astrological Angles

The astrological planets travel along a circular band in the sky known as the zodiac. This circular band is a 360° wheel, which is then divided into twelve equal parts of 30° each. This is where we get the twelve signs of the zodiac.

The number 360 is very special in that it is heavily divisible. When two planets interact with one another through one of these divisions, we say they are in aspect to one another. When this occurs, their energies are engaged in either harmonious or inharmonious ways.

In terms of divisibility, the astrological circle of 360° is divided into eleven different combinations. This is where we get the major and minor aspects within astrology. This book will only cover and utilize the five major aspects: the conjunction (σ), sextile ($\times$), square ($\square$), trine (Δ), and opposition (σ^o). However, in order to exhibit the fully divisible nature of 360, all eleven combinations are demonstrated below (Table II-3).

TABLE II-3. The Major and Minor Aspects of Astrology

EQUATION	DIVISION	NAME	GLYPH	MAJOR OR MINOR
360/1	**360° or 0°**	**Conjunction**	σ	**Major**
360/12	30°	Semi-Sextile	'	Minor
360/8	45°	Semi-Square	∠	Minor
360/6	**60°**	**Sextile**	$\times$	**Major**
360/5	72°	Quintile	Q	Minor
360/4	**90°**	**Square**	□	**Major**

EQUATION	DIVISION	NAME	GLYPH	MAJOR OR MINOR
360/3	**120°**	**Trine**	Δ	**Major**
360 x (3/8)	135°	Sesquiquadrate	⊡	Minor
360 x (2/5)	144°	Bi-Quintile	bQ	Minor
360 x (5/12)	150°	Inconjunct	⅄	Minor
360/2	**180°**	**Opposition**	☍	**Major**

Conceptualizing Aspects

In the past, astrologers have often used vague umbrella terms to define the difficulty or ease of an aspect. For example, easier aspects like the sextile and trine were considered *soft aspects*, and the difficult aspects like the square and opposition were considered *hard aspects*. This terminology is insufficient because not only should you take aspects on a case-by-case basis, but aspects are incredibly specified toward the overall picture of the birth chart. Thus, aspects should not be categorized as soft, hard, difficult, or easy. Instead, aspects simply are.

For example, squares are typically considered difficult, but if it is a square involving transiting Venus or Jupiter, then the effect of the square is weakened due to the fact that Venus and Jupiter are the two benefits within astrology. Similarly, if Venus is in a trine with Jupiter, which is usually considered an easy aspect, and yes, there are a lot of benefits to this trine, the person could also be prone to laziness, weight gain, and overindulgence.

A person's psychological makeup is so complex and unique that when you are studying a natal chart, you should be focusing on the entire picture, not just one aspect here and there. The good news is there is a way to determine the importance of an aspect by prioritizing aspects from the most significant and impactful to the least using orbs of influence. This method will be discussed toward the end of this section.

This is Just the Stepping Stone

We will be observing planetary combinations when it comes to the conjunctions, but keep in mind that the other various planetary combinations by aspect are beyond the scope of this book simply because there are already exemplary books out there on the subject. If you want to get a better idea of the planets' interactions by aspect, I would recommend the books *Planets in Youth* by Robert Hand and *How to Be a Great Astrologer* by James Braha for natal aspects, and *Planets in Transit* by Robert Hand for transit aspects.

☌ Conjunction (0°)

Keyword: Blending

When two planets are in conjunction, their energies blend together and become inseparable in the way they function. For example, if Mars conjoins Saturn in a natal chart (♂☌♄), Mars operates with the characteristics of Saturn and vice versa in the same way two molecules in chemistry can combine together and create a new molecule altogether. The only difference is, with planets in a conjunction, they become inseparable and are therefore infinitely and permanently bound to one another. Therefore, the planetary interactions within these various connections are constantly manifested and observed throughout one's life.

If the planetary energies are complementary, like the Sun and Mars (☉☌♂) or the Moon and Venus (☽☌♀), then the conjunction functions more soundly. However, if the planetary energies are less complimentary, like Mars and Neptune (♂☌♆), or Venus and Saturn (♀☌♄), then the conjunction will be a little more difficult to handle.

This is where Table II-1 comes in handy, because you can tell if planetary combinations are more harmonious than others by simply observing their natural temperaments. Let us expand upon Table II-1 and view the various conjunction combinations and whether or not they behave harmoniously, inharmoniously, or neutrally (Table II-4). [NOTE: This table does not include the outer planetary conjunctions because they are generational and/or rarely happen due to the slow movement of the outer planets. For example, the last time Neptune conjoined Pluto (♆☌♇) was in the late 1800s and will not occur again until well into the 22nd century.]

TABLE II-4. Various Planetary Conjunction Combinations and Natural Temperaments

CONJ	GLYPH	H/I/N	CONJ	GLYPH	H/I/N	CONJ	GLYPH	H/I/N
Sun/ Moon	☉☌☽	I	Moon/ Jupiter	☽☌♃	H	Venus/ Mars	♀☌♂	I
Sun/ Mercury	☉☌☿	N	Moon/ Saturn	☽☌♄	I	Venus/ Jupiter	♀☌♃	H
Sun/ Venus	☉☌♀	I	Moon/ Uranus	☽☌♅	I	Venus/ Saturn	♀☌♄	I
Sun/ Mars	☉☌♂	H	Moon/ Neptune	☽☌♆	H	Venus/ Uranus	♀☌♅	I
Sun/ Jupiter	☉☌♃	H	Moon/ Pluto	☽☌♇	H	Venus/ Neptune	♀☌♆	H
Sun/ Saturn	☉☌♄	N	Mercury/ Venus	☿☌♀	N	Venus/ Pluto	♀☌♇	N
Sun/ Uranus	☉☌♅	I	Mercury/ Mars	☿☌♂	N	Mars/ Jupiter	♂☌♃	H
Sun/ Neptune	☉☌♆	I	Mercury/ Jupiter	☿☌♃	I	Mars/ Saturn	♂☌♄	H
Sun/ Pluto	☉☌♇	I	Mercury/ Saturn	☿☌♄	N	Mars/ Uranus	♂☌♅	N
Moon/ Mercury	☽☌☿	N	Mercury/ Uranus	☿☌♅	H	Mars/ Neptune	♂☌♆	I
Moon/ Venus	☽☌♀	H	Mercury/ Neptune	☿☌♆	I	Mars/ Pluto	♂☌♇	H
Moon/ Mars	☽☌♂	I	Mercury/ Pluto	☿☌♇	N			

KEY: H=Harmonious, I=Inharmonious, N=Neutral

Do not take tables such as these to be completely set in stone. Remember, astrology is filled with paradoxes and caveats, which cause some exceptions to occur. For example, although Jupiter is a passive planet, it still reacts harmoniously with the majority of active planets because Jupiter is the "great benefic," making his presence relatively beneficial for the individual regardless of the other planet involved.

Similarly, the majority of Mercury conjunctions are neutral, but Mercury conjoined Neptune is inharmonious because the innate nature of Mercury is uncomplimentary to that of Neptune. Therefore, it is important to treat tables like these as starting points, but remember to treat every birth chart with the individuality and minuteness they require. As we will examine in Book II, the birth chart is never cut and dry.

Similarity: Same Sign

Conjunctions typically occur within one sign. Meaning, it is less about the signs in which they occur and more about the two planets involved. The way to observe how the sign influences the conjunction is to consider dignities and debilities (Part II-Section 4).

For example, with the Moon/Venus conjunction in Capricorn (☽♑☌♀♑), the harmony of Moon blending with Venus is slightly disrupted because the Moon is in detriment in Capricorn and is thus weakened, even though both of these planets are passive and therefore work harmoniously. We will cover all sign combinations for all other aspects, but for the conjunction, going into the details about each combination is beyond the scope of this book. I would recommend *Planets in Youth* by Robert Hand as a good starting point to further explore the various planetary combinations that can form a conjunction.

✶ Sextile (60°)

Keyword: Cooperation

It is all too easy to take for granted the amazing potential found within sextiles. Instead, we brush them off as minor windows of opportunity here and there, and nothing too serious or beneficial. However, with sextiles, we see a sort of alchemical process where two elements work together in harmony and therefore bring about the positive characteristics of the elements involved. Sextiles within the birth chart are inherent strengths that lay dormant within the individual. They can be very beneficial for the individual, but they require active and conscious utilization in order for the sextile to be properly expressed.

Similarity: Same Polarity

Fire and Air (Masculine/Yang/Active) or Water and Earth (Feminine/Yin/Passive) are the two combinations of sextiles. Air encourages Fire and helps to breathe more life into the flames. Fire encourages Air to keep going with their instincts. Water replenishes Earth and makes the garden grow. Earth feeds into Water, allowing for life to exist where it dwells. Sextiles embody these mutual and powerful relationships, but again, they require the individual to actively use these forces to their advantage else their potential benefits lay dormant.

Sextile Combinations

ARIES SEXTILE GEMINI (♈⚹♊), Active Participation

Aries encourages Gemini to continue with their findings and ponderings. Gemini loves to talk, and Aries loves to be heard. This sextile gives one the ability to keep conversations going, let opinions be heard, and have courage when it comes to meeting new people and situations.

TAURUS SEXTILE CANCER (♉⚹♋), Feminine Loving Energy

Taurus provides life for Cancer in her oceans, and Cancer provides life for Taurus through her rains. Both signs embody the ultimate loving feminine energy that exists on this planet. People with this sextile are caring, loving, and bountiful.

GEMINI SEXTILE LEO (♊⚹♌), Creative Brainstorming

Gemini helps Leo brainstorm his creativity. Leo is able to write and create works that reach his audience. These signs greatly aid in the creative and artistic process. People with this sextile are creative, clever, and charismatic.

CANCER SEXTILE VIRGO (♋⚹♍), Slow and Steady Improvement

Cancer tells Virgo that it is ok to be different and shy. Virgo tells Cancer that she does not mind Cancer's faults because she knows how much Cancer loves her in return. People with this sextile are gentle, hard workers that are invested in their output, and make great nannies/parents.

LEO SEXTILE LIBRA (♌✶♎), Artist with an Audience

Leo exchanges and connects his ideas with the audience of Libra. Libra admires Leo's skills and also hopes to create a personal relationship due to Leo's laid-back and authentic nature. People with this sextile are great at politics, know what the audience wants, and feel confident in who they are when others are around.

VIRGO SEXTILE SCORPIO (♍✶♏), The Best of the Best

Virgo does not feel afraid to tell Scorpio what they can be doing better, and Scorpio appreciates Virgo's honesty and bluntness. These two signs allow for no stone to be unturned, and people with this sextile are great with any detective work, occult knowledge, and finding beneficial master/apprentice relationships.

LIBRA SEXTILE SAGITTARIUS (♎✶♐), The Highest Rule of Law

Libra works with Sagittarius to make sure that people are working together toward a better society through the art of compromise. Sagittarius ensures that they are doing so for the betterment of human society. People with this aspect make excellent debaters, intelligent professors, and tend to see the best in people.

SCORPIO SEXTILE CAPRICORN (♏✶♑), Executive Powers

Scorpio's ability to handle other people's resources mixed with Capricorn's ability to be frugal and strategic makes this combination unstoppable in the corporate world. People with this aspect are great at calculating risks, obtaining wealth, and have strong abilities for self-analysis and self-improvement.

SAGITTARIUS SEXTILE AQUARIUS (♐✶♒), Human Progress

Sagittarius provides the institutions where humanity can create a world of elevated peace and cooperation. Aquarius ensures that these institutions and laws change with the times so that they are always adapting for the betterment of society. People with this aspect have a high faith in their fellow man, fight for minorities within the system, and have a finely tuned gauge of what is right and what is wrong.

CAPRICORN SEXTILE PISCES (♑⚹♓), Spiritual Discipline

Capricorn is the Guru that can lead you toward enlightenment. Pisces is the door-way to that spiritual knowledge. People with this aspect are highly psychic, can reach high states of consciousness, and can maintain equilibrium within entropy.

AQUARIUS SEXTILE ARIES (♒⚹♈), Revolutionary Courage

Aquarius is the injustice that sparks the revolution, and Aries is the brave patriot that has stood up against tyranny throughout the world's history. People with this aspect are true revolutionaries, not afraid to stand up for injustice, and are highly original.

PISCES SEXTILE TAURUS (♓⚹♉), Ultimate Healing

Pisces gives the person the connection to the spiritual and psychic realm, and Taurus allows for them to use their five senses in order to convey the messages that spirit wants to convey. These people have great talents in massage/reiki, energy work, and feng shui.

□ Square (90°)

Keyword: Unconscious

It should not be understated that squares are our most important karmic work in this lifetime. They are the self-destructive parts of our psychology that are so hidden, we are not even aware of their presence. With the square, you have two planets working with a lot of energy but at cross-purposes. Both planets want you to address their urges and demands, and their influences affect your ability to make lucid, coherent decisions in life.

By their very nature, squares require immense psychological intro-spection and observation because the first step is to simply put them on your radar. Once you have detected their sabotage, you can then begin to analyze, understand, and overcome. Squares require a lot of personal attention and perse-verance, but the more you work on overcoming them, the more you take yourself out of the karma that was given to you in this lifetime. This helps you to evolve your consciousness to higher realms because you are simply peeling off layers of previous karma that you were meant to address and overcome. In other words, you are doing the work you were meant to be doing and as a result, you are rewarded with inner peace because you are calming down the erratic, shadow energies inside of you.

Similarity: Same Modality

The reason for the square's confusing and unaccommodating nature has to do with the fact that squares involve signs of the same modality. That is, they are both either cardinal, fixed, or mutable. When you have two signs of the same modality, you have two signs that see life the same way, but due to them being different elements, they approach that similar worldview differently and cannot understand why the other is approaching life in that way.

This is echoed by the fact that squares involve elements of different polarities as well. For example, Aries squares Cancer. Both are cardinal, but Aries is Fire (Yang) and Cancer is Water (Yin). Another example, Virgo squares Sagittarius. Both are mutable, but Virgo is Earth (Yin) and Sagittarius is Fire (Yang). Signs and planets in a square look at one another and go "No! You are doing it wrong! It needs to be done this way!" When it comes to your psychology, you have these two aggressive forces unconsciously motivating you to act on their behalf. The problem is, because you have two signs and two planets telling you this, and because they are at cross-purposes to one another, self-destructive tendencies begin to arise.

The trick to squares is to catch them when they flare up, put them on your radar, work through them, talk to both of them, and consciously put an effort to not rely on their energies. Instead, use the energies in your chart that are more beneficial and are there to help you, like your trines, sextiles, and beneficial conjunctions.

Square Combinations

ARIES SQUARE CANCER (♈□♋), The Emotionally Insecure

Aries wants to proceed how it wants to proceed. Cancer wants to evaluate the situation first and see if they feel comfortable before they act. Aries is aggressive and inconsiderate. Cancer is too considerate and sensitive. People with this square can have issues connecting with their emotions, can be emotionally volatile, and can take things too personally.

TAURUS SQUARE LEO (♉□♌), The Battle of the Wills

Taurus and Leo both want to do what they want to do. The problem is, Taurus wants to stay at home and watch a movie with popcorn, and Leo wants to go out clubbing. Due to their fixed nature, it is impossible for the other to sacrifice their wants for the other, especially because they cannot understand why the other person wants what they want. People with this square fight introversion with extroversion, excitement with predictability, and taking a risk with playing it safe.

GEMINI SQUARE VIRGO (♊□♍), The Whirlwind

Gemini wants to talk and talk where Virgo wants to talk about something meaningful. Gemini relays fact after fact, and Virgo becomes overwhelmed with data. People with this square have a hyperactive brain, cannot stand still, and analyze before they get the entire picture.

CANCER SQUARE LIBRA (♋□♎), Same Relationship, Different Approach

Cancers and Libras both desire relationships with another. The problem is, Cancer's relationship is based on emotions and with Libra, it is based on an intellectual connection. Cancer wants to cuddle and coddle; Libra wants to chat and go out on dates. People with this square cannot seem to find the right partner, push their emotional insecurities onto their partners, and have a hard time with personal identity and autonomy.

LEO SQUARE SCORPIO (♌□♏), Light Versus Dark

Leo wants to approach life with vigor and brightness. Scorpio only sees the dark in everything and hates the spotlight. People with this aspect have issues with optimism and pessimism, background versus foreground, and are unable to enjoy the moment because they are always trying to downplay everything as happenstance.

VIRGO SQUARE SAGITTARIUS (♍□♐), Intense Deflation and Expansion

Sagittarius wants to think of all possibilities and outcomes. Virgo reminds Sagittarius that there is a big difference between what is possible and what is practical. Sagittarius wants to expand and reach out while Virgo wants to reel in and conserve. People with this square cut themselves down, dream big but have poor drive, and are not able to see the good times when they are to be had.

LIBRA SQUARE CAPRICORN (♎□♑), Daddy Issues

Libra wants to connect and relate. Capricorn does not believe in sharing one's feelings. Libra wants to learn from others, while Capricorn believes in self-sufficiency. People with this square are too serious to be casual, experience conflict with authority figures, and lack professional skills and professionalism.

SCORPIO SQUARE AQUARIUS (♏□♒), Two Different Types of Transformation

For both signs, transformation and change are important, but for Scorpio, it is more on the emotional and psychological side and for Aquarius, it is on the societal side. Both signs value freedom, change, and, most importantly, seeing to it that all justice is served but both disagree on how to get there. For Scorpio, this change is internal and deep, and for Aquarius, it is not emotionally deep but ideological instead. People with this square are social in the wrong crowds, see themselves as a victim of society, and have a hard time opening up emotionally.

SAGITTARIUS SQUARE PISCES (♐□♓), Both Sides of Jupiter

Sagittarius and Pisces have similarities because they are both ruled by Jupiter and are thus both signs of expansion and growth. With Sagittarius, this is expansion of knowledge, but with Pisces, it is expansion of consciousness. People with this square have a hard time releasing logic around spiritual endeavors, can be too in over their heads, idealize people and situations, can be hopelessly naïve and optimistic, and avoid confrontation at all costs.

CAPRICORN SQUARE ARIES (♑□♈), The Wonder Years

Capricorn tells the Aries that there are rules. Aries tells the Capricorn where he can stick it. Aries has no real prerogative except that of his own self-interest, and Capricorn is about being a responsible and reliable provider. People with this square can be bigoted, have issues around what the self wants to do versus obligation, and can have a very hard time with empathy.

AQUARIUS SQUARE TAURUS (♒□♉), Flight Versus Immobility

Aquarius wants to go out into the world and experience the adventures of life. Taurus wants to stay at home, watch a movie, and eat popcorn. Aquarius thinks outside the box and loves new ideas. Taurus is more interested in pursuits of the senses, not the mind. People with this square have a hard time with money, crave social gatherings but can be anti-social and secluded, and can lack motivation for their ideas which, if they were to pursue, would work out wonderfully for them.

PISCES SQUARE GEMINI (♓□♊), Too Much Confusion

Gemini is all about words and communicating. Pisces is about the lack of meaning and the abstract. Gemini continually craves connections where Pisces is too psychically open to be around too many people. People with this square are highly influenced by others around them, have trouble processing factual information, and, on the other hand, cannot sit still to meditate. They need to relax the mind as much as possible and be sure to keep their surroundings as calm and clean as possible.

Δ Trine (120°)

Keyword: Harmony

The trine is thought to be the strongest and most beneficial aspect within astrology. In a trine, the two planets in question are operating in highly agreeable ways, bringing about the most positive qualities of the planets and signs within the individual.

The trines in your chart are the skills, abilities, and attitudes that have positively shaped you into the person you are today. Unlike sextiles, trines act without provocation, and seem to always be present inside the person. It is here where we see the amazing benefits of the trine but also, the trine's biggest enemy: apathy. In other words, because trines are automatic and beneficial by their nature, one hardly notices their benefic influences and therefore, we can miss out on taking full advantage of the trine's power due to complacency.

For example, if you have Mars trine Saturn (♂△♄) it is very easy for you to gain muscle mass, maintain muscle mass, and to stay relatively healthy with a good amount of un-depleted energy. However, if you have Mars square Saturn (♂□♄), you can be prone to weight gain, have a lack of motivation, and become depressed about your lack of physical prowess or health.

The difference is that the person with the Mars/Saturn trine does not completely realize their full potential because the energy is automatic and effortless. Therefore, it is possible that they do not gain as much muscle or be as healthy as they can be. On the other hand, the person with the Mars/Saturn square has to consciously put an effort into maintaining good health and physique and therefore has a higher reverence for their struggle and for the rewards that it has bestowed onto them. It is important for us to not take for granted our trines and rest on their laurels. Instead, capitalize on their potential because they are the pillars of strength where our struggles fall upon. Without those pillars, our shadow side can, and will, get the better of us.

Similarity: Same Element

Planets in a trine share signs of the same element, which is how they get their increased power and fortune. Like energy attracts like energy is a universal truth, and we see this manifested in birth charts via trines where energies are manifested and magnified due to their complementary nature.

Trine Combinations

ARIES TRINE LEO (♈△♌), The Model

Aries is a risk taker and Leos are creative geniuses. These people are forces to be reckoned with and make great personal trainers, directors, and stunt men.

TAURUS TRINE VIRGO (♉△♍), The Finest Tastes

Taurus' keen eye for aesthetics with Virgo's eye for purity makes for immaculate tastes in the fine arts. These people are stunning, have talents in fashion and interior decorating along with any kind of craftsmanship.

GEMINI TRINE LIBRA (♊△♎), The Networker

Gemini knows what to say and Libra knows all the right people. This trine allows for the person to have impeccable communication skills with others along with talents in the media, mediation, and relationship counseling.

CANCER TRINE SCORPIO (♋△♏), The Gentle Psychologist

Cancer is caring and understanding, while Scorpio knows what you need to do to make yourself more psychologically sound. These people have a gentle way of helping others get through tough times and have an infinite amount of emotional support and love. They make great drug addiction therapists, real estate agents, and guidance counselors.

LEO TRINE SAGITTARIUS (♌△♐), The Ethical Politician

Leo is the leader, and Sagittarius is the platform for the leader. However, thanks to the trine, Leo's desire for tyranny is calmed down and focused into a more cooperative approach. These people are great at politics, judicial institutions, and universities, are immensely fair and ethical, and are pleasant to be around.

VIRGO TRINE CAPRICORN (♍△♑), The Decisive Strategist

Virgo does not let anything get past them, and Capricorns are brilliant at taking it one small step at a time. These people are able to stick to a plan and see it through, make effective bosses/union leaders that listen and care about their workers, and are confident in every step they take.

LIBRA TRINE AQUARIUS (♎△♒), The Egalitarian

Libra creates positive relations with others and Aquarius wants to be friends with the world and share their thoughts with everyone they meet. These people make excellent activists, have great friendships, and very few enemies.

SCORPIO TRINE PISCES (♏△♓), The High Priestess

The occult magic of Scorpio mixed with the spiritualism of Pisces creates a potent vessel for bringing those realms onto this planet. These people are energy healers both for humans and for the Earth. They are highly psychic, gifted in occult knowledge, and have a strong connection to spirits, angels, and God.

SAGITTARIUS TRINE ARIES (♐△♈), The Ultimate Manifester

Sagittarius' optimism for seeing all things as possible mixes with Aries' drive and self-motivation. These people are highly motivated, especially in academic pursuits, have great physical vigor, and inspire and influence others through their ideas and personal confidence.

CAPRICORN TRINE TAURUS (♑△♉), The Wise Parental Figure

Capricorn's ability to provide mixes with Taurus' appreciation and respect for what the Capricorn accomplishes. These people are immensely frugal, talented in woodwork, and are able to create legacies.

AQUARIUS TRINE GEMINI (♒△♊), The Profound Professor

The forward-thinking ideas of Aquarius mixes with Gemini's ability to share those ideas with others. These people are profound in thought and in word, make excellent writers and scientists, and are honest with themselves and with those that are around them.

PISCES TRINE CANCER (♓△♋), The Guru

Pisces' love for love mixed with Cancer's tenderness creates a well of feminine knowledge that is unparalleled. These people make caring parents and nurses, are able to channel higher realms, and allow for others to feel vulnerable around them.

☍ Opposition (180°)

Keyword: Midpoint

Oppositions may be complicated to control but are not complicated to understand. Unlike the square, where we have two opposing forces blind-sighted by the other, with the opposition, you are well aware of the two forces in play. The trick is to come to the middle of these two perspectives. This differs from the square because you are asked to listen to both sides and allow for both sides to be expressed consciously. Oppositions require the art of compromise between two forces. Sometimes, you favor *side A*, other times, *side B*. Either way, oppositions require you to sacrifice both sides in order to meet in the middle.

Similarity: Opposite Sign

It is true when we say, "opposites attract," and this truth is echoed within oppositions because opposite signs are surprisingly similar in many respects. Indeed, it is their commonalities that make them two sides of the same pole. The critical difference is that *sign A* seems to have what *sign B* is lacking and vice versa. Approaching oppositions this way makes them less intimidating and cryptic.

Opposition Combinations

ARIES OPPOSITION LIBRA (♈☍♎), Me vs. You

Aries thinks about his priorities while Libra thinks about the other. Both require the other person in order to function. Libra needs to learn how to be self-motivated with their own ideas and thoughts, and Aries needs to learn to compromise and meet others half-way.

TAURUS OPPOSITION SCORPIO (♉☍♏), My Needs vs. Your Needs

Taurus wants things to stay the same, while Scorpio wants things to change constantly. However, both involve the possessions and feelings of the other. Taurus need to learn to be more flexible and movable in their thoughts and perspectives, and Scorpios need to learn to relax and enjoy life.

GEMINI OPPOSITION SAGITTARIUS (♊︎☌♐︎), Simple vs. Complex

Gemini wants to look at the small picture, while Sagittarius is looking at the larger picture. They both involve obtaining some sort of knowledge and applying that knowledge toward their interests and understanding. Gemini needs to zoom out and think of larger concepts, while the Sagittarius needs to zoom in and see what they are missing.

CANCER OPPOSITION CAPRICORN (♋︎☌♑︎), What I Feel vs. What is Real

Cancer wants to live life solely based on their emotional perspective while Capricorn sees life as very matter-of-fact and does not let emotions get in the way of decision making. Both require stability and enjoy the idea of making a family and a legacy. Cancers need to learn to be motivated and take the personal out of business matters, and Capricorns need to open up to others, to themselves, and learn to enjoy the fruits of their labor.

LEO OPPOSITION AQUARIUS (♌︎☌♒︎), Singularity vs. Multiverse

Leo considers their personal expression to be the only one that matters, and Aquarius does not think that their individuality matters in the great sea of humanity. However, both involve social circles and creative outlets. Leos need to learn that they are not the only person on this planet, and Aquarians need to learn that their uniqueness is special and must be brought out into the world.

VIRGO OPPOSITION PISCES (♍︎☌♓︎), Meaning vs. Abstract

Virgo wants to figure out the meaning behind everything, and Pisces is the absence of meaning. They both involve improvement of the self. Virgo needs to learn to let go of meaning and understand that sometimes, there is such a thing as the unexplainable, and Pisces need to learn how to focus, make goals, and plan things out in order to achieve.

Orbs of Influence and Aspect Hierarchy

When it comes to aspects, not all of them are precise hits. For example, if Venus is at 12°♒ and the Sun is at 14°♒ we still say that these two planets are in a conjunction but with an orb (gap) of 2° (14°-12°=2°). Similarly, if Mars is at 26°♈ with Saturn at 20°♑, we still say that these two planets are in a square, but with an orb of 6° (26°-20°=6°).

When the orb is smaller, we say the aspect is tighter. When the orb is wider, the aspect is wider. The tighter the aspect, the more significant and intense it is for a person. There are just as many orb ranges as there are astrologers. Every astrologer has their own viewpoint, and it is up to you to find out what works. It appears, on average, most astrologers give an orb range as wide as 10° to still be considered valid. Personally, I tend to be more conservative with my orbs and only accommodate aspects with an orb of 6° or less to be of the most importance with my biggest perimeter extending to 8° and here is why:

(1)   Starting out, this gives you fewer aspects to analyze, making it less overwhelming at first. Furthermore, any aspect that is 6° or less is a great place to start because those aspects are clearly the most important for that person.

(2)   If you think about it, a 10° range is 1/3 of the 30° allotted to one sign, and in my opinion, if you were meant to have that aspect, you were meant to have that aspect.

(3)   When you focus on the tightest orbs first, you get to the heart of the chart and address the more relevant points with greater ease, as it tends to remove a lot of the guesswork.

My personal orb scale is as follows (Table II-5):

Table II-5. My Personal Orb Scale with Description

ORB RANGE	DESCRIPTION
0°-1°	These aspects are highly important for the individual and if it is a square, opposition, or a difficult conjunction, it is some of their most difficult hindrances in this lifetime. If it is a sextile, trine, or a beneficial conjunction, then those are the strongest resources the individual has in order to counter their more difficult aspects.

ORB RANGE	DESCRIPTION
1°-2°	These aspects are just as important and powerful, but orbs between 0°-1° should get priority.
3°-6°	Again, these aspects are important and significant, but not as tightly bound as other tighter aspects. Nevertheless, these aspects are still felt and are relevant for natal chart analysis.
6°-8°	Not felt as heavily, but can still have an influence for the individual.
8°-10°	Ignore any aspect that has this range.

Organizing your aspects from the tightest to the widest is a great way to approach a natal chart and is, in fact, one of the strategies we will cover in Book II in this book series. Approaching aspects this way takes an overwhelming map of aspects and helps you to break it down from the most relevant to the least.

Aspect Patterns

When certain aspects are formed in a pattern, their energies become amplified and can become more difficult or beneficial depending on the circumstance. I will be discussing the three main aspect patterns, although there are more than these three:

The Grand Trine

When three planets are all in the same element and all trine one another, they are in a grand trine. The grand trine is what I like to call "the spiritual safety net." These people are never able to reach rock bottom and because of this, their lives are always secure, which gives them plenty of free will to do as they choose. The issue is, when you have that much free will and life hands you benefits that easily, it is very hard to come up with a life direction. However, once these people follow a path, there is no stopping them.

The T-Square

When two planets are in an opposition and another planet is squared to the two planets that are in an opposition, they are said to be in a T-square. T-squares involve three out of the four signs of the same modality and thus, these energies are very intense and highly psychological in nature. The issues that involve the planets, signs, and houses of the T-square are incredibly significant for that individual's life path because there is a crystallization that forms, which makes these planetary energies difficult to thaw and uncover.

The Yod

The Yod is a little difficult to discover because it involves a minor aspect that was not covered: the inconjunct. The yod is when one planet is in inconjunct with two other planets, and those two planets are sextile to one another. This creates a sort of arrow image on the natal chart. The yod is nicknamed "the finger of God" because these people are very much tied down to their life path. Unlike the grand trine, which is ultimate free will, people with the yod have a very clear life path that must be experienced due to the laws of karma. The key is to accept whatever comes their way.

Aspects are the Rope that Binds

The aspects within the natal chart provide the essential fiber for the individual that they carry for the rest of their lives. The information they provide for you as an astrologer allows you to better determine an individual's most unconscious motivations and struggles along with the realms of fortitude that they carry in order to approach their darker self. Indeed, aspect analysis, in my opinion, constitutes the highest emphasis within the natal chart. All other components (i.e., Signs, Houses, Cardinal Points, etc.) simply paint the picture with a finer brush. They help to explain how these energies are manifested, but the aspects tell you what these energies are in the first place.

Up to this point in the book, we have now examined the Signs, Planets, and Aspects within Astrology. There are two final components to consider so that we have a full understanding of all the archetypal symbols found within the birth chart. The last two components of the birth chart are the most unique for the individual because they are computed by incorporating the birth time and birth location. These two data points are the most personalized for the individual and therefore it is where the birth chart receives its distinct uniqueness. Of course, I am referring to the Houses and Cardinal Points of Astrology.

SECTION 6 — THE HOUSES

The Wheels of Destiny

Think of the natal chart as two wheels on top of one another. The first wheel is the zodiac, the band of 12 signs around a 360° wheel. Remember, wherever the planets are located within this wheel, their location will be the same for everyone else that was born at that same exact moment in time. However, this wheel's orientation relative to the sky at the moment of birth depends on the birth time and birth location (latitude and longitude).

For example, let us say that *child A* is born in Oregon and *child* B is born in Florida at the same time. This means, both *child A*'s and *B*'s planets are located around the zodiac at the same location. However, if the parents of both *child A* and B were to look East, toward the horizon where Sun rises, they would be looking at two different signs (orientations) of the zodiac (Fig. II-5).

FIGURE II-5. Child A and B birth charts with East/Sunrise/Ascendant Indicated.

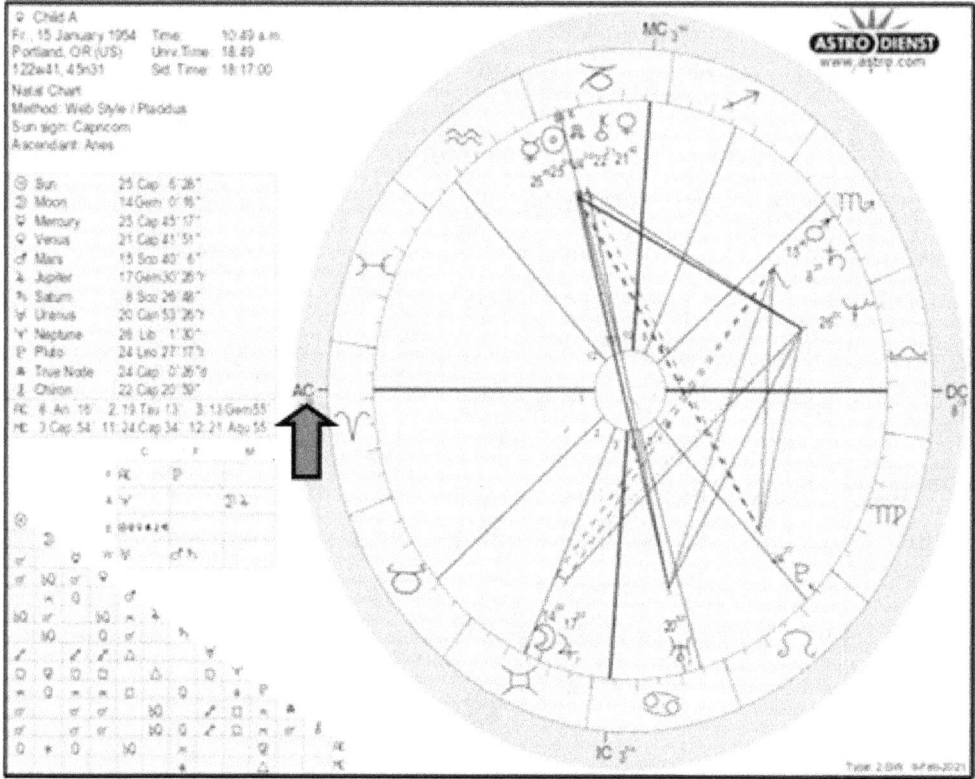

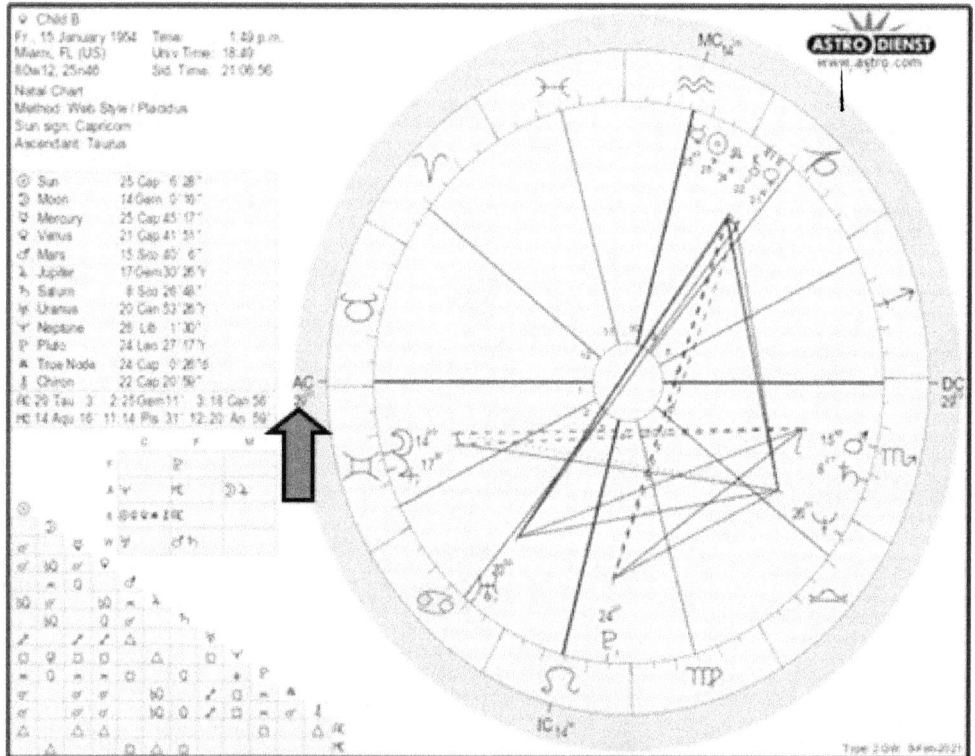

On the birth chart, East is the dark horizontal line pointing left, as indicated by the arrow. As you can see, for *child A's* parents, they would be observing the constellation of Aries, and for *child B's* parents, they would see the Taurus/Gemini cusp of the zodiac. We call this point the *Ascendant* (Asc) and its opposite point, West, the place of Sunset, the *Descendant* (Dsc). In every birth chart, this line will be completely horizontal and therefore acts as the foundation for which all other calculations and divisions of the sky map are determined.

Time to Get Three-Dimensional

Although the natal chart will always appear as a perfect circle, it is important to remember that the zodiac functions in a three-dimensional sphere. To this point, if the parents of either *child A* or *B* were to face East and with their finger traced all the way up to the highest point in the sky (the zenith), we would expect the zodiac band to exist at that point, but that is not the case. In fact, the zodiacal band is tilted and angled depending on the latitude and longitude and time of year of the birth (Fig. II-6A-C).

FIG. II-6A. Zodiacal Band Relative to the Horizon and Zenith (Side View)

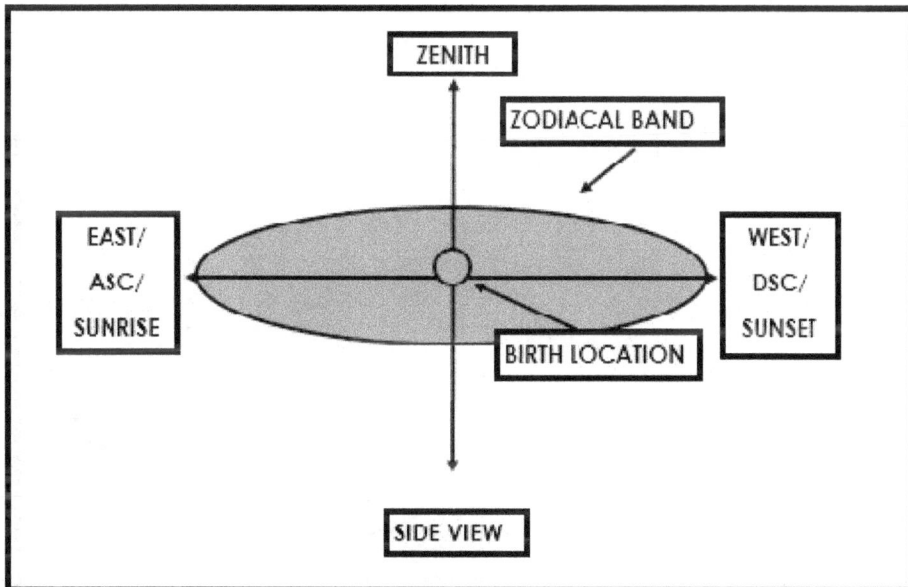

FIG. II-6B. Zodiacal Band Relative to the Horizon and Zenith (Shifted View)

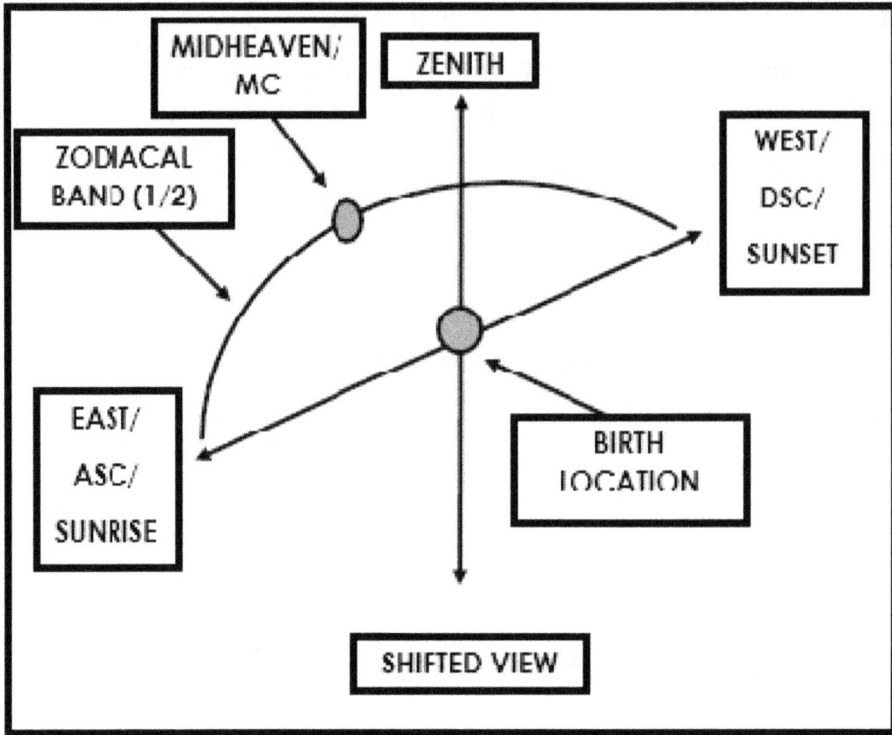

MIDHEAVEN/
MC

ZENITH

WEST/
DSC/
SUNSET

ZODIACAL
BAND (1/2)

EAST/
ASC/
SUNRISE

BIRTH
LOCATION

SHIFTED VIEW

FIG. II-6C. Zodiacal Band Relative to the Horizon and Zenith (Frontal View)

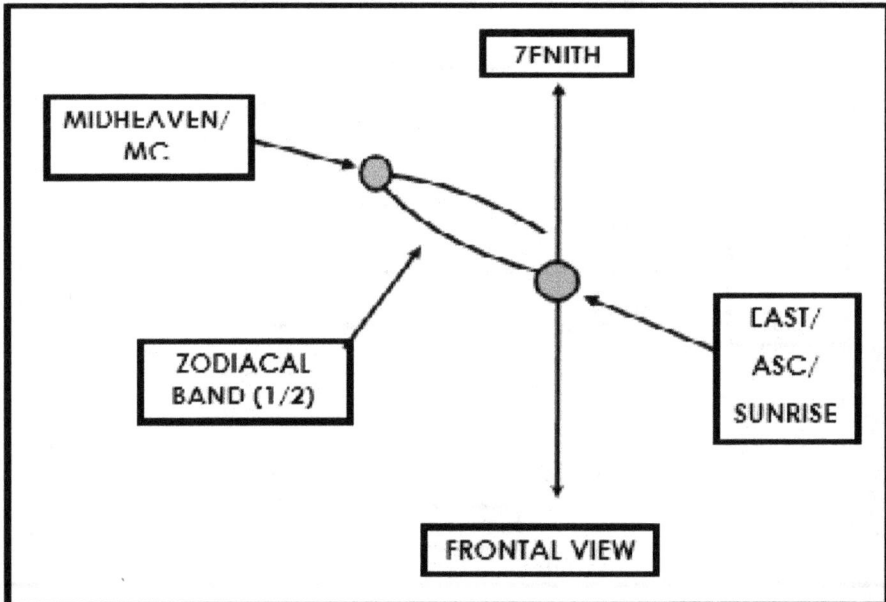

ZENITH

MIDHEAVEN/
MC

EAST/
ASC/
SUNRISE

ZODIACAL
BAND (1/2)

FRONTAL VIEW

By analyzing Figures II-6A-C, you can begin to notice that the highest point of the zodiac (Midheaven or MC) does not necessarily mean it is the highest point in the sky (zenith). Due to this fact, the perfectly circular band of the zodiac becomes slightly oval/parabolic.

The intensity of the parabola's compression or expansion, along with the location of the highest point of the zodiac (Midheaven/MC), is completely dependent upon the latitude and longitude of the birth location and birth time. Let us once again examine *child A* and *child B's* birth charts (Fig. II-7). Notice this time that the arrows are pointing toward the Midheavens.

FIGURE II-7. Child A and Child B's Birth charts with Midheaven (MC) Indicated

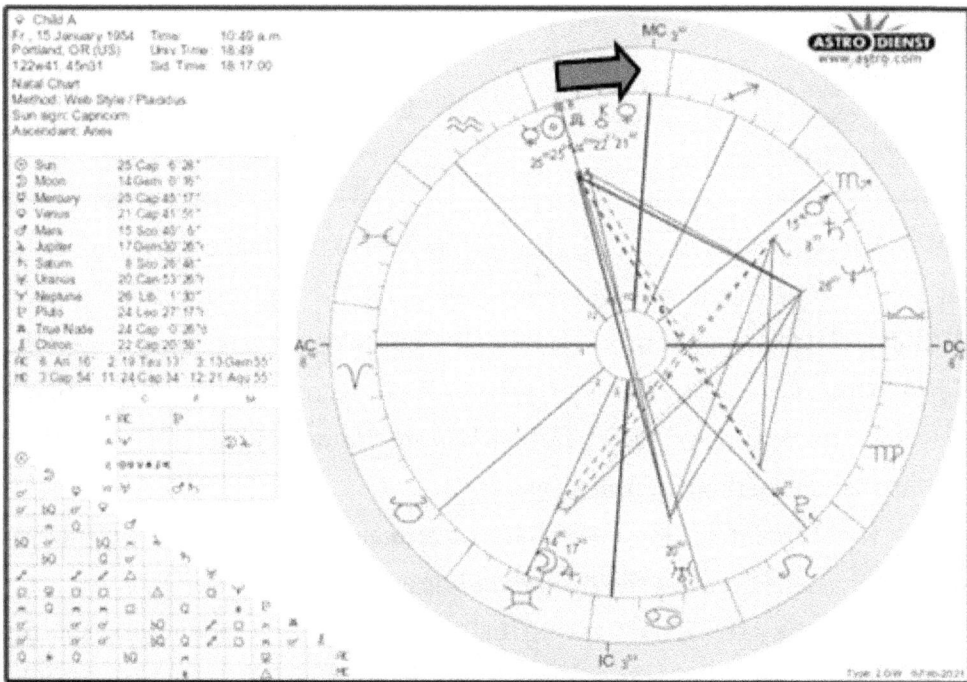

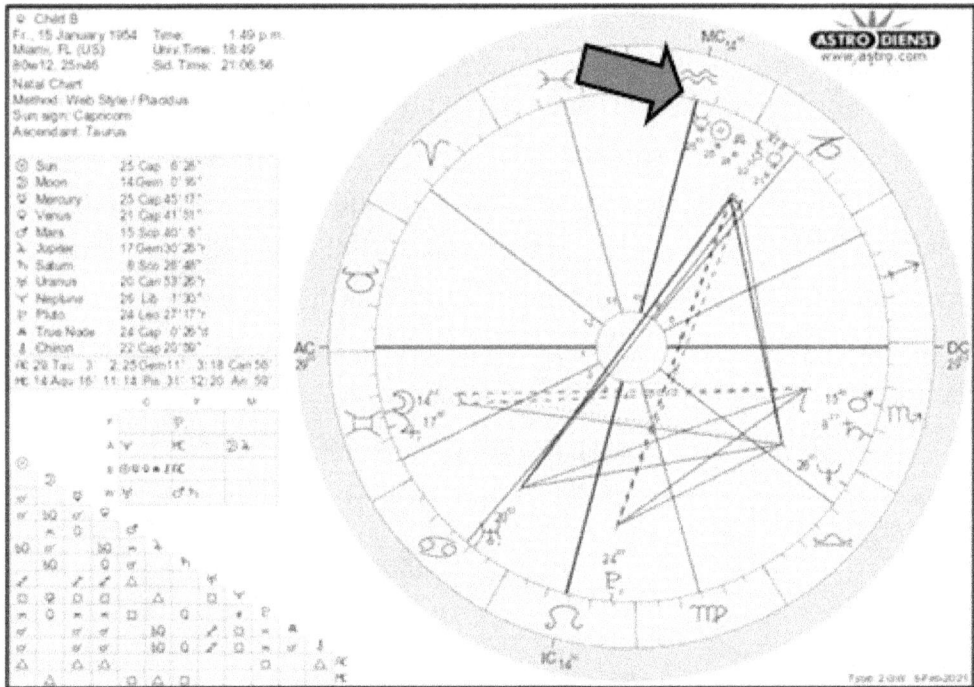

For both children, the Midheaven (arrows in the image above) are different relative to the center point because the parabolic equations differ for each child. For *child A*, their parabola is more "compressed" because they live further North on the globe where the sky's surface area is decreased, but for *child B*, who lives closer to the equator, their parabola is more thinned out and therefore closer to a circular shape than an oval shape.

To this point, examine the charts once again, but this time notice the various subdivisions between the *Ascendant* line and the *Midheaven* line. All that is happening is the Astrologer is taking that surface area of the zodiac and splitting it into equal parts. However, notice that *child A's* divisions are more lopsided and *child B's* divisions are slightly more symmetrical, although not completely equal (Fig. II-8). This is how astrology transforms three-dimensional space onto a two-dimensional birth chart.

FIG II-8. Sub-Division Lengths of Child A and Child B.

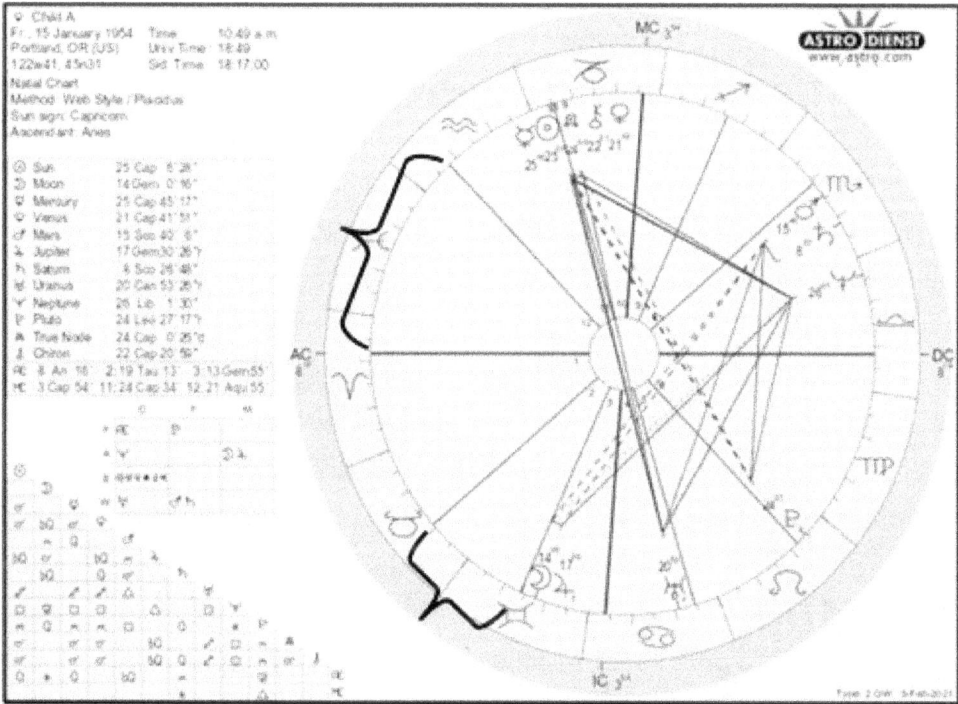

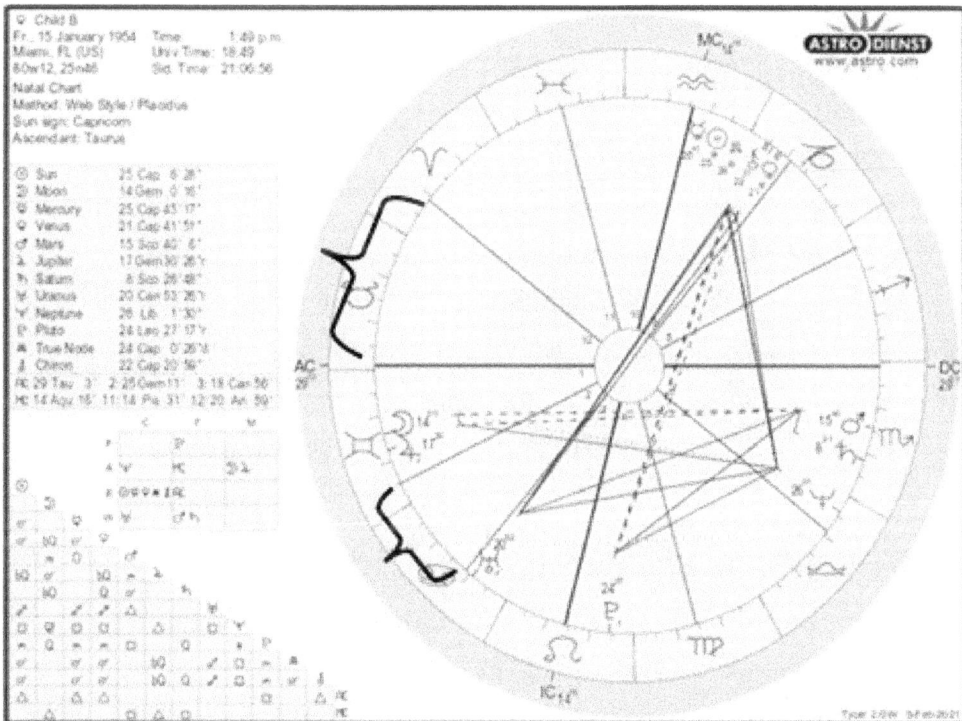

Welcome Home

These subdivisions of the zodiacal band are called the Houses of Astrology. There are twelve Houses which correspond to the twelve Signs of the zodiac and therefore the Houses represent similar themes. The Houses also indicate when certain areas of our lives will be emphasized or not depending on when transiting planets enter and exit a certain House (More on this in Book II). For now, we will examine each House individually in order to understand what themes are present in each House.

The Houses each represent a certain life stage along with qualities of the Sign that is originally associated with that House. Due to this fact, I always find it easier to remind myself which Sign has an authentic rule over which house. For example, instead of saying "The 1st House" I tell myself "The House of Aries," so I know that this House is associated with Aries themes. Or, instead of saying "The 10th House," I will acknowledge it as "The House of Capricorn," and so on and so forth. This way, your brain instantly connects themes associated with each House. Let us now take it one House at a time and learn more about each one.

THE 1ST HOUSE/THE HOUSE OF ARIES

Time of Development: Birth

The 1st House represents the exact moment we came into this world within this body. Once we have left our mother's womb, we are now autonomous, breathing entities whose life is now separate and independent from the mother's, even though both parents are involved with the conception and, often, the subsequent upbringing. Recall, the key phrase for Aries is "I am," and when we are born, it is the moment when we tell the world "Here I am! Ready to start my life on this planet."

Various Realms of Control

The physical body and its appearance, our vitality, our sense of ego and self-identity, personal boundaries, how we initiate things within our life, physical abilities, and first impressions.

THE 2nd HOUSE/THE HOUSE OF TAURUS

Time of Development: Toddler (0–2 yrs.)

Once we are born and our brain begins to develop, we start to get a better sense as to where our body ends, and other things begin. This spatial awareness is a key component of this stage of child development. We begin to think, "I am this, I am not this." It is also where we begin to utilize our five senses in order to map out our surroundings.

Various Realms of Control

Our possessions and outlook toward material objects, sense of style, the five senses (taste, touch, smell, sight, and hearing), artistic endeavors, our surroundings, overall temperament, and sense of self-worth.

THE 3rd HOUSE/THE HOUSE OF GEMINI

Time of Development: Pre-School (3–4 yrs.)

At this time in the story of life, the child is now beginning to communicate with their parents and others. They start to voice their preferences and opinions and are becoming quite fond of the word, "No!" The child is starting to get to an age where familial friendships, such as relating to siblings and cousins, begin. Additionally, this is the time where children are becoming skilled in locomotion through crawling and walking.

Various Realms of Control

Communication, mental capacities, short-distance traveling, mediums of communication and travel, language and writing abilities, siblings, and the press/journalism.

THE 4ᵗʰ HOUSE/THE HOUSE OF CANCER

Time of Development: Early Childhood (5–7 yrs.)

The time of the 4ᵗʰ House is when we begin to separate from our parents and home for the first time by attending school. We are taught how to be more comfortable within our own skin and learn about our sensitivities toward others and ourselves. We also begin to be nurtured more by the community via teachers, babysitters, neighbors, and extended family.

Various Realms of Control

The mother or the mother figure, home, being nurtured, food, family, ancestry, unconscious self, emotions, sense of security, emotional self-reliance, memories, personal foundation, local neighborhood, real estate, and traditions.

THE 5ᵗʰ HOUSE/THE HOUSE OF LEO

Time of Development: Middle Childhood (8–10 yrs.)

Now that the child is growing into their own, they are beginning to express themselves more freely and uniquely. They are beginning to show their likes, dislikes, hobbies, and interests. In general, individuals are simply enjoying the bliss of childhood. They begin to show their level of extroversion or introversion, and the personality of the child begins to shine through.

Various Realms of Control

Creative expression, theme parks and other places of recreation, vacations, hobbies. drama, innocence, leadership, children, desire for attention, courage, politics, figureheads, individuality, film industry, romance, and games.

THE 6ᵗʰ HOUSE/THE HOUSE OF VIRGO

Time of Development: Late Childhood (11–13 yrs.)

At this time, the child is now getting into the routine of school along with their extracurricular activities. Life becomes a little more sobering as the carefree nature of early childhood is now replaced with the need to focus on learning and getting a decent education. This is a time when thinking processes adjust and improve as our learning styles begin to be fully utilized.

Various Realms of Control

Elementary education in general, teachers, routines, domesticated pets, daily work, service-oriented professions, health, nutrition, detailed and hard work, skillsets and specialized training, digestion, dexterity, and analytical abilities.

THE 7ᵗʰ HOUSE/THE HOUSE OF LIBRA

Time of Development: Early Adolescence (14–17 yrs.)

Now that the child is reaching the age of puberty and leaving the elementary education system, they are beginning to relate with others on a more intimate basis. They begin to create closer bonds with their friends and start to branch out of their normal social circles. Their interests and preferences change as they start to accept their individualized nature because they now have more freedom to be who they are.

Various Realms of Control

Relationships, personal and professional partners, diplomacy, quality of married and romantic life, our social nature, debate, the law, resolutions, maintaining equilibrium, agreements, and mediation.

THE 8ᵗʰ HOUSE/THE HOUSE OF SCORPIO

Time of Development: Middle Adolescence (18–21 yrs.)

With the individual now having experienced puberty with even more autonomy as a legal adult, boundaries are pushed even more, and individuals begin to have sexual encounters, along with trying drugs and alcohol for the first time. This is also when individuals need to consider how to make a living and therefore begin to rely on the resources of others to provide access to funds.

Various Realms of Control

Sexuality and the reproductive system, occult subjects, secrets, inheritance, death (more metaphorical as opposed to literal), cycles of transformation and rebirth, joint finances, resources and ventures, debt, regeneration, and intimacy.

THE 9ᵗʰ HOUSE/THE HOUSE OF SAGITTARIUS

Time of Development: Late Adolescence (22–25 yrs.)

During this stage of life, the individual is expanding their mind by either attending college or by simply experiencing the world as a young adult. Their worldview, ideologies, and opinions are likewise adjusted due to this new exploration. They start to examine the diversity of various cultures, lifestyles, and upbringings.

Various Realms of Control

Institutions (academic, governmental, religious, and judicial), higher-education, long-distance traveling, philosophy, wisdom, good fortune, foreign affairs and cultures, belief systems, ethics, long-term goals and plans, ideologies, wisdom, and professors.

THE 10ᵗʰ HOUSE/THE HOUSE OF CAPRICORN

Time of Development: Adulthood (25–40 yrs.)

This is the time when individuals begin to "settle down" into realms like marriages, careers, and having children. Roots are beginning to take hold due to hard work and past experiences as the individual begins to become a functioning member of society. Naturally, younger people begin to look toward them for guidance and wisdom.

Various Realms of Control

Career, achievements, ambitions, authority, father or the father figure, status, long-term investments and planning, limitations, restrictions, government, integrity, mastery, state officials, and aspirations.

THE 11th HOUSE/THE HOUSE OF AQUARIUS

Time of Development: Late Adulthood (40–55 yrs.)

By now, the individual is reaping many fruits of their labors from their adult-hood, which finalizes at the second Saturn return at around sixty years of age. At this point, Saturn (the traditional ruler of Aquarius) asks for us to take stock of our lives, as awareness into one's inevitable passing from this Earth becomes an unavoidable topic. Hopefully, through introspection and understanding, a sort of optimism grows as the bigger picture of life begins to make more sense, having now lived for so many years.

Various Realms of Control

Civic organizations, friends and acquaintances, legislative branches of government, daydreams, communities, like-mindedness, non-profits, fruits from your labors, hopefulness, fraternities and sororities, and flashes of insight.

THE 12th HOUSE/THE HOUSE OF PISCES

Time of Development: Elder (55–80 yrs.)

We are now headed toward the twilight of an individual's life as they become that of the wise old hermit. They rely on the charity of humanity, as they will now have to ask for those younger than them to take care of their ailments. The moment of ultimate surrender, death, begins to befall us. As the body approaches this inevitability, the beauty in it all is that it is merely a repetition of the oldest story ever told: the cycle of life.

Various Realms of Control

Psychic abilities, meditation, religion, refuge and where we seek seclusion, addictions, healing abilities, peace of mind, conclusions and endings, hospitals and clinics, retirement life, bluffing and thievery, and large animals.

Everything in the Birth Chart is Connected

Every individual has all twelve houses within their birth chart. It is only a question of how activated or inactivated these houses are, depending on the malefic or benefic statuses of the planets that rule them within the birth chart, and the planets that are placed or not placed within. For example, if the planet that rules the 9th House is powerful but also inharmonious, then realms related to the 9th House will similarly be affected. Or, if a planet is working harmoniously and resides in the 2nd House, even if it does not rule the 2nd House, 2nd House realms will still feel the beneficial nature of the planet in question. We will cover this more in greater detail in Book II.

This same concept can also be applied to transiting planets when they enter and exit house after house. Similarly, the nature of the planet, along with the energy of the House they are about to enter, shifts the experience for the individual during the entire time that planet resides within that House. More on this in Book II.

If you recall, at the start of this section, the various subdivisions of the parabola that constitute your House sizes and placements is heavily determined by your birth time and location. In other words, your House placements and sizes are the most individualized part of your birth chart, even more than your Sun and Moon placements. You will certainly see this in action when you learn how to work with transits in Book II. Before we get there, let us dive deeper into our House divisions by examining the four most important points within: the cardinal points.

SECTION 7—THE CARDINAL POINTS

Astrology's Compass

If you recall from the previous section, we discussed how there are two main points along the zodiac that establish all of the other House locations: the Ascendant, the point located east at the horizon, and the Midheaven, the highest point of the zodiac. Remember, just because the Midheaven is the highest point along the zodiac does not necessarily mean that the Midheaven is also the zenith, the highest point in the sky located directly above you. It is this slanted feature that creates variations in House sizes and shapes. The Ascendant and Midheaven anchor the birth chart and the various House subdivisions.

The four cardinal points are associated with the two solstices and equinoxes of the yearly astrological calendar. These are pivotal moments during the year that signify when the start of a new season is underway. The major shifts to the environmental climates during the solstices and equinoxes parallel shifts in individual priorities. As such, they indicate major vortexes within us that heavily dictate our character, both on an external and subconscious level.

The four cardinal points show us how we portray ourselves out into the world (The Ascendant), how has persona is perceived by the world (The Descendant), our highest ambitions (The Midheaven), and the deeply hidden psychology that governs it all (The Imum Coeli (IC)). Suffice to say, the various planets and signs that rule the cardinal points within a birth chart are heavily emphasized within their respective realms. Furthermore, if natal planets are connected to the cardinal points via aspects, this also manifests specific details into their varying conditions and the ways in which they are expressed. We will cover this more in Book II. Let us now examine each of the cardinal points in greater detail.

The Ascendant (Asc): The Mask We Wear

When we think of the Ascendant, it is easy to assume that it represents who we are as a person, but this is not entirely true. Instead, the Ascendant shows us the person we portray out into the world, not necessarily the person we truly are. Remember, within astrology, our unique individuality stems from our Sun and Moon, where the Sun represents our external character, and the Moon represents our internal wellbeing.

In other words, the Sun and Moon constitute our personal psychology, but the Ascendant is the persona that we project out into the world. For example, if I was a Cancer rising, I would come off as timid and shy at first, but if my Sun was in Leo, this would be slightly contrary because the Leo Sun indicates that I desire some form of sociability and individual expression. As such, it could be possible that the person is incredibly shy at first (Cancer Rising) but once someone becomes their friend, they in turn become comfortable, which allows for their extroversion to come forth (Leo Sun).

As is true for all cardinal points, the overall condition of the planet(s) that rule the signs involved are vitally important in demonstrating how these various energies manifest. With the Ascendant, it shows whether the person's actual psychology is in harmony with the person they portray; the actor in the show of life. In fact, many astrologers emphasize the planetary ruler(s) of the Ascendant to be the *chart ruler(s)*, which adds emphasis toward the entirety of the birth chart.

The Ascendant demonstrates the qualities of the person we become when we are out there within society. How planets are aspected to the Ascendant line itself also indicates if the actual psychology and outward persona are working in harmony or at cross purposes. In this way, it can also show the difficulty or ease for an individual to let go of their self-image for the sake of psychological evolution. The Ascendant is the mask we put on with the hope that others will accept our mask, along with the individual behind its façade. How others react to this mask is determined by the Ascendant's opposite pole, the Descendant.

The Descendant (Dsc): How We Relate to Others and Vice Versa

Whenever we encounter anyone within the world, they see our Ascendant and we see theirs. How we both react to one another and toward any sort of personal interaction is indicated by the Descendant and its planetary ruler(s). The Descendant shows the second part of the Ascendant's story. For example, if we are too abrasive due to our Ascendant, others might be apprehensive to engage with us. Or, if we are charming with charisma due to our Ascendant, then this would naturally lead to pleasant personal interactions, which again would be demonstrated by the Descendant.

Due to this fact, if planets aspect our Ascendant they also aspect our Descendant. For example, if a planet is sextile to the Ascendant, it is simultaneously in a trine to the Descendant and vice versa. Similarly, if a planet forms a conjunction to the Ascendant, then they also form an opposition to the

Descendant and vice versa. Lastly, if a planet is in a square to the Ascendant, they are similarly in a square to the Descendant (Fig. II-9).

FIG. II-9. How Planets interact with both Poles of the Cardinal Points

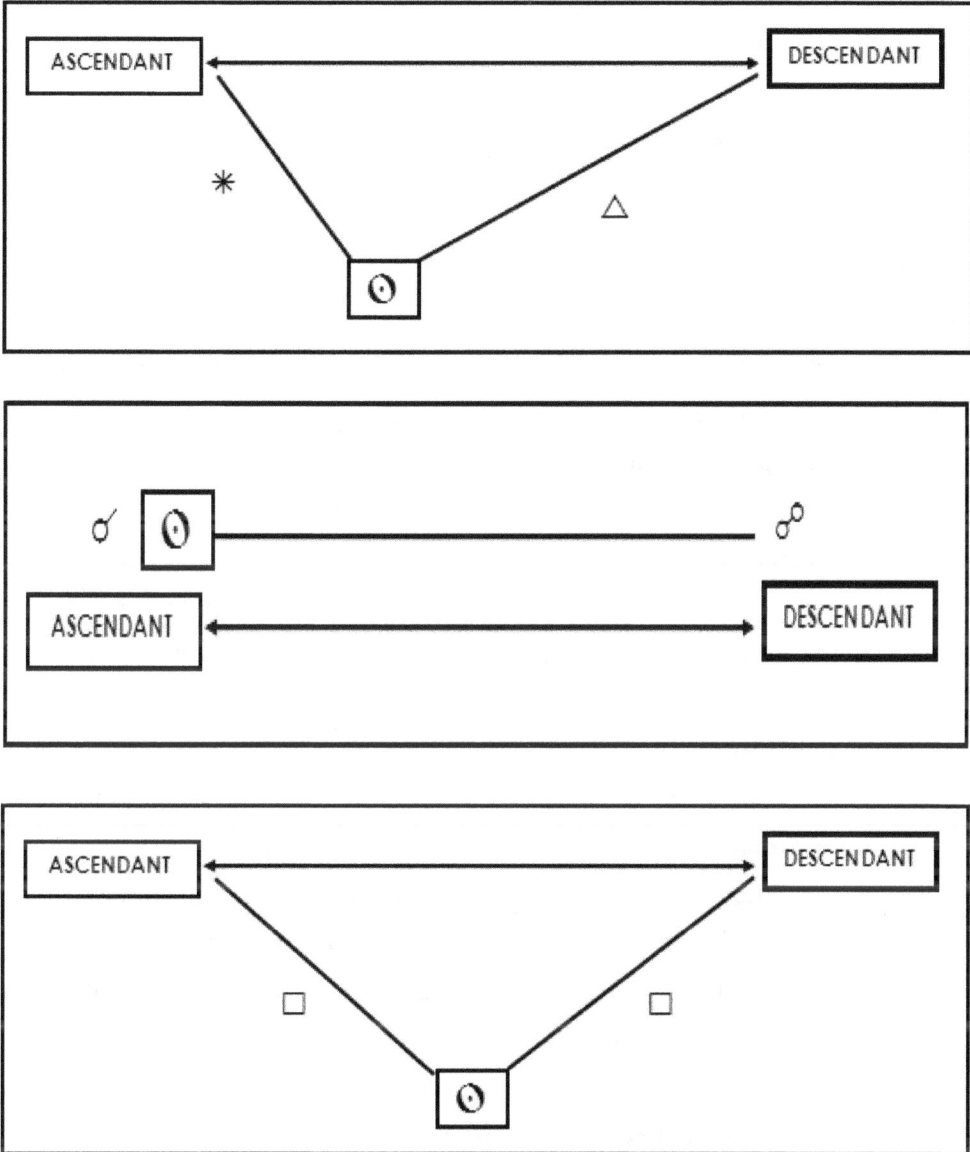

By this logic, it is easy to see how the person we portray (Ascendant) affects our interpersonal relationships (Descendant). The various aspects to both would logically affect both for better or worse.

Be that as it may, the Descendant line and its planetary ruler(s) show us how well we are received by others, how well we receive others, and if this is due to a personality that is true to the actual self or due to a front that was created to hide our true nature based on the condition of the Ascendant or Descendant. Therefore, if planets are in difficult connection to the Descendant or Ascendant, this can indicate possible areas of trauma that cause the individual to not be truthfully expressive.

The Midheaven (MC): Our Highest Goals and Ambitions

The Midheaven indicates our highest aspirations and our means of obtaining them. It indicates our sense of motivation, dedication, and overall approach toward success. It also represents our major purpose that we have been set out to do in this world. As the highest point of the zodiac during our moment of birth, the types of people and stories we look up to for inspiration are also indicated by the Midheaven.

Just how it was with the Ascendant/Descendant (Asc/Dsc) line, planets can make aspects to the Midheaven/IC line, which would subsequently alter their manifestations. Additionally, the planetary ruler(s) of the Midheaven and their condition demonstrates various manifestations of the Midheaven. Our vocations and personal dignity are also tied into these matters.

Just as psychological trauma toward the expression of our personality and its connection to our actual psychology is tied into the Asc/Dsc line, reasons for dysfunction into our sense of self-worth and ambitions can also be affected by poorly aspected planets to the MC/IC line. For example, we could be self-destructive or overly ruthless toward our personal objectives and this could be due to past trauma, leading to a dysfunctional way of responding to our place within the professional world and adult society. Consequently, our integrity and place within society is also dictated by the Midheaven.

The Imum Coeli (IC): Our Unconsciousness

Imum Coeli is Latin for "bottom of the sky" and is the least known of the four cardinal points. This makes sense, given that the IC is representative of our deepest, most unconscious parts of our being. Our ancestry and previous experiences (whether in this life or in previous lives) are tied down to the IC and essentially show us the psychological and karmic *baggage* of these previous experiences and that of our familial karma.

According to theories of twentieth-century psychological astrology, children are typically born at the expense of unprocessed karma of the parents involved. Therefore, parents tend to place a lot of their personal issues onto their children for better or for worse. This cycle is multi-generational, and psychologists along with doctors can attest to the genetic connection between mental and physical disease. In this same light, astrology, specifically the IC, shows us those various genetic connections that have now been placed onto us for us to transmute or further repress. Suffice to say, the quality of our upbringing, parents, and family life are all tied to the IC.

The pool of our unconscious can either be deep or shallow, understood or ignored. The IC demonstrates these varying degrees of our most hidden psychology. It also shows us the type of strengths and weaknesses that arose out of past action. In some ways, the entire birth chart can be seen as a story of the karma that we have obtained from past action, but the IC explains why and how we have obtained this karma and have yet to release its hold. Metaphysically speaking, even if the IC condition is harmonious, any sort of karmic ties, good or bad, still tie us down, nevertheless. In other words, if we come into this life with more fortunate karma than others, this does not necessarily mean we have an overall advantage because we are still being tied down to attachment through the IC one way or another.

The Core DNA of a Person

As we will see in Book II, the condition of the cardinal points and their planetary ruler(s) provides a foundational core into the individual and how they express that personality into the person they truly are, along with the aims they strive to attain. Additionally, they indicate our deepest unknown aspects of ourselves, along with how other people interact with our persona. Indeed, many astrologers put great emphasis into the cardinal points in addition to the natal Sun and Moon and consider these factors to be the core structure of an individual.

Time to Put Theory into Practice

Part II of this Book has been the bulk of the important and various astrological symbols and archetypes that you will encounter during your exploration. Now that you have a firm foundation into the various astrological energies, and the nature in which they react to one another, it is time to put all of that theory into actual practice through the various ways one can. We will start by observing the daily, weekly, and annual phenomena that affect all individuals on the planet regardless of their birth chart. All of the events that occur in Part III engage with the entire human race from day to day, month to month, and year to year as the astrological calendar.

PART III

THE
ASTROLOGICAL
CALENDAR

"I know that I am mortal by nature and ephemeral, but when I trace at my pleasure the windings to and from of the heavenly bodies, I no longer touch earth with my feet. I stand in the presence of Zeus himself and take my fill of ambrosia."

—Ptolemy

A Calendar That's Rooted in Ancient Times

Recalling from Part I-Section 1, annual sun-calendars became important for humanity as early as the farming communities c. 2500 BC, and moon calendars were invented and functional even earlier than that with Aurignacian cultures c. 32,000 BC.

The Sun and the Moon are the Driving Force of the Calendar

The yearly astrological calendar consists of 360 days where the Sun travels along the 360° of the zodiac at an approximate rate of 1° per day. Each year begins a 0° Aries, also known as the Spring Equinox, and each month within that year is equally divided into twelve equal months of 30°/thirty days each. In other words, each sign of the zodiac would incorporate one month during the astrological year, which is heavily tied to the natural energies of the seasons that coincide with those respective months.

The Moon cycle is approximately twenty-eight days and serves a multitude of roles during the monthly, yearly, and daily cycles. Daily cycles are primarily affected by Void of Course Moons which will be discussed in Part III-Section 2. Yearly influences involve the semiannual eclipse events which is the discussion of Part III-Section 3. Finally, the Moon's influence toward monthly energies and biorhythms will be discussed in Part III-Section 1.

Hours are Also Part of the Astrological Calendar

Planetary hours were developed by ancient Greek astrologers. In Part III-Section 5, we will learn how they computed the hours of the day and how you can use their energies toward everything you do in life from appointments to parties to annulments.

Retrogrades are Frequent and Shift the Energy

In addition to the Moon and Sun primarily acting as the driving force for our celestial calendar, retrograde periods of the inner planets: Mercury, Venus, and

Mars, are just as influential toward the energies that are felt by everyone, regardless of where they are located on planet Earth. These retrogrades are the topic of Part III-Section 4.

Aligning Your Body to the Tempo of the Universe

When you begin to align your life toward these various subtle forces of nature, you will begin to notice an immediate change. This is mostly due to the fact that you are no longer accidentally going against the natural current of time and space. Countless times, individuals plan events during inopportune moments, which causes unnecessary stress and frustrations. When you work with astrology as a calendar, you eliminate these avoidable mishaps.

It's Important to Be Inactive at Times

The Moon cycle is incredibly important because it indicates when it is a time for activation or a time for recuperation. Two weeks out of every month, we are asked to slow down and consolidate our energies and projects, but instead, most individuals are constantly on the go or they are constantly listless and do not act when they should. The astrology calendar teaches you the important lesson of patience and releasing control.

Your Turn to Experiment

I encourage you to experiment and try to see what happens to events that you have no control over, but you were able to observe using your astrological calendar. This is a game of trial and error, but when you get the hang of it, you will observe literal manifestations of the rules that are established in this part of the book. With that, let us begin with the Moon and all her facets as a working calendar.

SECTION 1—THE MOON CYCLE

The Real Month

The moon travels approximately 27–28 days during its monthly cycle. During this cycle, it makes one full rotation around the entire zodiac. This means the Moon resides in each sign for approximately 2.5 days per monthly period. At the start of every moon cycle, the Moon will begin its cycle within one different sign per month. For example, if the Sun is in Taurus, sometime during those thirty days, there will be a new moon in Taurus. During the next month, Gemini, there will be a new moon in Gemini and so on and so forth. By this logic, if we pay close attention to each new moon, we are able to make twelve distinct intentions every year as each sign of the zodiac tends to represent a certain facet of the human experience.

12 Months, 12 Intentions

When the new moon is in Aries, this is a good time for intentions regarding the body and the year ahead. Taurus is for relaxation, enjoyment of the arts, and improving upon what we own. Gemini is a time to improve upon how we communicate, how we process, and how we interact. Cancer is a time to get in touch with our feelings and become introverted. Leo is a time for recreation, hobbies, and for taking pleasure in life. Virgo is for hard work, reassessing, taking care of your health, and organizing. Libra's intentions are ones involving relating with others, creating strong bonds, and resolving conflicts. Scorpio is a time for change, intimacy, and deep reflection. Sagittarius is for expanding your knowledge and awareness, travel, and creating abundance for yourself.

Capricorn is a time for achievement, discipline, and working toward long-term goals. Aquarius is a time for friends, social endeavors, and harnessing intuition and empathy. Pisces is a time for spiritual practices, meditation, and embracing unconditional love.

During every moon cycle, these new intentions go through a time of testing, reward, climax, integration, and rest, through what we call the eight stages of the lunar monthly cycle. If you recall, in Part II-Section 5, there are five major aspects within astrology. Now, it is time to learn that these aspects are, in fact, cyclical in nature.

Aspects Play a Part

Aspects involve a planet to planet connection. When we are comparing two planets in transit, the faster planet is revolving around the slower planet. In the case of the moon cycle, the faster planet (the Moon) is revolving around the slower planet (the Sun). This is how the Moon receives its various shading of light and darkness because of her rotation relative to the Sun (Fig. III-1). The eight primary moon phases parallel the eight stages of the aspect cycle (Table III-1).

FIGURE III-1. Various Moon Phases are due to the Aspect cycle.[37]

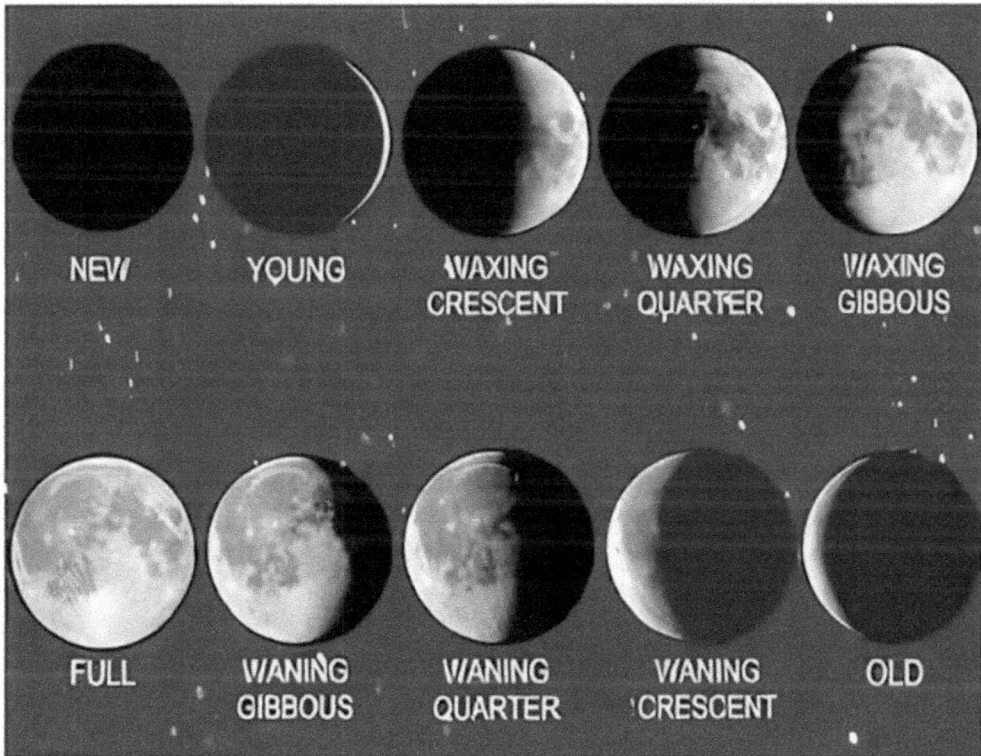

37   Walberto Martinez, *Moon Phases All*, June 16, 2012, Photograph, Archived January 12, 2019 at https://web.archive.org/web/20190112025517/https://www.flickr.com/photos/walberto_fotos/7380282754/.

Table III-1. Aspect Cycle with Corresponding Moon Phase

#	STAGE NAME	GLYPH	MOON PHASE
1/8	Birth/Conjunction	☌	New Moon
2/8	Opening Sextile	✳	Waxing Crescent
3/8	Opening Square	□	Waxing Quarter
4/8	Opening Trine	△	Waxing Gibbous
5/8	Climax/Opposition	☍	Full Moon
6/8	Closing Trine	△	Waning Gibbous
7/8	Closing Square	□	Waning Quarter
8/8	Closing Sextile	✳	Waning Crescent
1/8	Birth/Conjunction	☌	New Moon

We will discuss the aspect cycle in greater detail in Book II. For now, let us now observe each stage of the Moon and Aspect cycle one event at a time.

STAGE ONE: The New Moon/Conjunction

Every cycle begins at the conjunction with the new moon. This is the time to think about your intentions for that month based upon the sign of the new moon and the house where it is placed within your natal chart. Usually, new moon energy lasts up to three days after the new moon occurs.

For example, let us say it is the new moon in Aries (☽♈) and we decide to start an exercise routine to get back into shape. You begin to make a plan, gather the supplies you will need to accomplish this goal, like weights or gym clothes, and begin to start working out daily.

STAGE TWO: Waxing Crescent/Opening Sextile

This is a time to adjust your intentions slightly, depending how the story is unfolding. The sextile is cooperative and helpful, which gives you a sense of optimism. Therefore, during this time, you will most likely find an opportunity that will steer your intentions into the right direction. The catch is you have to put in the effort in order to obtain the benefits.

With our example, during this time you might find a nice discount for a gym membership during the waxing crescent while the Moon is in Gemini, the opening sextile. Or you find a friend that wants to be your fitness partner and offers to join you on your daily runs. Again, we only reap the rewards of the sextile if we actively take what is offered to us.

STAGE THREE: Waxing Quarter/Opening Square

During this time of the moon cycle, the amount of light and dark seen on the moon is 50/50, which is reflected toward the square aspect within astrology. Recall from Part II-Section 5, squares involve two opposing forces that have the same amount of energy and drive but are working at cross purposes. Naturally, this is a time of conflict.

This is now the time when the universe tests you to see if you are keeping up with your end of the bargain. The moon cycle's manifesting powers do not come about without you demonstrating that you are willing to make the appropriate sacrifices.

Back to our example, with the new moon in Aries, this would occur when the moon ingressed (entered) into Cancer. This would be the time when you are starting to become more lax with your gym attendance. Or maybe you are starting to eat the wrong things again. In any case, your goals become more difficult during this time of testing.

The answer is to introspectively address your motivations and be willing to adjust. If you can admit that you should not be eating poor foods and instead should be going back to the gym, that takes a lot of admission of your own self-destructive actions. If we work through the dilemmas brought on by the square, we emerge stronger because we have a better understanding into why we were not progressing in the first place. This is the ultimate lesson found within squares, and one of the most important struggles within astrology.

STAGE FOUR: Waxing Gibbous/Opening Trine

After the time of conflict and tribulation, you are rewarded with the opening trine of the moon phase which, in the case of the Aries new moon, would occur when the moon ingressed into Leo. If you stuck with your goals and fought through the struggle of the first quarter moon, you are rewarded during this time. Maybe you begin to see results on your body from your hard work, or perhaps your workouts are getting easier to handle because you are becoming more fit. In either case, this is a time to look back and congratulate yourself on the hard work you have done.

STAGE FIVE: Full Moon/Opposition

The opposition is a time of climax and culmination. Your goals have now reached their peak, and you are experiencing the fullest expression of the fruits of your labor. The sign where the full moon occurs is relevant because it ties back to the sign of the new moon as its opposition. So, if you had an intention of getting fit during the Aries new moon, during the full moon in Libra, you might find that our new self-confidence (Aries) has attracted the attention of others (Libra). Either way, this is a time of high energy.

STAGE SIX: Waning Gibbous/Closing Trine

Once the full moon occurs, we then transition from the waxing (developing) period into the waning (disseminating) period. When we switch into the waning phase, energy starts to dwindle and slow down over time. This is critical to understand, as most people will have the hardest time with the waning period because we are constantly encouraged by our society to be active, go-getting, and yang oriented. However, there are two weeks out of every lunar month where we are asked to slow down, relax, and become tranquil and reflective instead.

During the waning gibbous, we experience the closing trine. In the case of the Aries new moon would be Sagittarius. Now that you have experienced the highest climax from the full moon, and assuming you were attentive and doing everything to the best of our abilities, everything becomes easier and more routine because you have been instilling good habits.

During the closing trine, going back to the workout analogy, this is not a time to push yourself too hard at the gym, and your diet also becomes manageable as everything has now fallen into a comfortable routine. Nevertheless, progress and results are still apparent because you have been going at it for almost three weeks now, and your body is now used to the regimen.

STAGE SEVEN: Waning Quarter/Closing Square

The closing square, which would occur in Capricorn during the Aries new moon, is a time for permanent integration and instillation of these better habits so that they may go beyond the current moon cycle and into the future. You are able to firmly cement your habits into permanency during this time. This could be difficult because out of all of the positive progress you have now seen, it might be hard to continue because you have now witnessed a good amount of success already. Still, one must keep in mind that continuing our good practices over time yields even greater results because we are pursuing goals for longer periods.

To our analogy, your body and overall health are looking good, but yet again, you can be tempted to eat poorly or skip a workout. However, this conflict is easier to handle because you have already experienced this conflict with the opening square. Only now you have more to show for it, which makes the right decision easier to make.

STAGE EIGHT: Waning Crescent/Closing Sextile

During this time, the moon phase is winding down in preparation for the next one. This is a time for rest and relaxation as the entire energy surrounding the moon for that month is almost gone completely. With the Aries new moon, this is when the moon ingresses into Aquarius, making it a good time to be social and outgoing with your fresh, healthier body and vitality. It is important that we take it easy because the overall energy is very low during this phase. Nevertheless, these are the ultimate "treat yourself" days because the only thing left to do with this lack of energy is to take it easy.

Your Personal Biorhythms

While the Moon travels along her monthly journey, she is simultaneously creating aspects to every one of your natal planets in the process. Therefore, it is easy to tell if your natal planets in your chart are working in harmony or disharmony with the Moon depending on the day. You can easily discover your monthly biorhythms for every single planet in your chart, but for the sake of simplicity and importance, I would only compare the transiting Moon to your natal Sun (☉), Moon (☽), Ascendant (ASC), and Midheaven (MC) because these are the four main important points within your birth chart. Simply determine their signs and follow the table below as the moon phase progresses through the zodiac from month to month (Table III-2).

TABLE III-2. Personal Bio-Rhythm Tracking Chart

Personal Planet/ Cardinal Point Location	Stage 1: New Moon	Stage 2: Waxing Crescent	Stage 3: Waxing Quarter	Stage 4: Waxing Gibbous	Stage 5: Full Moon	Stage 6: Waning Gibbous	Stage 7: Waning Quarter	Stage 8: Waning Crescent
♈	♈	♊	♋	♌	♎	♐	♑	♒
♉	♉	♋	♌	♍	♏	♑	♒	♓
♊	♊	♌	♍	♎	♐	♒	♓	♈
♋	♋	♍	♎	♏	♑	♓	♈	♉
♌	♌	♎	♏	♐	♒	♈	♉	♊
♍	♍	♏	♐	♑	♓	♉	♊	♋
♎	♎	♐	♑	♒	♈	♊	♋	♌
♏	♏	♑	♒	♓	♉	♋	♌	♍
♐	♐	♒	♓	♈	♊	♌	♍	♎
♑	♑	♓	♈	♉	♋	♍	♎	♏
♒	♒	♈	♉	♊	♌	♎	♏	♐
♓	♓	♉	♊	♋	♍	♏	♐	♑

Now, using your celestial calendar datebook, every time you see the moon in one of these signs, you can then understand how your own personal energies are being affected.

This is the first part of the puzzle when it comes to observing the Moon's influences on a monthly and daily basis. The next piece involves determining when the Moon is Void of Course (VOC) because, regardless of the waxing or waning periods, these are moments where we need to be mindful as they can occur during any part of the moon cycle.

SECTION 2—VOID OF COURSE MOONS

Red Light, Green Light

The monthly Moon cycle lasts approximately twenty-eight days, with the Moon residing in each sign of the zodiac for approximately two and a half days. While the Moon is traveling around the zodiac, she is making various aspects with the other planets in transit. However, when she ingresses (transitions) from one sign to the other, there is a moment when these aspect connections are no longer made with the other planets. When this occurs, the moon is said to be Void of Course (VOC).

Think of the VOC period like a light switch and the aspects the moon makes to the other planets as the electrical cord that gives the light switch its power. When the Moon is VOC, the cord detaches, and the light switch turns off, cutting out the power. Because aspects and planetary positions are mathematical in nature, these VOC periods are mathematically predictable and accurate. VOC periods can occur during the waxing or waning phase and can be as short as a few minutes or, in some instances, as long as thirty hours. In other words, VOC may seem arbitrary, but they are scientifically predictable.

When the moon is void of course, the mantra is: "nothing will come of it." Starting new endeavors, making purchases, or plans during void moons simply do not end up working out. Observe the table below for a more comprehensive list as to what one should or should not do during a VOC moon (Table III-3).

TABLE III-3. Do/Do Not List for VOC Period

DO DURING VOC MOON	DO NOT DURING VOC MOON
• Meditate/Yoga	• Parties or planning of parties
• Clean house/cleaning in general	• Make plans or have plans
• Organize/Sort	• Purchases of any kind
• Review/Edit	• Meet new people
• Brainstorm	• Initiation of any project
• Cancel things/Endings	• Meetings (unless brainstorming)/Presentations
• Exercise with no specific planning/routine	• Planning/Scheduling for the future
• Leisure	• Correspondence
• Sleep In/Take a nap	• Begin a new job/Interview/Send out Resumes
• Things you do not want to develop into anything	• Judge people or situations too quickly as judgment is clouded
• Keep life as simple as possible. The more you plan, the more your plans get foiled	• Medical procedures or professional testing

The more you pay attention to void moons, the more you will realize that people who are out of synch with their own lives tend to unconsciously plan things against this natural flow of energy. Void moons are more common than we realize, and when you put them on your radar, you are able to align your body and your life to the natural flow of this planet. This greatly helps in your endeavors and your own wellbeing because you are eliminating unnecessary chaos that can easily be avoided by simply waiting for the active time when the Moon is out of the void.

When you purchase an Astrological calendar, make sure it includes the VOC periods and mark them with a highlighter or a pen so you can easily see when they will occur. Now that we understand VOC periods and the monthly moon cycle, the last lunar observation involves the semiannual eclipse cycle with the Sun.

SECTION 3—ECLIPSES

The Dark Times

Twice every year, we experience a complete moon cycle as an eclipse period. Eclipses occur when the orbital planes of the Earth, Moon, and Sun are parallel, lining up with one another. They always occur in pairs of two: Solar to Lunar or Lunar to Solar.

Solar eclipses occur on the new moon when the Moon is in front of the Sun, blocking out the Sun while the Moon travels across. Normally, the Moon would be invisible because the Sun's light is covering up its surface. Only this time the opposite is true, and the Sun becomes engulfed by the moon. Lunar eclipses happen on the full moon when the Moon is opposite the Sun. This time, the Earth is sandwiched between them, blocking out the Sun's light onto the full moon. The shadow that you see on the Moon during a lunar eclipse is actually the shadow of the Earth as it travels between them.

How We Calculate Eclipse Locations

Astrologically, there is a way to determine when and where an eclipse will occur by observing the North Node (☊) and South Node (☋). The nodes are there to tell us, "If an eclipse were to happen, around here is where it would happen along the zodiac." Now, keep in mind that some eclipses do not occur on that precise spot. The range in which an eclipse can occur is very wide and sometimes, we only receive a penumbral eclipse, which are ones that occur but are not exact. We will cover nodes in more depth in Book III.

A Bridge to the World Before and After This One

Some astrologers believe that during eclipses, the Earth receives a sort of "karmic exchange" when the old souls and energies that have passed away are able to leave the Earth plane, and the new souls that are entering begin to integrate into their earthly bodies. To this point, some astrologers like to look at the "pre-natal eclipse" in natal charts as part of their studies. This is based on a theory that whichever eclipse occurred before your birthday is the time when your soul entered your body inside of your mother's womb.

A Time to Tread Lightly

During eclipses, we experience a time of testing. A time when there are two distinct roads to take: face whatever comes your way with a clear head in order to release anxiety, or get swept into the chaos and build up anxiety and undesirable situations around yourself. When eclipses occur, you need to be incredibly alert, sober, and cautious.

Try not to react to things suddenly, arrive at any conclusions, or make definitive plans that would drastically alter your life direction or circumstance. Any agitation or stress you feel during an eclipse is your unconsciousness showing you what needs to be worked out. Essentially, your inner fears are emerging and taking hold, which can cause you to act incorrectly because you become frightened. Instead of acting on these fears, the point is to understand and process.

Eclipses are Tied to Our Ancient Ancestors

Eclipses of the Sun and Moon are very much an Earthly phenomenon that have been going on since time immemorial. For millennia, humanity has been witnessing eclipses and the energies they bring. In order to better understand this global context, we need to put ourselves in the shoes of our ancient ancestors.

Picture a time when our concept of the universe was still primitive. No major cities or empires have yet to emerge, and humanity is mostly made up of small farming communities that worship the Sun as the eternal life-giver and the Moon as the nurturing mother.

Now, imagine you and your farming friends are out in the field one day, just like any other day, but then something strange begins to happen. You look up and you see the Sun, the god that you worship, the god that makes the crops grow and provides heat and light, becomes engulfed and swallowed up by who knows what! Imagine the confusion, chaos, and the lack of understanding that every member of the community must have felt. Although humanity now is more advanced in our ways of thinking, these inherent and anxious energies are still prevalent during eclipses even within our modern-day society because eclipses are a global and eternal phenomenon.

Eclipses Require Calmness

Regardless of the time in history, during eclipses, fear takes over. Fear takes over because we do not know which way is up. The Sun, the king of the solar system, is being swallowed, engulfed, and we are now left alone with our unconscious anxieties. During eclipses, you are being asked to understand what fears you have been neglecting so that you can overcome them. Eclipses, in this way, are very positive and beautiful in that you are able to face what you fear head-on, but more often than not, individuals react to these stressors and make regrettable decisions.

Do not let these anxieties run the show. If you do, not only will you understand them less, you will build up unwanted situations by acting upon these impulses. Many times, I have witnessed friends make drastic life decisions like moving into another state, changing occupations, or selling property, only to find out that it was a huge mistake to do so after the fact. These apparently obvious mistakes only become apparent after the eclipse cycle is over and the fog finally lifts.

The mantra during an eclipse is: "Wait and see." Even when we want to act, and during an eclipse, it is incredibly tempting to act, we are nevertheless doing so out of our unconscious ego drive. Therefore, during each eclipse cycle, all of us have a choice to either be the Prince Igor in our own story and follow our egos toward destruction, or to act as his wife and tap into our intuition instead and subdue the ego flair-ups that occur during eclipses.

During the eclipse, you literally think to yourself, "how can this possibly go wrong?" Once the eclipse disappears, you are literally no longer eclipsed yourself, and all of the reasons as to why it would not work out becomes painstakingly clear. This is why it is better to simply "wait and see," instead of finding yourself in a hole that you need to now dig yourself out. The table below shows the eclipses up to 2030 (Table III-4).

TABLE III-4. Upcoming Eclipses

FIRST ECLIPSE (TYPE)	SECOND ECLIPSE (TYPE)	LOCATION	CLARITY DATE
MAR 14 2025 (L)	MAR 29 2025 (S)	VIRGO/ARIES	APR 13 2025
SEP 7 2025 (L)	SEP 21 2025 (S)	PISCES/VIRGO	OCT 7 2025
FEB 17 2026 (S)	MAR 3 2026 (L)	AQUARIUS/VIRGO	MAR 19 2026
AUG 12 2026 (S)	AUG 28 2026 (L)	LEO/PISCES	SEP 11 2026
FEB 6 2027 (S)	FEB 20 2027 (L)	AQUARIUS/VIRGO	MAR 8 2027
AUG 2 2027 (S)	AUG 17 2027 (L)	LEO/AQUARIUS	AUG 31 2027
JAN 12 2028 (L)	JAN 26 2028 (S)	CANCER/ AQUARIUS	FEB 10 2028
JUL 6 2028 (L)	JUL 22 2028 (S)	CAPRICORN/ CANCER	AUG 5 2028
DEC 31 2028 (L)	JAN 14 2029 (S)	CANCER/ CAPRICORN	JAN 30 2029
JUNE 12 2029 (S)	JUNE 26 2029 (L)	GEMINI/ CAPRICORN	JUL 11 2029
DEC 5 2029 (L)	DEC 20 2029 (S)	SAGITTARIUS/ GEMINI	JAN 4 2030
JUN 1 2030 (L)	JUN 15 2030 (S)	GEMINI/ SAGITTARIUS	JUN 30 2030
NOV 25 2030	DEC 9 2030	SAGITTARIUS/ GEMINI	JAN 8 2031

KEY: L=Lunar Eclipse, S=Solar Eclipse

The clarity date is the time when the solutions surrounding the eclipse become apparent. This is the time when our mistakes during the eclipse bear fruits, and not tasty ones. Be patient and aware during eclipses and this will take out a lot of chaos in your life.

SECTION 4—INNER PLANETARY RETROGRADES

Two Steps Forward, One Step Back

With the exception of the Sun and the Moon, all planets within Astrology turn retrograde relatively frequently. The outer planets, Jupiter, Saturn, Uranus, Neptune, and Pluto, tend to change directions every five months or so. The inner planets, Mercury, Venus, and Mars, have shorter episodes with more frequent intervals. A lot of this section can be applied toward all retrogrades, but we will be focusing mostly on retrogrades of the three inner planets: Mercury, Venus, and Mars (TABLE III-5).

TABLE III-5. Summary of Inner Planetary Retrogrades

PLANET	FREQUENCY AND LENGTH	DOMAINS
MERCURY ☿	3 Times Per Year for 30 Days	Communication Negotiations Travel
VENUS ♀	Every 20 Months for 40 Days	Romance Leisure Cooperation
MARS ♂	Every 2 Years for 80 Days	Drive Conflict Agitation/Aggression

A Shift in Focus

Retrogrades are not a time when the energy seems to be completely shut off like during a void moon. Instead, energies shift toward a different focus in that we are asked to process instead of progress. An easy guide for any retrograde is to observe the themes in the domain column from the table above, and consider any word that has the re- prefix. For example, retrogrades are a time to reevaluate, revisit, reconnect, rekindle, rejuvenate, reassess, review, reorganize, etc., etc.

Certain individuals, emotions, and circumstances that have yet to be removed out of your psychic clutter seem to reappear during this time, reminding you that you still have work to do. Just like eclipses, this is not a time for action or making plans, as they will similarly fall through or become thwarted. Instead, take this time to gear up for the future, when the planet will no longer be in retrograde, because that will be the time to act. The retrograde, is a time to clean up the excess junk that has been holding you back.

Anatomy of a Retrograde (℞)

Astronomically, retrogrades are a visual phenomenon where the planet appears to be moving backward in our sky, when in fact, the Earth's orbit has either jumped ahead or behind the other planet's orbit, giving it the optical illusion of going backward from our perspective here on Earth.

Every retrograde consists of five phases: Shadow I, Stationary Retrograde, Retrograde, Stationary Direct, and Shadow II (Fig. III-2). The shadow periods are when the planet is going direct (the astrological word for "forward motion") through the zodiacal degrees that the planet is going to pass through during the retrograde. The stationary periods are when the planet slows down to a grinding halt so that it may switch directions. The retrograde period is when the planet is appearing to move backwards relative to our observations here on Earth, but it is traveling at the same speed as it normally would if it was going direct.

FIGURE III-2. Anatomy of a Mercury Retrograde from 16°Ⅱ – 7°Ⅱ

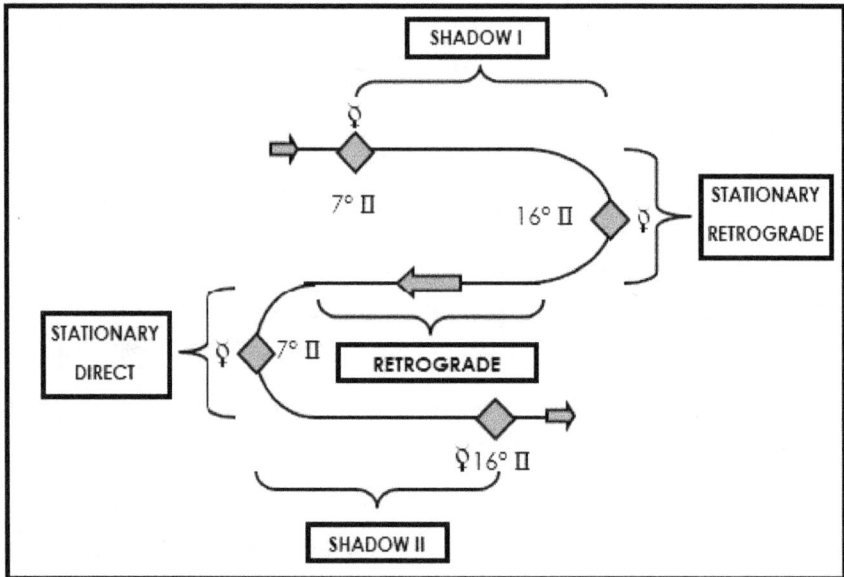

PHASE #1: SHADOW I

During this time, you will start to experience the themes of the upcoming retrograde because the planet will revisit these degrees while it is traveling backward. In our example, Mercury will be traveling in retrograde from 16°II–7°II which means when the planet is traveling forward from 7°II–16°II prior to the retrograde it indicates the Shadow I period.

PHASE #2: STATIONARY RETROGRADE

Think of stationary periods like changing directions in a car. Before you can go from forward to reverse, you first need to slow down, stop, change from forward to reverse, and then accelerate once again. This same concept applies to stationary periods because this is the time when the planet slows down, stops, and then speeds up only in the opposite direction.

Stationary periods are the most stressful and intense part of the retrograde period because any movement, even if it is backward, is better than no movement at all. Therefore, it is important to be mindful of when they occur so you can be more prepared.

PHASE #3: RETROGRADE PERIOD

This is the more familiar phase of the retrograde, when the planet is traveling backward for an extended amount of time. During the retrograde period, the energies of the retrograde are in full expression and you should respond accordingly, following the guidelines outlined in this section.

PHASE #4: STATIONARY DIRECT

Just as it was with the stationary retrograde, the planet slows down only to stop and then pivot toward the opposite direction. Again, these are intense moments when you should take care and wait until the stationary period is over before you react.

PHASE #5: SHADOW II PHASE

Once the planet has finished traveling in retrograde, it is time for it to change back into direct motion. It will cover the same ground that was covered during the Shadow I phase, only this time, the planet will continue to proceed along the zodiac until the next retrograde period. This is the time when you should be wrapping up the retrograde themes and act upon what you have learned during the retrograde period in order to make the appropriate adjustments.

Retrograde Timing

When it comes to the stationary periods, Mercury stations are felt for a week before it turns retrograde, a week after it turns retrograde, a week before it turns direct, and a week after it turns direct. Venus stations are felt 1.5 weeks before it turns retrograde, 1.5 weeks after it turns retrograde, 1.5 weeks before it turns direct, and 1.5 weeks after it turns direct. Mars stations are felt 2 weeks before it turns retrograde, 2 weeks after it turns retrograde, 2 weeks before it turns direct, and 2 weeks after it turns direct. These, of course, are approximations. Once you learn how to read an Ephemeris in Book II, you will be able to obtain precise dates for these stationary periods. In the meantime, follow the table below in order to get a running start on this data (Table III-6A-C).

TABLE III-6A. Upcoming Mercury Retrogrades and Stationary Periods

ZODIACAL RANGE	Stationary Rx Start	Mercury Retrograde	Stationary Rx End	Stationary Direct Start	Mercury Direct	Stationary Direct End
9°♈—26°♓	MAR 11 2025	MAR 15 2025	MAR 19 2025	APR 3 2025	APR 13 2025	APR 15 2025
15°♌—4°♌	JUL 14 2025	JUL 18 2025	JUL 25 2025	AUG 8 2025	AUG 11 2025	AUG 20 2025
6°♐—20°♏	NOV 6 2025	NOV 9 2025	NOV 14 2025	NOV 27 2025	NOV 29 2025	DEC 6 2025
22°♓—8°♓	FEB 21 2026	FEB 26 2026	MAR 1 2026	MAR 15 2026	MAR 20 2026	MAR 25 2026
26°♋—16°♋	JUN 23 2026	JUN 29 2026	JUL 5 2026	JUL 18 2026	JUL 23 2026	JUL 29 2026
20°♏—5°♏	OCT 18 2026	OCT 24 2026	OCT 30 2026	NOV 8 2026	NOV 13 2026	NOV 19 2026
5°♓—20°♒	FEB 6 2027	FEB 10 2027	FEB 15 2027	FEB 27 2027	MAR 3 2027	MAR 9 2027
6°♋—27°♊	JUN 5 2027	JUN 11 2027	JUN 17 2027	JUN 30 2027	JUL 4 2027	JUL 13 2027
4°♏—19°♎	OCT 2 2027	OCT 7 2027	OCT 13 2027	OCT 25 2027	OCT 28 2027	NOV 1 2027

ZODIACAL RANGE	Stationary Rx Start	Mercury Retrograde	Stationary Rx End	Stationary Direct Start	Mercury Direct	Stationary Direct End
19°♒—4°♒	JAN 20 2028	JAN 24 2028	JAN 29 2028	FEB 9 2028	FEB 14 2028	FEB 21 2028
16°♊—7°♊	MAY 16 2028	MAY 21 2028	MAY 28 2028	JUN 8 2028	JUN 14 2028	JUN 22 2028
18°♎—3°♎	SEP 14 2028	SEP 19 2028	SEP 27 2028	OCT 6 2028	OCT 12 2028	OCT 17 2028
3°♓—17°♑	JAN 3 2029	JAN 7 2029	JAN 12 2029	JAN 22 2029	JAN 27 2029	FEB 2 2029
26°♉—17°♉	APR 29 2029	MAY 1 2029	MAY 9 2029	MAY 19 2029	MAY 25 2029	JUN 2 2029
1°♎—17°♍	AUG 28 2029	SEP 2 2029	SEP 8 2029	SEP 21 2029	SEP 25 2029	OCT 2 2029

TABLE III-6B. Upcoming Venus Retrogrades and Stationary Periods

ZODIACAL RANGE	Stationary Rx Start	Venus Retrograde	Stationary Rx End	Stationary Direct Start	Venus Direct	Stationary Direct End
10°♈—24°♓	FEB 23 2025	MAR 2 2025	MAR 15 2025	APR 5 2025	APR 24 2025	APR 24 2025
8°♏—22°♎	SEP 25 2026	OCT 3 2026	OCT 13 2026	NOV 6 2026	NOV 14 2026	NOV 25 2026
19°♊—3°♊	APR 30 2028	MAY 10 2028	MAY 21 2028	JUN 13 2028	JUN 22 2028	JUL 4 2028
24°♑—8°♑	DEC 2 2029	DEC 16 2029	DEC 31 2029	JAN 17 2029	JAN 26 2029	FEB 5 2029

TABLE III-6C. Upcoming Mars Retrogrades and Stationary Periods

ZODIACAL RANGE	Stationary Rx Start	Mars Retrograde	Stationary Rx End	Stationary Direct Start	Mars Direct	Stationary Direct End
6°♌—17°♋	NOV 24 2024	DEC 6 2024	DEC 21 2024	FEB 12 2025	FEB 24 2025	MAR 16 2025
10°♍—20°♌	DEC 27 2026	JAN 10 2027	FEB 3 2027	MAR 15 2027	APR 2 2027	APR 17 2027
13°♎—25°♍	JAN 28 2029	FEB 14 2029	MAR 7 2029	APR 23 2029	MAY 5 2029	MAY 24 2029

Affected Domains During the Retrograde

Mercury retrogrades affect areas of communication, traveling, efficiency, and negotiations. It is hard to explain yourself during this time and can have cases of "it's on the tip of my tongue," along with misunderstandings. Messages, emails, and packages get lost or take longer to be delivered or answered. Commuting to work takes longer, and there are unexpected mishaps with traffic and public transportation. Take care if you are naturally accident prone or a poor car driver. This is a good time to edit, clear out junk, make processes more efficient, read contacts but do not sign them, review for exams, brainstorm, and turn off the mental functions through meditation.

Venus retrogrades affect romance, aesthetics, one-to-one relationships, and leisure. Old romances can reappear, or you can find that your feelings for an ex have changed. Breakups and reevaluating current relationships are also possible. Individuals are more sensitive to *Feng Shui*. Therefore, your living environment can become more stressful. It is easier to disagree with coworkers, romantic partners, children, and bosses. It can also be difficult to simply relax. This is a good time to make amends, move around furniture, clean out your wardrobe but do not dedicate yourself to a new style just yet, think about your tastes, and ponder if every acquaintance you have in your life is good for you in the long run.

Mars retrogrades affect action, movement, aggression, and conflict. In fact, Mars retrogrades are the most difficult because Mars is the planet of forward motion, so when he is not allowed to move in the direction he wants, he becomes highly irritable. There can be shorter tempers and sudden acts of violence or personal injuries/accidents. It is hard to get anything off the ground and you have to contend with feelings of impatience. This is a good time for addressing anger, slow breathing techniques, outlets that allow you to release your pent-up physical energy, and to observe your sense of self-esteem and confidence.

SECTION 5—PLANETARY HOURS

It's All Greek to Me

When the ancient Greeks, along with the various cultures that existed alongside them and before them, were working with Astrological systems, their understanding of the solar system only extended to Saturn because it is the last outer planet that can be viewed without the help of modern-day telescopes. These seven planets each ruled a day out of the seven-day week. These daily rulerships were so deeply ingrained within Greek and Latin culture, that it has influenced not only our modern use of the seven-day week, but the words that are used to signify which planet rules which day is still apparent (Table III-7).

TABLE III-7. Planetary Day Rulers in English and Spanish (A Latin-Based Language)

PLANET	GLYPH	NAME IN ENGLISH	NAME IN SPANISH
MOON	☽	**MON**DAY	**LUN**ES
MARS	♂	TUESDAY	**MAR**TES
MERCURY	☿	WEDNESDAY	**MIÉR**COLES
JUPITER	♃	THURSDAY	**JUEV**ES
VENUS	♀	FRIDAY	**VIERN**ES
SATURN	♄	**SATUR**DAY	**SÁBA**DO
SUN	☉	**SUN**DAY	DOMINGO

The Daily Ruler Gets the Torch

When considering the days of the week in this respect, certain energies are emphasized and become available for us depending on the day. On Monday, emotions are heightened, and it is a time to relax, get groceries, and stay home. No wonder people have "a case of the Mondays;" we are starting the work week on possibly the worst day! It would make more sense to have the week begin on Tuesday because this is the day of Mars, which makes it good for initiation and physical vigor. Wednesday, Mercury's day, is the best time to write correspondences, have meetings, run errands, and short-distance traveling. Thursday, Jupiter's day, is the day to take a chance and plan events that you want to work out favorably. Venus rules Friday and it is no wonder we call it "TGIF." This is the day to relax and save your hard work for the next day, Saturn's day, or, Saturday. Sunday should be "your day" where you plan and do whatever your heart desires.

Applying the Day to the Hour

When it comes to the planetary hours, these same energies still exist, only during a shorter window throughout the day. For example, if it is Monday, the day is ruled by the Moon, then anything you do that is Moon-themed on the hour of the Moon doubles the power behind the intention. On the other hand, if you plan something during the Mercury hour and it is during a time when Mercury is in retrograde, then this could have the same powerful effect but in the opposite direction.

There are countless phone apps and websites that calculate planetary hours, but it is still important to understand how the hours are calculated. The twenty-four-hour day we are familiar with is evenly divided into a twelve-hour day period and a twelve-hour night period. Planetary hours are similarly divided into a day period and night period as well, but the time allotted for each depends on the time between the sunrise and the sunset. In other words, daytime is from sunrise to sunset, and nighttime is from sunset to the sunrise of the next day. The time between these two events are calculated and divided into twelve "hours" using the table below (Table III-8).

TABLE III-8. Planetary Hour Rulers

DAY	DAY HOURS (SUNRISE TO SUNSET)											
	1	2	3	4	5	6	7	8	9	10	11	12
SUN	☉	♀	☿	☽	♄	♃	♂	☉	♀	☿	☽	♄
MON	☽	♄	♃	♂	☉	♀	☿	☽	♄	♃	♂	☉
TUES	♂	☉	♀	☿	☽	♄	♃	♂	☉	♀	☿	☽
WED	☿	☽	♄	♃	♂	☉	♀	☿	☽	♄	♃	♂
THUR	♃	♂	☉	♀	☿	☽	♄	♃	♂	☉	♀	☿
FRI	♀	☿	☽	♄	♃	♂	☉	♀	☿	☽	♄	♃
SAT	♄	♃	♂	☉	♀	☿	☽	♄	♃	♂	☉	♀

DAY	NIGHT HOURS (SUNSET TO SUNRISE)											
	1	2	3	4	5	6	7	8	9	10	11	12
SUN	♃	♂	☉	♀	☿	☽	♄	♃	♂	☉	♀	☿
MON	♀	☿	☽	♄	♃	♂	☉	♀	☿	☽	♄	♃
TUES	♄	♃	♂	☉	♀	☿	☽	♄	♃	♂	☉	♀
WED	☉	♀	☿	☽	♄	♃	♂	☉	♀	☿	☽	♄
THUR	☽	♄	♃	♂	☉	♀	☿	☽	♄	♃	♂	☉
FRI	♂	☉	♀	☿	☽	♄	♃	♂	☉	♀	☿	☽
SAT	☿	☽	♄	♃	♂	☉	♀	☿	☽	♄	♃	♂

According to this method, there will always be twelve hours of daytime and twelve hours of nighttime, but these "hours" could last approximately fifty-four to sixty-three minutes, depending on when the Sun would rise and set relative to the location of the individual. This means that every latitude and longitude has varying planetary hour lengths throughout the year, but there will always be twelve hours per night and day, nevertheless. For example, individuals living in Alaska will have immensely short day hours during the winter because there is very little sunlight, but will have very long day hours during the summer because the time of daylight is very long.

Monitoring planetary hours gives you an hourly and daily basis for auspicious timing to activate certain planetary energies (Table III-9). Try to experiment and observe how certain events unfold during certain hours.

Table III-9. Recommended Activities During a Planetary Hour

HOUR	GLYPH	RECOMMENDED ACTIVITIES
SUN	☉	Personal hobbies, Events with children, Presentations, Recreation, Brainstorming, Acting upon what you want to do in the moment
MOON	☽	Eat and make food, Counseling, Taking showers and baths, House cleaning, Events involving the mother
MERCURY	☿	Correspondence, Traveling and commuting, Breathing exercises, Mental puzzles and games, Making lists, Studying
VENUS	♀	Relaxation, Spa and skin treatments, Making amends, Going on a date, Mediation, Romance
MARS	♂	Exercise, Anything requiring expedience, Sexual encounters, Physical labor, Strategic moves
JUPITER	♃	Present and take up opportunities, Spiritual and academic pursuits, Taking chances, Any form of growth or expansion

HOUR	GLYPH	RECOMMENDED ACTIVITIES
SATURN	♄	Activities involving focus and tenacity, Events involving the Father, Career and Long-Term decisions, Dedicating to something or someone, Disciplined activities

Multilayered Daily Living

You now have the tools and know how to follow the astrological calendar on a yearly, monthly, and even hourly basis. The more you work and observe astrology in motion, the more astrology reveals its abilities to you. Experiment with the calendar, take risks, and also trust when it's time to hold off. This won't say that life will suddenly become perfect and pleasant forever, but you will at least take out a lot of unnecessary stress, chaos, and guesswork out of your life.

CONCLUSION
(and a note from the author)

A New Approach to an Old Tradition

You made it through the first book!

As mentioned in the Introduction, I'm writing this series to completely redefine how we conceptualize astrology and "bring it down to Earth". Integrating metaphysics, mathematics, and mythology, we have established astrology as a viable working system that both unveils our complete and unique character and provides a working calendar based on the unceasing motions of the celestial bodies within our solar system.

You've now learned about the various archetypes within astrology and how they manifest from a more theoretical and academic perspective. But there's so much more . . .

Time for that Second (and Third) Cup of Coffee

Grab that extra shot of espresso! In Book II, we'll fully integrate your new knowledge through multiple facets, including natal chart and transit analysis. You'll learn valuable skills that you can apply to your own chart (as well as those of others if you decide to become an astrologer yourself).

Starting from basic natal chart interpretation, I'll share my own top secret until now step-by-step process to break the overwhelming nature of astrology into smaller, more digestible chunks. We'll explore the ethics of astrology readings and how the planets and signs manifest in various and unique ways using case studies of actual astrology clients.

Warning: I'm about to use two words that may seem scary, but I promise I'll be right there with you to make them as painless as possible . . .

Astrological Mathematics

Don't give up just because I said mathematics. Give me a
chance to explain.

First, if you do decide to become a certified astrologer, you will need to learn some form of astrology math and this basic lesson will put you ahead of the curve. Second, this type of math is very simple algebra and is not only interesting, but it also shows you just how precise and accurate astrology is, grounding you more to the true inner workings of astrology. (Still, if math isn't your thing, you can always skip this section and have plenty of other experiences to focus on.)

From there things get even more exciting as we learn the main method astrologers use to predict future events: Transits. We will explore how transits are determined and then analyze them (again using case studies to show how it works in the real world).

When you've completed Book II, you will be ready to give your first astrology reading with confidence, using a workable step-by-step system that takes out the guesswork.

Until then, keep reading, keep exploring, keep growing, and watch the intimate story of you unfold right before your very eyes.

Until next time,

BIBLIOGRAPHY

Bartlett, Kenneth. "Education in the Renaissance." *The Great Courses Daily.* 2016. https://web.archive.org/web/20170601225458/http://www .thegreatcoursesdaily.com/education-in-the-renaissance/.

Braha, James. *How to Be a Great Astrologer: The Planetary Aspects Explained.* Hermetician Press, 1992.

Brown, Jeffrey M. and Terence P. Hannigan. "An Empirical Test of Carl Jung's Collective Unconscious (Archetypal) Memory." *Journal of Border Educational Research.* 2006. Vol. 5.

Campion, Nicholas. *A History of Western Astrology, Volume 1: The Ancient Word.* Continuum International Publishing Group, 2008.

Campion, Nicholas. *An Introduction to the History of Astrology.* ISCWA, 1982.

Cicero, Marcus Tulius. *De Senectute De Amicita De Divinatinoe, Book 2, Section 95, With an English Translation.* Translated by William Armistead Falconer. Harvard University Press, 1923.

Cramer, Frederick. *Astrology in Roman Law and Politics.* American Philosophical Society, 1954.

Cybermetrics Lab. "Ranking Web of World Hospitals." Archived 2015 at https:// web.archive.org/web/20150206120833/http://hospitals.webometrics.info/.

Dasa, Shyamasundara. *A Brief History of Jyotish.* 2021. https://shyamasundaradasa .com/jyotish/what_is_jyotish/jyotish_history.html.

Davis, Matt. "What is the Cosmic Web?" Big Think. Archived September 29, 2020. https://web.archive.org/web/20200929020109/https://bigthink.com /surprising-science/cosmic-web?rebelltitem=5#rebelltitem5.

Economist, The. "Astrology is Booming, Thanks to Technology and Younger Enthusiasts." January 15, 2025. https://www.economist.com/culture

/2025/01/15/astrology-is-booming-thanks-to-technology-and-younger
-enthusiasts.

Enyart, Bob. *An Original 360 Day Year.* 2018. "An Original 360 Day Year, Was There
One?" 360 Day Year. Archived January 20, 2018. https://web.archive.org
/web/20180120122832/http://360dayyear.com/.

Exploring Your Mind. "Carl Jung and Astrology in Psychoanalysis." 2018. Archived
March 18, 2025. https://web.archive.org/web/20250318044441/https://
exploringyourmind.com/carl-jung-astrology-psychoanalysis/.

Forrest, Steven. *What is Evolutionary Astrology?* 2021. https://www.forrestastrology
.com/pages/what-is-evolutionary-astrology.

Hand, Robert. *Towards a Post-Modern Astrology.* 2005. https://www.astro.com
/astrology/in_postmodern_e.htm.

Herlihy, Anna. "Renaissance Star Charts" in *History of Cartography, vol.* 3. University
of Chicago Press, 1998.

Hunger, Hermann, ed. *Astrological Reports to Assyrian Kings.* vol. 8. State Archives
of Assyria, 1992.

Jarvis, Dennis. *Italy-3104 – Apollo.* October 22, 2010. Photograph. https://www
.flickr.com/photos/archer10/5378415112.

Jung C.G. *Civilization in Transition, Second Edition.* Princeton University Press. 1970.

Kepler College. "Kepler's History." Archived June 19, 2021. https://web.archive
.org/web/20210619041944/https://www.keplercollege.org/index.php
/about/history.

Koch-Westenholz, Ulla. *Mesopotamian Astrology.* Vol. 19. Museum Tusculanum
Press, 1995.

Magner, Lois. "Astrology and Medicine." *Science and Its Times: Understanding
the Social Significance of Scientific Discovery.* https://www.encyclopedia
.com/science/encyclopedias-almanacs-transcripts-and-maps/astrology
-and-medicine.

Martinez, Walberto. *Moon Phases All.* June 16, 2012. Photograph. Archived January
12, 2019. https://web.archive.org/web/20190112025517/https://www.flickr
.com/photos/walberto_fotos/7380282754/.

McCann, Maurice. "The Secret of William Lilly's Prediction of the Fire of London." *Astrological Journal* 32, no.1(1990).

Moesgaard, K. P. "Ancient Ephemeris Time in Babylonian Astronomy." *Journal for the History of Astronomy*. 1983. 14(1). https://doi.org/10.1177/002182868301400104.

Ostermeier, Dr. Eric. "Presidents Day Special: The Astrological Signs of the Presidents." Smart Politics. 2010. Archived November 1, 2020. https://web.archive.org/web/20201101065750/https://smartpolitics.lib.umn.edu/2010/02/15/presidents-day-special-the-ast/.

Pesce, Joe. "Researchers PROVE Time Travel Mathematically Possible." *Rising with Krystal and Saagar*. Posted Nov. 26, 2020 on The Hill. Youtube. 5 min. 42 sec.

Plumer, Brad. "We've Been Using the Gregorian Calendar for 434 Years. It's Still Bizarre." Vox News. Archived October 5, 2016. https://web.archive.org/web/20161005130206/https://www.vox.com/2016/10/4/13147306/434th-gregorian-calendar-anniversary-google-doogle.

Rayburn, William F. MD, et al., "Multiple Gestation: Time Interval Between Delivery of the First and Second Twins," *Obstetrics & Gynecology, 63(4),* April 1984, 502–6. https://journals.lww.com/greenjournal/abstract/1984/04000/multiple_gestation__time_interval_between_delivery.12.aspx.

Ripat, Pauline. "Expelling Misconceptions: Astrologers at Rome," *Journal of Classical Philosophy* 106, no. 2, (2011):115-54, https://www.journals.uchicago.edu/doi/10.1086/659835.

Saliba, George. *A History of Arabic Astronomy: Planetary Theories During the Golden Age of Islam.* New York University Press, 1994.

Science Source. Guido Bonatti: Italian Astronomer and Astrologer. 2025. https://www.sciencesource.com/2009908-guido-bonatti-italian-astronomer-and-astrologer-stock-image-rights-managed.html.

Solar System Exploration Research Virtual Institute. "The Oldest Lunar Colanders." 2021. https://sservi.nasa.gov/articles/oldest-lunar-calendars/.

Tobar, Germain and Fabio Costa. "Reversible dynamics with closed time-like curves and freedom of Choice." *Classical and Quantum Gravity*. vol. 37 no. 20. https://doi.org/10.1088/1361-6382/aba4bc.

Weizmann Institute of Science. "Quantum Theory Demonstrated: Observation Affects Reality." ScienceDaily. February 27, 1998. www.sciencedaily.com /releases/1998/02/980227055013.htm.

World Counts, The. "How Many Babies are Born Each day?" 2025. https://www .theworldcounts.com/stories/how-many-babies-are-born-each-day.

Zeevveez. Urania Zodiac Albrecht Durer. September 30, 2008. Photograph. Archived August 7, 2020. At https://web.archive.org/web/20200807160624 /https://www.flickr.com/photos/zeevveez/2900531631/.

Can't Wait for Book II?

You don't have to!

We've set up a special gift for you.

Visit kyleukesastrology.com for a

sneak peek.

While you're there, download your

FREE Quick Analysis of Natal

Conjunctions to analyze your own

chart conjunctions!

(We'll do a more in-depth analysis

in Book II coming soon.)

Kyle Ryan Ukes

ABOUT THE AUTHOR

Kyle is an NCGR-PAA-certified professional astrologer and has been a counselor, teacher, volunteer and writer since 2012. The primary focus of his practice is to understand and improve the human condition through astrological comprehension and self-empowerment. His writing has appeared in local and national NCGR journals, and he was a co-author of "The Daily Scope" in Vogue magazine. Kyle also teaches classes in astrological mathematics and beginning-to-advanced levels of chart interpretation.

For more about Kyle or to schedule speaking engagements or private readings, email KyleUkesAstrology@gmail.com or visit KyleUkesAstrology.com.

ABOUT NEWHOUSE CREATIVE GROUP

Founded by Keith Newhouse and his father Mark Newhouse in 2017 on the principle that every story has a purpose, Newhouse Creative Group (NCG) aims to educate and innovate through its authors and their work. Since then we've expanded to over 20 traditionally published authors and have helped numerous others with publishing and marketing services, online courses, coaching, consulting and more!

Whether looking for a novel to curl up with, an educational experience for your child, or a chance to live out your dream of being a writer, we hope that you'll become a part of the NCG family.

Newhouse Creative Group . . . Inspiring the Readers and Writers of Today and Tomorrow!

ABOUT HASTINGS HOUSE PUBLISHERS

Hastings House was founded in 1936 for the purpose of telling the world about America. Hastings has grown from a one-book, one author operation into an international publishing house with the rights to over 2700 books. Since Walter Frese founded Hastings House (as he lived in the suburb of Hastings-on-Hudson), the publisher has been a part of some of the country's largest literary undertakings including:

- The WPA Writers' Project (A federally-funded New Deal program designed to keep writers from starving during the Great Depression)

- The American Guide (A 1948 one-volume guide to the United States which became Book-of-the-Month Club's most successful work up to that time)

- The American Procession Series (A significant literary venture of dramatic non-fiction books that center around the epic episodes in our history and cultural growth that until then had not been adequately told)

- The Daytrips Series (A series of travel guides that are still popular to this day)

Since Walter Frese retired in 1985, the firm was acquired by different publishing executives until it was moved to Florida by Peter Leers and his wife Dee.

In 2024, Hastings House Publishers was acquired by Newhouse Creative Group in hopes of reinvigorating this almost 100-year-old brand.

MORE FROM HASTINGS HOUSE PUBLISHERS AND NEWHOUSE CREATIVE GROUP

Inspiring the readers and writers of today and tomorrow!

Visit HastingsHousePublishers.com for more books and other products from Hastings House and the rest of the Newhouse Creative Group family!

www.ingramcontent.com/pod-product-compliance
Lightning Source LLC
Chambersburg PA
CBHW080458110426
42742CB00017B/2928